CYBERCULTURE COUNTERCONSPIRACY

A STEAMSHOVEL WEB READER

Kenn Thomas, Editor

Volume One

Cyberculture Counterconspiracy • Vol One

ISBN 1-58509-125-1

LAYOUT AND DESIGN

Tedd St. Rain

COVER DESIGN

Kevin Belford

"UNTHINKABLE COMPLEXITY"
by Kenn Thomas

"The matrix has its roots in primitive arcade games," said the voice-over, "in early graphics programs and military experimentation with cranial jacks." On the Sony, a two-dimensional space war faded behind a forest of mathematical - ly generated ferns, demonstrating the spa[t]ial possibilities of logarithmic spi - rals; cold blue military footage burned through, lab animals wired into test sys - tems, helmets feeding into fire control circuits of tanks and war planes. "Cyberspace. A consensual hallucination experienced daily by billions of legit - imate operators, in every nation, by children being taught mathematical con - cepts...A graphic representation of data abstracted from the banks of every computer in the human system. Unthinkable complexity. Line of light ranged in the nonspace of the mind, clusters and constellations of data. Like city lights, receding...."

— William Gibson, Neuromancer —

The durability of Gibson's description of the internet testifies to the writer's talent. He wrote it in 1983 and now, in 1999, it's only beginning to seem dated, even though consumer computer technology has evolved through many gener- ations. More advanced military technology still awaits transfer down to the cyberpeonage. *Steamshovel Press* has telegraphed suggestions of it in reports on topics like the PROMIS backdoor variations (1) found on web browsers, and the super-surveillance ECHELON satellite system, portrayed but not named in the movie *Enemy of the State* (2). Gibson's elegant description, of course, has yet to catch up with William S. Burroughs' *Interzone* visions, Burroughs dead since 1997, and cohort Tim Leary, the true champion of the cyberculture, years gone now as well.(3)

Their presences still beam, however, as *Steamshovel Press* readers jacked into the grid await further surprises from the developing technology. It came as no surprise that the Heaven's Gate webmasters were Steamshovel fans. The group's combination of UFO obsession and alienation from the mainstream cul- ture fit the reader profile, albeit in a fatally exaggerated form (4). For the more typical reader, Steamshovel's pulp-paper presence began on the newsstands in 1992, although as a small zinelet it's history extends back to 1988. It circulated among the other bygone zines with names like *Ganymedean Slime Mold, Popular Reality, Crash Collusion,* Jim Keith's old *Dharma Combat*, and Greg Bishop's still current *Excluded Middle,* produced by bright minds, anarchists, fanboys, varieties of sex maniacs, religious cultists, and really good graphic artists and writers, already going nuts with the technology of cheap, easy paper reproduction. Those familiar with this history know that this creative frenzy of small publishers blossomed into the *Factsheet Five* phenomenon, and remains quite a contrast to the vapid media dross hardcopy on the magazine stands but rushed also to the new electronic playground. As that activity and energy enlivened the developing electronic technology, *Steamshovel* began to develop its web presence even as it became more of a newstand magazine. The *Steamshovel Press* web site resides at **http://www.umsl.edu/~skthoma**.

The volumes of *Cyberculture Counterconspiracy* collect material posted to the web by *Steamshovel Press* over the past several years. This material has been removed from the web now to make the site less cumbersome, and to make these volumes unique. Appropriately enough, *Cyberculture Counterconspiracy* uses one of the new digital technologies for books, the laser book imprint.

These web pages have been submitted to the digital system of a major distributor, where they remain on file until orders come in. *Steamshovel* may print copies one at a time but also can produce thousands of copies for bookstore distribution. At present, this process remains more expensive than regular printing and distribution, but it provides a degree of flexibility unavailable the old fashioned way. *Steamshovel* produces only what it needs to satisfy demand, and the book never goes out of print.

The first volume of *Cyberculture Counterconspiracy* collects the most prominent feature of the *Steamshovel* web site, a column called "The Latest Word." Changed sometimes as frequently as every week, this column includes short informational features, interviews and editorials, by writers like Jim Keith, Len Bracken and Adam Gorightly, and others whose longer pieces often appear in the newsstand *Steamshovel*. It chronicles the Clinton conspiracy era, beginning with the White House report using *Steamshovel* material that led to the coining of the phrase "Vast Right Wing Conspiracy." It includes Peter Dale Scott's definitive analysis of the Lewinsky matter as a military intelligence operation. Some reports, like that on the murder of former White House intern Mary Caitlin Mahoney, include the relevant hyperlinks as inserts on the page. Other insights gathered here involve mind control, Wilhelm Reich, Czechoslovakian spy activity connected to Beat poet Allen Ginsberg, possible alien mathematics secretly coded into the daily *New York Times*, obits for Carlos Castaneda and Kerry Thornley (a long, revelatory interview accompanying the latter), remote viewing and much else.

Volume two contains book, movie and electronic media reviews from the "Offline Illumination" column from the website and "Things Are Gonna Slide", a column, assembling parapolitical news items and theory. Both cover the same period of recent history as the first volume. "Offline Illumination" gives a capsule view of the best literature and electronic media productions of the counterconspiracy culture. It is highlighted by the contributions of Rob Sterling, whose Konformist newsletter (**www.konformist.com**) has risen to the top of conspiracy news reporting on the web; and Acharya S who carries on a web discussion about religious conspiracy (**www.truthbeknown.com**). New essays by Sterling, Acharya, Greg Bishop (whose *Excluded Middle* zine now has a web presence at **www.primenet.com/~exclmid/**) and Richard Metzger (his *Infinity Factory* webcast, on the *psuedo* network or via Metzger's **www.disinfo.com** has become a regularly watched program on the desktops of many conspiracy students) are absolutely unique to this second volume--never on the *Steamshovel* web page, never in the hard copy *Steamshovel*. *Steamshovel* takes great pride in having these writers as contributors and web allies. As dharma combatants in the cybersphere, their historical insights are unparalleled.

The all-new section of volume two also highlights the talents of Kevin Belford, an artist whose work has adorned pages of the hardcopy magazine. *Cyberculture Counterconspiracy* includes two of his remarkable graphic presentations, "The Rosetta Solution: The Murder of Officer Tippit" and "The Manson Family Who's Who."

Steamshovel Web readers go to the "Things Are Gonna Slide" column for raw data about the conspiracy culture, as much as possible unfiltered by political, religious or personal agendas. The column's title comes from a Leonard Cohen song, "The Future", which ironically laments the passing of the pre-information age era: "Give me back the Berlin Wall/Give me Stalin and St. Paul/I've seen the future, brother/It is murder/Things Are Gonna Slide/Slide in All Directions/Won't Be Nothin'/Nothin' you can measure anymore…"

Steamshovel shares both the sentiment and the irony of Cohen's intent (5).

The info-abyss of cyberspace, was imagined early by Harry Truman's scientific adviser, Vannevar Bush, and *Steamshovel* also shares his observation that "Presumably man's spirit should be elevated if he can better review his shady past and analyze more completely and objectively." (6) It offers the two volumes of *Cyberculture Counterconspiracy*, and the continued work on the *Steamshovel* web page, in that spirit.

Kenn Thomas
July 4, 1999

Notes:

1. The story of the PROMIS software, stolen from the Inslaw company and sold illegally by the US to police agencies around the world with a secret built-in capability to spy on those agencies, is told best in *The Octopus: Secret Government and the Death of Danny Casolaro* (Feral House). Casolaro's biography reads like a cyberpunk novel, with protagonist Casolaro lost, and ultimately killed, while delving into the PROMIS cyber environs.

2. Conspiracy topics now proliferate in Hollywood. Oliver Stone used the interest to help create the JFK Assassination Materials Review Board, but by and large this interest has served little social good. *X Files* and Mel Gibson's *Conspiracy Theory* movie continued Steppin' Fetchit-type stereotypes of conspiracy students. Many actors, notably Will Smith, now use the label "conspiracy theorist" as part of their public image. That Smith's movie, *Enemy of the State*, did not contain the word "ECHELON" in any of its script speaks volume. The title of the movie refers to a phrase, "enemies of the state", usually applied to Stalinist ethnic resettlement programs, source of the civil war in the Russian republic of Chechnya. In December 1998, Chechen rebels beheaded three employees of the telecommunications firm Granger Telecom. Rumors circulated widely that the rebels caught the men installing an ECHELON satellite aerial.

Oliver Stone tried to continue his filmic foray into conspiracy with a documentary television program entitled *Oliver Stone's Declassified* for the entertainment division of the ABC network. The program was dropped when Stone insisted on a segment detailing the theory that a missile downed TWA Flight 800 in 1996. *Time* magazine (11/9/98) reported that pressure from "aviation-industry sources" caused ABC's news division to apply enough pressure to have the show canceled before it aired. Interesting, too, that the subject of Stone's *JFK* movie, Jim Garrison, felt that Kennedy was a victim of the aerospace industry. (See *Maury Island UFO*, IllumiNet Press, 1999.)

3. Perhaps Dr. Leary would have appreciated the irony that the FBI continued its smear against him by releasing on the internet selected documents from his time in prison, when he provided the Bureau with some information. Leary long acknowledged that he did this, just as he gave due credit to the CIA for helping usher in the psychedelic era. However, it became "news" once again in the Summer of 1999 when a website called *Smoking Gun* posted files documenting that time released to it through the Freedom of Information Act.

Dr. Leary discusses it in his 1983 autobiography, *Flashbacks*, and it's discussed in the Leary/G. Gordon Liddy debate movie, *Return Engagement*. According to Leary, the only people harmed by anything he said were some scumbag lawyers who deserved it. The FBI make an effort to exaggerate this and turn it into a "snitch jacket" for the sake of ruining Leary's future credibility. In fact, while Leary was doing his "informing", several people organized a press conference, PILL (People Investigating Leary's Lies), to denounce it and the situation that had been forced upon him. Allen Ginsberg spoke at this conference. None of the conference organizers were compromised seriously by what Leary said and many remained his friends until his death. Leary knew everyone. If he had "snitched" anything of significance, this would be a much bigger deal than it is.

The allegations had a strange afterlife, however. Walter Bowart, for instance, transformed them into an entirely imaginary scenario of Leary returning to his cell one night after a lobotomy, with blue streaks painted across the temples of his shaved head, now a total mind control slave. This came in a particularly ungracious obituary Bowart wrote for Dr. Tim, Leary's reward for one having given some lurid details about his intelligence community connections for Bowart's book, *Operation Mind Control*.

Another author, Mark Reibling, in a 1994 book called *Wedge: The Secret War Between the FBI and the CIA*, tried to make the case for Leary having been an informant before prison, during his years in exile. I checked Reibling's government document sources and they did not match the details of Leary's biography. Reibling also tried to make the case that Bob Woodward's Deep Throat was actually Cord Meyer, ex-husband of famous Leary gal pal Mary Pinchot Meyer.

The February 1999 issue of *Flatland* recounts my own petition for Leary's FOIPA file. The FBI is still doing its best to make sure that the full file is not released, only "summaries" to a chosen few in the media. The files posted on the web by *Smoking Gun* make every effort, by selection and interpretation, to put the worst possible spin on this episode in Leary's life. For instance, a statement Leary makes about his plans for public life after prison, in most contexts a heroic ambition for him considering the circumstances, has been placed before other testimony about one of those lawyers. This has been done "for clarity"--to make it "clear" that Leary was simply finking for the sake of his own freedom.

4. *Steamshovel* was one of a small number of newspapers and magazines that ran ads paid for by the group containing rants that explained their philosophy.

5. Richard Belzer, whose show business career stretches back to the 1971 *Groove Tube* movie of 70s and forward to his role as Detective John Munch in the TV show *Homicide: Life in the Streets*, once interviewed Leonard Cohen for his old talk show, *Hot Properties*. He asked Cohen about his favorite band. "Foetus On Your Breath" came the response. Belzer didn't miss a beat with his follow up question about the name of the band's hit song. "My Gums Bleed For You", said Cohen. Belzer's book, *UFOs, JFK and Elvis: Conspiracies You Don't Have To Be Crazy To Believe*, came out in 1999.

6. The essay, "As We May Think," was written at around the time of the Roswell crash and Vannevar Bush's signature can be found on the notorious MJ12 documents. Bush helped frame the developing technology, but his 1947 description of personal computers remains uncanny, especially in its acknowledgement that it is based on projections about the then current technology, as if he has an awareness of an alien technology that he's trying to match to the technology he is familiar with.

Bush says: "Consider a future device for individual use, which is a sort of mechanized private file and library. It needs a name, and to coin one at random, 'memex' will do. A memex is a device in which an individual stores all his books, records, and communications, and which is mechanized so that it may be consulted with exceeding speed and flexibility. It is an enlarged intimate supplement to his memory. It consists of a desk, and while it can presumably be operated from a distance, it is primarily the piece of furniture at which he works. On the top are slanting translucent screens, on which material can be projected for convenient reading. There is a keyboard, and sets of buttons and levers. Otherwise it looks like an ordinary desk.

In one end is the stored material. The matter of bulk is well taken care of by improved microfilm. Only a small part of the interior of the memex is devoted to storage, the rest to mechanism. Yet if the user inserted 5000 pages of material a day it would take him hundreds of years to fill the repository, so he can be profligate and enter material freely.

Most of the memex contents are purchased on microfilm ready for insertion. Books of all sorts, pictures, current periodicals, newspapers, are thus obtained and dropped into place. Business correspondence takes the same path. And there is provision for direct entry. On the top of the memex is a transparent platen. On this are placed longhand notes, photographs, memoranda, all sort of things. When one is in place, the depression of a lever causes it to be photographed onto the next blank space in a section of the memex film, dry photography being employed.

There is, of course, provision for consultation of the record by the usual scheme of indexing. If the user wishes to consult a certain book, he taps its code on the keyboard, and the title page of the book promptly appears before him, projected onto one of his viewing positions. Frequently-used codes are mnemonic, so that he seldom consults his code book; but when he does, a single tap of a key projects it for his use. Moreover, he has supplemental levers. On deflecting one of these levers to the right he runs through the book before him, each page in turn being projected at a speed which just allows a recognizing glance at each. If he deflects it further to the right, he steps through the book 10 pages at a time; still further at 100 pages at a time. Deflection to the left gives him the same control backwards.

A special button transfers him immediately to the first page of the index. Any given book of his library can thus be called up and consulted with far greater facility than if it were taken from a shelf. As he has several projection positions, he can leave one item in position while he calls up another. He can add marginal notes and comments, taking advantage of one possible type of dry photography, and it could even be arranged so that he can do this by a stylus scheme, such as is now employed in the telautograph seen in railroad waiting rooms, just as though he had the physical page before him.

All this is conventional, except for the projection forward of present-day mechanisms and gadgetry."

THE DIVINE MR. MORTON

UFO Magazine Volume 10, Number 4 (July/August 1995) prints a letter from *Steamshovel* editor Kenn Thomas defending UFO lecturer Sean Morton, who was labeled as a cultist in the previous issue of UFO. The letter pointed out that a critic of Morton's, Russ Estes, was proven wrong on the Montel Williams Show when he claimed that Morton did not have the undergraduate degree from USC he claims. Morton proved the claim by insisting that Montel's post-production people electronically splice in a copy of the degree on subsequent broadcasts. Estes now admits that Morton has the degree--although he complains he was cut off by Montel before he could fully articulate his charge that Morton lied about it (cut-off or not, this was clearly Estes' message). Readers remain in the dark about Estes' other charge, that Morton doesn't have the Doctorate of Divinity from The Berachah University because "The Berachah Church of Houston, Texas does not issue ANY degrees of that type." Are Berachah University and Berachah Church different institutions? Did Morton go through a course of study at one or the other that was a non-degree conferring institution's equivalent to a doctorate program? Estes answers neither question.

And just how divine does one have to be to speak frankly about alternative views of the UFO phenomenon? Thomas' letter makes the glib observation that divinity degrees can be had from the classified ads in Rolling Stone. Estes argues with Morton's credentials, not with his claims, ideas or the interpretation of the video documentation of UFOs he brings to his lectures. He presents his audiences with unusual data, tells them what he knows and what he thinks, and lets them make up their own minds. He does not demand the blind obedience of followers. Estes' response notwithstanding, *UFO Magazine's* characterization of Morton as a cult leader is still wrong.

This should not dissuade readers from picking up the new issue, however. It concentrates on a "UFO and War" theme and includes several articles reflecting good research and fascinating anecdotes, including research director Don Ecker's Vietnam encounter with the infamous black helicopters. In a field rife with disinformation, little doubt remains that *UFO Magazine* is a standard bearer for credible research. Surely this is part of the reason that it is quick to point a nervous finger at someone with Sean Morton's unusual sensibilities.

(Also, poor editing marred Kenn Thomas' letter to UFO, turning the word "geo-psychic" into the nonsensical "geo-physic", for instance. The entire letter is reproduced below.)

Dear *UFO*:

I feel obliged to come to the defense of Sean Morton, someone *UFO* identified as a cult leader in its current issue ("Cults...Or Cutting Edge?", *UFO Magazine*, Volume 10, Number 3, May/June 1995.) The *UFO* article left the impression that Sean delivers the dicta of Tibetan monks and Native American spirits to worshipful and incredulous followers. I have met Sean many times and interviewed him once for *Steamshovel Press* and I can attest that this is far from the case.

I am sure that Sean wouldn't deny anyone the right to regard what he says as hooey on the scale of the Republican's Contract On America. I also know that he brings some fascinating video documentation to his lectures and workshops on the UFO circuit and never fails to discuss their merits (or lack thereof) in Q&A's with the audience. Moreover, he has done a great deal to bring the Area 51 situation to the attention of the public, even if one views his work only as theater.

However, my understanding is that the only pre-requisite to joining Sean Morton's group, Delphi Associates, is to pay the newsletter subscription cost. It does not even require the belief that certain divination techniques (as with the "earthquake sensitives"--people who seem to have the apprehensions that some animals have prior to a quake--that Sean networks with) have information value. Also, Sean's reality paradigm includes the notion of geo-psychic mediation (my term, not Sean's); meditation and prayers can alter the events he "predicts". This renders the success rate of his prophesies, actually quite impressive at times despite what was reported in UFO, a relatively inadequate measure of his work.

Also, I don't know that Russ Estes disproved Sean's assertion of holding a Doctorate of Divinity (why hoax it? aren't these available through the classified ads in *Rolling Stone*?), but I do know that when Estes challenged the existence of Sean's undergraduate degree at USC on the Montel Williams show, he was proven wrong. Montel did not allow enough time for Sean to defend himself, but Sean insisted that the program flash the actual degree on the screen in post-production. It goes by in a flash, and without explanation, but it's there and I'll be happy to copy the videotape for doubters.

Best,

Kenn Thomas

Editor/Publisher

Steamshovel

STEAMSHOVEL PRESS

FUSION PARANOIA

I: Of Norman Olson, Wilhelm Reich, Robert Fletcher, *Steamshovel* and the New York Press

Steamshovel Press editor Kenn Thomas was visiting Washington, DC on June 15 when militia members gave statements to a Senate hearing concerning the militia movement. Norman Olson, whose re-presentation of Debra Van Trapp's take on the OKC bombing got him kicked out of the Michigan militia, provided the most direct verbal attack on government corruption. Olson angered chairman Sen. Arlen Specter (R-Pa.) into demanding proof for the accusations. Olson also took the opportunity to grab what should have been much bigger headlines by uttering three simple words: Magic Bullet Theory. The Magic Bullet Theory provides a convoluted, implausible scenario supporting the lone nut view of the JFK assassination. Critics widely regard it as an assault on physics and common sense, a piece of lawyer work intended only to obfuscate real understanding of JFK's murder and support the mistaken conclusions of the Warren Report. Arlen Specter authored the theory, and shortly thereafter his political fortunes brightened and he became a district attorney for Philadelphia. Specter is now running for president as a pro-choice Republican.

Perhaps Norman Olson did not underscore the importance of a *Steamshovel* subscription in dealing with issues like this. *Steamshovel*, for instance, could have provided historical background to Olson's claim of government abuse of weather modification technology, a claim roundly ridiculed by the mainstream press. Government interest in weather control is, in fact, well documented and played a prominent role in the persecution and imprisonment of Wilhelm Reich, regularly the subject of *Steamshovel* articles. Interested readers should also seek out the latest issue of *Flatland*, which contains fascinating interviews with Reich's daughter Eva; the man who occupied a cell next to Reich the day Reich died; and Orson Bean, the TV personality who underwent Reichian therapy and applied Reich's ideas on childhood education in a school environment. It also includes *Flatland* editor Jim Martin's new research on Reich's weather control "cloudbusting" work. *Flatland's* homepage can be contacted via a link on the list below.

Another person testifying at the Senate hearing, Robert Fletcher, was the subject of an article by Michael Kelly in the June 19 edition of *New Yorker* that also mentioned *Steamshovel*. Jonathan Vankin's analysis of Kelly's idea of "fusion paranoia", the coming together of leftist and rightist conspiracism, appears on the *50 Greatest Conspiracies of All Time* homepage. *Steamshovel* would appreciate response from readers, to Kelly's article, Vankin's rejoinder and another brief article on the topic appearing in the June 4 edition of the *New York Times Magazine* ("Not All The Same Nuts", p. 19) for a possible forum on the topic in the next issue.

II: Burden Squares Off With PARANOIA

Steamshovel contributor Jack Burden writes: "the fact that some conspiracy theories are lies meant to advance fascist agendas of course doesn't discredit all conspiracy theories"...but! Burden explores issues surrounding the left-right debate within the conspiracy research community. PARANOIA editors Al Hidell and Joan D'Arc also respond to the criticism. Steamshovel Press urges its readers to read and respond to this correspondence for the sake of a forum it plans in the next issue, collecting the most insightful responses. (Note: This forum never appeared. --kt)

Dear John,

Your point on the historical use of conspiracy theories to justify reprehensible acts is well-taken, and I certainly agree that ethnic scapegoating is wrong. But what does this have to do with *PARANOIA*? The views of Linda Thompson which we published seem to me to be based on a healthy concern over governmental threats to individual rights, and an understandable disgust with America's corrupt politics-as-usual. In her statement, she was advocating a government by and for the people. She thinks the government has become too powerful, John. If you think that's a tenet of fascism, neo-or otherwise, then you have a very twisted understanding of the term.

It's fine if you want to criticize particular *PARANOIA* articles because they have a ludicrous premise or are poorly-written, or whatever. But your generalized criticism of *PARANOIA* seems to be based mainly on what you believe to be the political ideology of certain article writers! *PARANOIA* a tool of the Right? Well, I could label Prevailing Winds a tool of the Left, but that seems to me to be a pointless and unfair criticism.

Your suggestion that *PARANOIA* might as well be written by Lyndon

LaRouche because of all the space we devote to "patriot-oriented spew" betrays your ignorance of both *PARANOIA* and the LaRouche philosophy. In nine issues, *PARANOIA* has devoted a grand total of one single-page article to the views of LaRouche. (Five pages, if you include the Schiller Institute article. By the way, we did identify the author as an associate of LaRouche. But, you may ask, isn't the Schiller Institute a "LaRouche front"? Face it, John: ALL think-tanks are "fronts" to the extent that they are funded by individuals with political viewpoints, including those of the Left.) And we've featured a total of three pieces on the views of Linda Thompson, one of which was focused on her critique of the government actions at Waco. And, for the record, LaRouche thinks the militia-types are simply the ignorant tools of the British Crown.

Quite simply, we don't think all conspiracy theories are "equal." This charge implies that we exercise no discrimination in the selection of articles, which is untrue. I think you'd agree if you could see the pile of stuff we've decided NOT to publish. And, as I've said before, I personally do not believe everything we publish. But I've decided to evaluate articles on how interesting and/or entertaining I think our readers will find them, not on my own biased ideological filter. (For the record, our recent cover article on pro-choicer Bill Baird and the conspiracy against abortion rights didn't go over very well among some of our readers. Likewise, one article's references to "the gassings at Auschwitz" prompted an angry letter from people who apparently believe that such gassings never happened.)

You say you object to "right-wing" propaganda that is masked as conspiracy theory. (I guess if its from the right, it is by definition propaganda.) Well, to paraphrase a recent positive review of *PARANOIA*, I object to left-wing propaganda that's masked as objective analysis. Face it, the left contains among its ranks people with an agenda, too.

Just who is "exploiting" our "hippy dippy postmodern interest in High Weirdness"? What exactly is their agenda? In fact, what exactly is a "hippy dippy postmodern interest in High Weirdness"? If you're speaking of the UFO-related stuff, I don't see why the likes of Rush Limbaugh and his "propaganda machinery" would be very interested in financing such articles. (P.S. Attention, attention: This is not "the Age of Reagan and Rambo." Ronald Reagan is no longer President. The mindless militarism of Rambo is no longer chic. It's more like the Age of Bill Clinton and Forrest Gump, which I find equally disturbing.)

Finally, you say it's apparently easier for *PARANOIA* to just "reprint without commentary, a press release from the *Spotlight* about Jews and the UN." What the hell are you talking about? We've never published anything, from the *Spotlight* or any other source, about "Jews and the UN." At least get your facts straight before you criticize us for something we didn't do.

You want us to print more left-wing perspectives? Fine. We'd have no problem being an "organ of the Left," if they'd just submit some articles! People like Michael Parenti and John Judge do incredible work and research, and we'd love to print more of it. But, so far, they haven't expressed an interest.

And, somehow, I don't think your unfair labeling of *PARANOIA* as a right-wing propaganda machine will give them much encouragement to do so.

Al Hidell

Dear John,

Although we're getting quite used to hearing mainly from asswipes, it would be nice to get a pat on the head once in a while--good doggy.

How do you define your terms? What is "the right" and what is "the left"? Your dis-course is extremely simplistic and impossible to argue without definitions. One attempt I might try is that there are, in your words, "serious motherfuckers with serious agenda, bank accounts and battle plans" coming at us from all sides! How can today's extremely compli-cated political situation be adequately explained using two categories? Even if it could, your blanket statement "the people with the megabucks propaganda machinery are not, to put it mildly, on the left" is convoluted. The "left" is extremely dangerous right now. Just look at how they've got everybody scapegoating the "right"! The green movement is funded by Laurance Rockefeller and the CIA! Ditto for the feminist movement! The "progressive" media is anything but! Mr. Kimsey is doing some serious motherfucking "lumping" of ter-minology which is very difficult to counter. Is he really Chip Berlet incognito? Is he talking about the Patriarchal Christian Fortune 500 Companies? Is he talking about the militia movement in general? Does he think that any article that has a religious basis is automati-cally on the right? Did he even read the Bill Baird abortion conspiracy article, for which we may have lost many Christian readers?

To top it off, your lowbrow solution to this potentially explosive situation is to "shut-up" and not help them along. So apparently, censorship is the solution! Isn't that a fascist solution?

The basic ideal here which I oppose is that "ideas are dangerous." It's the so-called pro-gressive left which dangerously affirms the attitude that people are too stupid to incorporate ideas from all sides and make their own decisions based on innate intelligence. I know that people have been seriously "dumbed down," and that's part of the conspiracy, but it's not our job to spoonfeed people. Most people I have met in my life are perfectly capable of imput-ing information, processing it, and deriving meaning for themselves. It's not my job to assess ahead of time how something may be construed by someone else and then to go about "childproofing" it so that there is no possible way someone could get hurt by it. That is exactly what Jim and Debbie Goad are going through right now. Yes, certain rhetoric is unpleasant to the ears. But that is what free press and free speech is all about.

You know what I'd like to have done once and for all? I'd like to form an independent committee where "blind" copies of articles from various conspiracy magazines (not just *PARANOIA*) are given to people to read and they would judge them "left" or "right" utiliz-ing set definitions and parameters. Al and I have been asked many times by readers to "bal-ance" the magazine in this way and we believe that we have attempted to do that, not inten-tionally in response to such requests, but by our own sensibilities. If certain articles in *PARA -NOIA* are construed (or misconstrued) as coming from an unpleasant avenue of thought, I don't think its presence there is a right-wing conspiracy. I think the reader is a repressed wannabe fascist dictator who thinks there should be more laws to save the human race from extinction. I prefer the anarchist solution: less laws to save the human race from distinction. People need to cultivate new ways of assessing information as it comes at us faster and faster. And they need to cultivate a sense of humor as well. If they could see us chuckling over some of this stuff, the light in the attic might go on!

Your ludicrous suggestion that we might be LaRouchies or may be funded by some nefarious "They" makes it obvious who is the paranoid here. We are people with day jobs who fund this magazine with our own money, as well as newsstand sales and subscriptions. Second, if you had actually read a few issues of *PARANOIA*, you would know that we've featured many stories which cannot in any way be considered "right wing.' Among those are stories on the Leonard Peltier case, the CIA at Chappaquiddick, UFOs and Virgin Mary sightings, and the conspiracy against abortion rights. Bill Baird, Robert Cutler, Alan Cantwell, Loren Coleman, Monte Evans, George Andrews, and others, should be extreme-ly insulted by your blanket assertion that *PARANOIA* is a "right-wing" conduit.

Perhaps you would be better served by a magazine of left-wing political commentary.

Joan d'Arc

III: Adam Parfrey on the topic

#From Adam Parfey's Cult Rapture, now available from Feral House Press,: "The *New Yorker* accused Feral House of indulging in 'fusion paranoia,' a phrase conjured to castigate those who research conspiracies using information from both Left and Right. The *New Yorker* seemed flabbergasted that we weren't yoked to the Democrat/Republican, Right/Left paradigm like all "responsible" journalists. I am not alone in regarding the two-party system as a false stratification, a dumb-show concocted for the public as a means to distract attention from the ruling elite. This *New Yorker* piece proves why it receives so many ads for sixty thousand dollar watches and full-length furs. It's where the elite goes to confirm its preconceptions."

IV: View from a Gemstoner

From "American Militia Papers," by Gerald A. Carroll, author of Project Seek, a book on the Gemstone File:# "Like many other mainstream journalists, Michael Kelly [in coining the phrase 'fusion paranoia' in *New Yorker*] is catching up to the story that this current militia fervor is nourished by much more than just gun control or wild New World Order conspiracies. Genuine people with genuine fears are being hurt in a variety of ways by what they feel is an unfeeling, mechanical government apparatus that has run amok... Kelly's piece represented a departure from the New York literati norm of lampooning the militia movement and its ancillary "conspiracy researchers." Anybody who has ever read the publications to which Kelly refers--i.e. *PARANOIA*, *Flatland*, *Steamshovel Press*, et al--much of that material is rooted in fact, not "theory." It is a matter of giving the "conspiracy researchers" like Robert Fletcher or anyone else at least marginal credit for collecting and interpreting a maze of the government's own documentation that clearly points to counterrevolutionary/reactionary activity by the current administration." "American Militia Papers" are available from gerald-carroll@uiowa.edu.

Photo of a young Mary Pinchot Meyer with then husband Cord Meyer.

V: Cord Meyer and the New World Order

A recent discussion on **Rob Sterling's** *Konformist* e-newsletter about **Mikhail Gorbachev's** current role as a Green globalist--a promoter for an ostensibly pro-environment international lobbying effort--led to the following contribution to the on-going fusion paranoia debate. Although it begins with a discussion of Gorbachev, it moves more into a look at **Cord Meyer,** a famous spook who worked as an organizer for one-world government idealists in the late 1940s and touches also on the role of drug traffic in the New World Order.

Readers interested in a free subscription to *Konformist*, a veritable feast of con deconstruction delivered direct to your cyberhood, should e-mail Robalini@aol.com with a subject heading of **I NEED TO KONFORM** or some such.

Dear *Konformist*:

I saw Gorbachev do the the "end of the iron curtain" speech in Fulton, MO, where Churchill first popularized the phrase "iron curtain," a term which had previously been coined by Joseph Goebbels. It wasn't too much later when I found myself in San Francisco at the protests against Zhirinovsky speaking at a posh supper club-- November 11, 1994, actually. The trip from Soviet thaw to old-time ethnic bigotry in Russia seemed quick.

Recently, though, I learned something interesting about globalism from the new issue of Lobster. Lobster is a highly recommended conspiracy analysis magazine in England published by Robin Ramsay (214 Westbourne Avenue, Hull, HU5 3JB, UK). The current issue deals with how the new British prime minister Tony Blair is beholden more to transnational investment corporations than British self interest. A sidebar to this discussion includes an anecdote from a conservative MP named Richard Body, who co-chaired an anti-European Economic Community referendum. He reports that infamous spook Cord Meyer, "not a normal CIA man...well known in the Federalist movement", was being brought to England in part to help subvert the anti-EEC campaign.

Cord Meyer, of course, was at one time married to Mary Pinchot Meyer, who gave LSD and sex to JFK in the White House, bless her heart. Cord Meyer was a founder of the World Federalist movement in the late 1940s, but he had forsaken it and later described that time in his autobiography as the naive liberalism of his youth. And yet here he is in 1975 using that background on assignment to derail the anti-ECC movement. I thought that was a good example of "fusion paranoia" that *New Yorker* wrote about.

Then the paranoia fused in the other direction. *The Lobster* article shed new light on some 1948 correspondence over Cord Meyer's lecture visit to St. Louis. Manuscript archives include a letter on that lecture sent back to Meyer afterwards with a list and some descriptions of the people who attended. This could have just been follow up work to tap potential donors, but it always looked all the world like a vacuum cleaner operation. Meyer's covert mission could have been to collect the data on people who would come out to something like a World Federalist meeting. The possible duplicity there seemed more plausible after reading *Lobster*.

In a 1990 book about POW/MIAs called *Kiss The Boys Goodbye* by Monika Jensen-Stevenson and William Stevenson (Dutton: New York): "Cord Meyer was such an old hand in diplomacy and intelligence that the *New York Times* had profiled him on January 7, 1973, as a man who had made a long journey from idealistic hopes for world unity to `the Department of Dirty tricks.' Newspapers had quoted Meyer as talking openly about his success in carrying out a CIA assignment to discredit a book alleging CIA involvement in illegal drug trade."

This was the 1972 book *The Politics of Heroin in Southeast Asia* by Alfred W. McCoy (Harper and Row: New York). In light of the *San Jose Mercury News* revelations about CIA drug traffic in south central LA, I thought this made a good comment about how transnational conspirators really see the global government working.

Kenn Thomas

Anarchy After Leftism by Bob Black (C.A.L Press, c/o AAA, P.O. Box 11331, Eugene OR 97440 $7.95 + $2.05 s&h) reviewed by John Filiss

Bob Black's *Anarchy After Leftism* is a seminal work from one of the seminal figures in the anti-authoritarian milieu. Written as a response to Murray Bookchin's abrasive *Social Anarchism or Lifestyle Anarchism: An Unbridgeable Chasm* (AK Press, P.O. Box 40682, San Francisco, CA 94140-0682), Black revives a type of intellectual exchange all but moribund in our modern era of encapsulated thought and belief: he

"Work is the source"

attacks his opponent not at his weakest points, but at his *strongest*. Not only is it marvelous critique on its own, it remains so with the object of critique next to it—the written works of Murray Bookchin.

Social Anarchism or Lifestyle Anarchism was written as a rather personal attack on the views of a number of contemporary anarchist authors who actually took the idea of anarchy, or freedom from rule, seriously. Whether it be the mystic flights of Hakim Bey, John Zerzan's critique of symbolic culture, or *Fifth Estate*'s search for useful concepts within primitive lifestyles, Bookchin attacks with an ire which does little to support his occasionally valid points. Interestingly, it is often where Bookchin founders in his attempts to bring down his opponents at all costs that the poverty of the prevailing vision—both his and his target's—is made most apparent. To give one example, Bookchin states:

"Ironically, even the collective that produces *Fifth Estate* found it could not do without a computer and was `forced' to purchase one—issuing the disingenuous claimer, `We hate it!' Denouncing an advanced technology while using it to generate antitechnological literature is not only disingenuous but has sanctimonious dimensions". (p.49)

Though the weakness of Bookchin's argument for a moralistic purity of the means of expression is all too obvious, being read as it is on paper and ink doubtless created through capitalist and ecological exploitation, it shows as well *Fifth Estate*'s own puritanism, a tendency to retreat from this world into restrictions and modes, rather than an uninhibited search for a utopia to supersede the current nightmare. The question is not whether new technology generally excels and surpasses within the limited spheres that technology creates (I'll take my modern word processor over my turn-of-the-century Oliver typewriter any day), but whether we can create a world where the processing of words is needless for our fulfillment.

When *Social Anarchism or Lifestyle Anarchism* first came out, I had mixed reactions towards it. While disliking Bookchin's (unwarranted) smugness and tone of debate, I granted it had, again, some valid points, and hoped that at some level it would foster intelligent input on issues which *need input*, and from as broad a spectrum of thought as possible. After reading *Anarchy After Leftism*, I realized above all else that we do not need to be ridiculed, not in an era where the most tiresome and inane proponents of the existing order pose as its iconoclasts. With Bob Black as defender of many of the most liberatory tendencies within modern anti-authoritarian thought, it is an issue which will surely come up with decreasing frequency in the years ahead.

The reasons for this are well known to Murray Bookchin. Black is a gifted satirist, whose penchant for pugnaciousness occasionally spills over into his writing, as well as being a much talked about aspect of his private life (an area I am hardly qualified to discuss or pass judgment on). Though as well or better known than anyone mentioned in *Social Anarchism or Lifestyle Anarchism* as a major theorist of the more radical of anarchist tendencies (e.g., having written *the* essay on zero-work), Black is nowhere mentioned in the book, certainly an attempt by Bookchin to escape Black's wrath.

And yet it is Black in this instance who comes off as being chivalrous in his critique. Though *Anarchy After Leftism* is cutting and sometimes merciless (and frequently hilarious), not one statement seems unwarranted against Bookchin, who gives us such gems of constructive and thoughtful criticism as "I would love to see the Bey and his disciples surface at an 'old-time libertarian picnic'!"(p. 24) Further, Black has enough respect for his readers and possible detractors to furnish an index, absent in Bookchin's book.

Incidentally, another book has recently been published in response to Bookchin: George Bradford's *Beyond Bookchin: Preface For A Future Social Ecology* (contact *Fifth Estate*, 4632 Second Ave., Detroit MI 48201). Though certainly of interest to those who have long dwelled upon the thought of Murray Bookchin, it hardly ranks with Black's effort. Bradford's ponderous overstriving for eloquence and lack of concision—he never uses one sentence where three will do— will unfortunately turn off the majority of readers merely curious about the debate. If not one in ten of those who buy Bradford's book will actually finish it, Black's book, by contrast, will be passed from friend to friend. Black's writing has the uncanny charm of awakening interest in topics previously thought to be of no interest.

Bradford's efforts are somehow tragic, as his writing shows some insight, and it seems that with a little effort, he could improve upon it dramatically. Black, too, has all too frequently done less than he is capable of, among other things directing his scathing wit at individuals w.ho could hardly be expected to match his skill at satire or polemic. *Anarchy After Leftism* is Black at his best, a lengthy yet stimulating dissection and critique of a multifaceted and intelligent thinker, Murray Bookchin, placed within a broader critique of the intellectual currents which made a Bookchin possible. Black bites hardest when he bites with ideas, which he does with elan.

As important as are its contents, just praise must be given to its format. Personalizing a debate, yet staying within appropriate boundaries, and making the core of the critique the ideas propounded by one's opponents, is a superb and too-little-used method of bringing one's viewpoints to a broader audience. Exposing as intellectual sham a trite, yet undeservedly cult figure within a given circle, whose members have probably had little or no exposure to the most emancipating concepts of modern anarchist thought ... brilliant, Bob. I only hope he continues to ripple in ever-larger circles, with an ever-growing audience. I would love to see a similar book on Chomsky.

In short, *Anarchy After Leftism* is an important part of the growing effort to wean anarchy off of leftism, with-a future none can easily foresee; an attempt to create something unique, wonderful, and ultimately real.

I realize, dear reader, that so far it seems I have only discussed this book in superlatives, and have done little of the critiquing here or there which gives a review an air of objectivity. Be that as it may. I haven't written a book review in two years and wouldn't have bothered now if I weren't so impressed. If you have any interest in the doctrine of social ecology, in primitivism, the abolition of work, or simply anarchy—*qet this book!*

John Filiss Port Jervis, NY

REICH AND LITTLE ROCK

Brave young black students comprised the Little Rock Nine, a group that integrated Central High School in Little Rock, Arkansas in September 1957, flanked by jeering white racists on one side and a cold military presence on the other. US president Bill Clinton created a dramatic scene of his own last Thursday when he greeted the now adult nine at the school with a grip and a grin, and directed them through it's glass doors as a cheering crowd looked on. The White House had orchestrated a warm celebration of school integration, a social engineering triumph. Dogs sniffing for bombs in Ryder trucks at nearby abortion clinics, however, provided a measure of how the psychological, emotional and social dimensions of racism in the US still have been left unaddressed.

The plight of the Little Rock Nine was not the only social oppression that America suffered in 1957, of course. Wilhelm Reich had been thrown in jail for daring to explore human energy potential and therapeutic techniques not approved by the Food and Drug Administration. He had been condemned as a medical quack, his books had been burned and his orgone boxes were destroyed. Reich had harmed no one and, indeed, had helped many with his understanding and manipulation of "life energy." The FDA never truly followed Reich's scientific protocols and convicted him only on technical violation of its injunction to stop distributing orgone boxes. Authorities threw him in a prison cell in Lewisberg, PA from which he did not emerge alive.

In memos to the prison chaplain before his death, however, Reich continued to write passionately about the social situation of his adopted homeland. His note from September 1957 even includes reference to the disturbance at Little Rock Central High School. He emphasized the very psychological and emotional undercurrents he felt were being ignored in the broader social arena of conspiratorial 1950s America:

"I am merely fulfilling my public duties as a U. S. citizen and worker in planetary affairs if I continue to point out where the *true* danger to our social and personal existence is placed: its is *Emotional Poisoning*: disruption through sowing distrust throughout our society, doping and drugging of our population, espec. our YOUTH; draining us financially through areas [...]race, a camouflage of the true menace, the *Emotional Poisoning* a la Little Rock racial upheavals; keeping our high placed officials at bay through fear of sexual scandals, railroading efficient men and women into prisons or lunatic asylums through [?] up there environments; subverting justice by whispered little lies & frightening or using judges. Doing all this destruction unnoticed as it were by all those responsible. It was clear from the very beginning that [?] and now lyrics were subverted by such use of *stupidities & evasions* on our part, especially by the staid reluctance to talk bluntly and take the bull by the horns. The bull is really no more tan a few *slimy tape worms* eating away at our emotional guts. It is high time to start giving social power to the established functions of Love, Work & Learning as bastions against the tapeworms."

(The prison memo form includes this banal and perhaps prescient statement: "Your failure to specifically state your problem may result in no action being taken.")

Reich's imprisonment was in part the end result of mis-reporting on him that

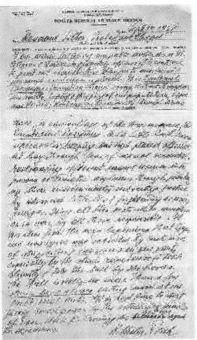

appeared in the *New Republic* under the editorial leadership of a now-confessed spy named Michael Straight (see "Toxic Disinformation" below; for information on Straight, see *Steamshovel Press* #8). *New Republic* made its own pronouncement about Little Rock in its July 7, 1958 edition, complaining about the Supreme Court's failure to stop legal challenges that were slowing down the integration process. The Supreme Court, opines *New Republic*, "must stand the ground they themselves have assumed, or the grand experiment they inaugurated will end in bitter farce, with consequences for the state of the union that stagger the mind." Clearly the magazine had a better view of the possible consequences of Supreme Court actions than it did on its own.

The consequences of Reich's work, on the other hand, and the implications of the study of character structure on the understanding of race issues has continued over the years. Writing in a chapter called "Racism and Slavery" in *The American Slave: A Composite Autobiography* (Westport, Connecticut: Greenwood Publishing Company, 1972), historian George Rawick notes the impact of "that great underground classic of modern thought, Wilhelm Reich, *Character Analysis*, 3d ed. rev., first published in German in 1933, and its less well-known but significant companion, Wilhelm Reich, *The Mass Psychology of Fascism*, first published in German in 1933. While I cannot subscribe to all of Reich's system, this chapter could not have been written without his monumental attempt to relate Marx and Freud which loosened the ideological armouring of Western rationalism for me and many others."

—Kenn Thomas

MORE ON MEYER

Steamshovel Press has in its files videotape from 1982 of the late, great Timothy Leary sitting in the "Crossfire" between Patrick Buchanan and Tom Braden, the original talking heads on that still popular CNN debate program. In the end they agree that Dr. Leary had led a "wasted life" (Braden's phrase). Years later Leary would complain that the full spectrum of political views on the program ran from left-wing of the CIA to the right wing.

The behind-the-scenes connections were more interesting than the program. Leary had been a friend of Mary Pinchot Meyer, JFK's last lover and the one who turned him on to psychedelic drugs. Braden had been in the same business as Cord Meyer, Jr., Mary's ex-husband. Cord Meyer

Cord Meyer, Jr., 1948

succeeded Braden as the chief of International Organizations Division. IOD was a CIA sponsored front for manipulating international groups. It served as part of the covert arsenal to engineer the New World Order.

Meyer's name has come up several times recently. According to J. Orlin Grabbe, Meyer recruited Bill Clinton for covert work while stationed in London. *Lobster* presented some new information on Meyer in its latest issue, and that led to some correspondence on this web site (see "Cord Meyer and the New World Order" in *Previous Latest Words* page.) This provides the opportunity below to direct *Steamshovel* reader attention to a new Feral House book by Alex Constantine, *Virtual Government*. The book is a remarkable study of CIA psyops and mind control and comes highly recommended. It includes discussion of Cord Meyer's role in a mass mind control program called Operation Mockingbird.

Meyer's work for the "liberal" cause to create a world government is everywhere tinged with "conservative" cause of the covert world. In a conversation with Burton Hersh about Cord Meyer's relationship with the infamous James Jesus Angleton, Tom Braden once said "Jim sucked Cord Meyer in, in my view. Cord Meyer became not only a great admirerer, but also believer." (*The Old Boys, 1992*) Hersh also had this to say about Mary Pinchot Meyer's murder:

Angleton's obsession with nurturing his friends started people referring to him quite openly as "Mother." "When Cord Meyer's ex-wife Mary was mur-dered while exercising on the path next to the Potomac canal," one bystander alleges, "Angleton had already let himself into her house with a key he kept to the place even before the cops turned up. I think he was after paper he knew she kept in her bedroom which had to do with her affair with John Kennedy."

For a more in-depth view of both Cord Meyer, Jr. and Tom Braden, *Steamshovel* presents an excerpt from U. S. Foreign Intelligence by Charles D. Ameringer (Lexington, Massachusetts: Lexington Books, 1990.)

STEAMSHOVEL PRESS

From *U.S. Intelligence Foreign Intelligence: The Secret Side of American History* by Charles Ameringer, Lexington Books: Lexington, Massachusetts, 1990.

In much the same way, the International Organizations Division used private international organizations-a number of them based in the United States-as instruments of covert action in foreign policy. These organizations, representing such diverse interests as students and youth, labor unions, community development, health care, and freedom of the press and human rights, were rarely aware of CIA sponsorship. In fact, many of them were part of the non-Communist Left and strongly opposed certain foreign governments that were considered U.S. allies at the time. The contradiction between official U.S. foreign policy and the one being carried out by the IOD caused consternation and controversy when the American public became aware of it in the mid-1960s.

The IOD provided funding to organizations that were outspoken in their criticism of U.S. foreign policy and that would have been outraged to know that they were receiving CIA support (although in some cases insiders knew what was going on). In order to conceal its involvement, the IOD devised the "pass-through," a means of channeling money through several conduits before it reached the intended beneficiary. The CIA would create a phony foundation that was little more than a post office box; it would contribute funds for a particular purpose to a legitimate foundation that was known to support certain causes and to have the necessary connections; the legitimate foundation finally passed the money to the organizations that the CIA wanted to favor in the first place.

Since the IOD seemed to be fomenting change in countries where the United States was officially supporting the status quo, the purported split between "DDI liberalism" and "DDP/DDO conservativism" was not really that clean. From 1950 to 1954, the chief of the IOD was Tom Braden, a former OSS operative and liberal journalist. (Thirty years later, Braden sat "on the left" in the Cable News Network program Crossfire.) His successor for the rest of the 1950s and into the 1960s was Cord Meyer, who had lost an eye in World War II combat and came out of the war dedicated to the cause of world federalism. Ray Cline, who became DDI in 1961, had earlier been station chief in Taiwan.

But there was less doubt about where the Special Operations Division stood politically.

***

In Albania, Kim Philby betrayed the U.S.-British infiltration teams even before they left their base in Malta, resulting in the ambushing and killing of many brave men. Yet if Philby was a monster of sorts, the CIA's Eastern European programs themselves had particularly malodorous features. Frank Wisner, who was in charge of the Office of Policy Coordination (the forerunner of the DDP), ran the programs with the collaboration of General Reinhard Gehlen. Gehlen was a German officer who had been responsible for Soviet intelligence during the war; he had planned his own capture by American forces in the closing days of the war and had brought his files with him. Gehlen aided Wisner in assembling "a cadre of German specialists on the Soviets [but] without regard for their pasts; some of his best experts were in fact former Nazis. This and similar Army connections with Nazis would prove embarrassing for the United States many years later."

Conducting guerrilla operations behind the iron curtain was infeasible, and the situation in Western Europe was improving in any case through conventional diplomacy. So Clandestine Services shifted its attention to parts of the globe where there was unrest. Events in China and Korea helped focus attention beyond Europe and broadened the cold war to the world arena. Some foreign affairs specialists questioned whether every coup or insurgency in Asia or Latin America was Moscow-inspired, but the American president did not have to worry about public debate in using his new secret weapon. Employing covert action, the CIA replaced the marines as the instrument of "Yankee interventionism."

The chart in figure 19-1 lists the places-where the CIA has intervened since its beginning. It is not exhaustive and has been compiled exclusively from published sources and public documents, but it serves to indicate the extent of the "new interventionism" and to identify the various covert action tactics used.

In the rich variety and broad extent of its deployment, covert action produced a new American personality: the "swashbucklers of secret wars," such as Edward Lansdale, Kermit "Kim" Roosevelt, John Peurifoy, Cord Meyer, William Colby, and Oliver North. Though there have been many others, these persons are associated with some of the CIA's most sensational episodes. Marchetti and Marks suggested that Lansdale's work was the "proto-type" for CIA covert operations during the 1950s: "His exploits under agency auspices, first in the Philippines and then in Vietnam, became so well known that he served as the model for characters in two best-selling novels, *The Ugly American* by William J. Lederer and Eugene Burdick, and *The Quiet American* by Graham Greene. In the former, he was a heroic figure; in the latter, a bumbling fool."

In the list of covert operations, Lansdale figured in the very first episode outside Europe, which occurred in the Philippines in 1949. Lansdale, an air force colonel, assisted Philippine leader Ramon Magsaysay in putting down the rebellion of the Communist Hukbalahaps, or "Huks." He was one of the earliest advocates of counterinsurgency warfare, or the use of guerrilla tactics to defeat guerrillas. Lansdale's mission enabled Magsaysay to win popular support by providing effective propaganda and by secretly providing funding for economic and social reforms. It ended when Magsaysay was elected president in 1953.

BALTIC STATES 1948-54; THE UKRAINE 1948-54; ALBANIA 1949-1954; THE PHILIPPINES 1949-53; KOREA 1950; VIETNAM 1954, 1955, 1963; CHINA/TAIWAN 1951-54, 1967; BURMA 1952-61; TIBET 1959-69; THAILAND 1960-73; LAOS 1962-71; INDONESIA 1958; IRAN 1953; GUATEMALA 1954; COSTA RICA 1955, 1959-61; HUNGARY 1956; CAMBODIA 1958-59; THE DOMINICAN REPUBLIC 1960-61; CUBA 1960-65; BRITISH GUIANA (GUYANA) 1963-64; CHILE 1962-73; ECUADOR 1960-63; URUGUAY 1964-66; MEXICO 1967-68; BOLIVIA 1967; THE CONGO/ZAIRE 1964; GHANA 1966; ANGOLA 1965/1975; WEST GERMANY 1963; THE UNITED STATES 1952-67; IRAQ (KURDS) 1972-75; AFGHANISTAN 1979-89; LIBYA 1981/1984; EL SALVADOR 1980; NICARAGUA 1981-87;

FIGURE 19-1. CIA COVERT OPERATIONS

Lansdale's success in the Philippines inspired President Eisenhower to have him try the same tactics in Vietnam. Although Eisenhower warned against getting involved in a "land war" in Asia, the CIA's proprietary airline CAT airlifted supplies to the beleaguered French at Dien Bien Phu in 1954. After the French were defeated and Indochina was divided in compliance with the Geneva Accords, the Eisenhower administration concentrated on South Vietnam as the place to stop "the dominoes from falling." Lansdale gave his support to Ngo Dinh Diem, an anti-Communist leader who had also opposed the French and Japanese, and engineered his election to the presidency in 1955. But Diem was no Magsaysay. He and his brother, Ngo Dihn Nhu, proved to be corrupt and repressive. This led to Lansdale's departure and created in time a made-to-order situation for the Communist Viet Cong and the North. Moreover, the usually astute Lansdale had intervened in favor of a Roman Catholic in a predominantly Buddhist nation. On November 1, 1963, as U.S. involvement in Vietnam was deepening, Diem and his brother were overthrown and subsequently assassinated. The CIA had put Diem in power and had now removed him after secretly conspiring with a group of army generals.

***

The CIA intervention in Guatemala stirred up a great deal of ill will toward the United States in Latin America. Even moderate, pro-United States leaders in the region, who had shunned the Arbenz regime, now complained about a Yankee double standard that used "free world" rhetoric against communism but that ignored the transgressions of right-wing tyrants. President Jose Figueres of Costa Rica, for one, urged the United States to stop arming dictators and to fight communism by eradicating poverty and injustice in Latin America. His urgings led to his becoming involved with the CIA as a target of intervention himself and, then, as an "agent of influence."

In the mid-1950s, Figueres was one of the Caribbean's few progressive leaders to hold office. He condemned the region's dictators and permitted political exiles to engage in conspiratorial activities on Costa Rican soil. Figueres's policy riled Nicaragua's Somoza, who, encouraged by the events in Guatemala, decided it was time to get rid of his annoying neighbor. Citing evidence that Figueres had abetted an assassination attempt against him in April 1954, Somoza helped Figueres's enemies launch an invasion of Costa Rica from Nicaragua in January 1955. Figueres had played a dangerous game, but he had also abolished the Costa Rican army, which forced him to appeal to the Organization of American States to protect his country from Somoza's aggression. The OAS, with the concurrence of the U.S. representative, ordered a cease-fire and sent a delegation to Costa Rica for an on-site investigation.

At that point, Somoza realized that he had to act quickly. He called in his IOU from the CIA. He had permitted the CIA to use Las Mercedes Airport, outside Managua, as a base for its P-47s during the Guatemalan intervention. Now he wanted the planes that were parked there to help him in his feud with Figueres. On

January 15, three days after the OAS action, a P-47 Thunderbolt violated Costa Rican airspace and bombed and strafed a number of Costa Rican towns. Figueres, alarmed by this escalation, pointed out that Costa Rica had no defense against "modern weapons" of this kind and again appealed to the OAS. The council of the organization immediately authorized the United States to sell four F-51 Mustang fighters to Costa Rica for a dollar apiece. The State Department, responding to pressure from certain U.S. congressmen and sensing an opportunity to improve America's image in Latin America after Guatemala, came to the rescue and preserved the Caribbean's "lone democrat." Its gesture ended the "invasion," and the State Department scored one over the CIA.

But the roles were soon reversed. Within the State Department, Assistant Secretary of State for Inter-American Affairs Henry F. Holland considered Figueres a "troublemaker." He rebuked him for his interventionism and refused to take seriously his warning of "reform now, or revolution later." Meanwhile, the CIA acting covertly hedged its bets when Latin American dictators started to slip toward the end of the 1950s and after the rise of Fidel Castro. Cord Meyer, chief of the DDP's International Organizations Division, was already intervening in behalf of the non-Communist left and extended CIA support to Figueres in the wake of the so-called Nixon riots in the spring of 1958.

Americans were shocked by that series of hostile demonstrations during Nixon's "goodwill" tour of Latin America. They climaxed in May in Caracas, where a mob stoned and spat upon the vice president's motorcade and threatened his life. At the invitation of Representative Charles Porter of Oregon, Figueres (at the time, just out of office) came to Washington to explain what had caused these events. "People cannot spit on a foreign policy," Figueres told a House committee, "which is what they meant to do." Figueres insisted that Latin America supported the United States in the cold war, but he asked, "If you talk human dignity to Russia, why do you hesitate so much to talk human dignity to the Dominican Republic?" He testified that the United States must change its policy in Latin America and that it could not sacrifice human rights for "investments."

But the best that Figueres could do was to induce the CIA to help Latin America's liberals secretly. The CIA gave him money to publish a political journal, Combate, and to sponsor the founding meeting of the Institute of Political Education in Costa Rica in November 1959. The institute was organized as a training school and a center for political collaboration for political parties of the democratic left, principally from Costa Rica, Cuba (in exile), the Dominican Republic (in exile), Guatemala, Honduras, Nicaragua (in exile), Panama, Peru, and Venezuela. The CIA concealed its role from most of the participants except Figueres. Its funds passed first to a shell foundation, then to the Kaplan Fund of New York, next to the Institute for International Labor Research (IILR) located in New York, and finally to San Jose. Socialist leader Norman Thomas headed the IILR. After the CIA connection was revealed, Thomas maintained that he had been unaware of it, but the IILR's treasurer, Sacha Volman, who also became treasurer of the institute in San Jose, was a CIA agent. The CIAused Volman to monitor the institute, and Meyer collaborated directly with Figueres.

Meyer came to San Jose sometime in the summer of 1960. He and Figueres created the Inter-American Democratic Social Movement (INADESMO), which was nothing more than a front. A flier describing the idealistic purpose of INADESMO carried the same post office box as Figueres's personal letterhead. The INADESMO setup enabled Meyer to disperse funds more directly, without having to bother with conduits or the accounting procedures of the institute. For example, INADESMO contributed $10,000 to help finance the First Conference of Popular Parties of Latin America in Lima, Peru, in August 1960.

The following May, Meyer returned to San Jose for a more urgent purpose. In the wake of the Bay of Pigs failure, he provided Figueres with INADESMO funds to sponsor a meeting at his farm (May 12-20) between the leaders of the principal Dominican exile movements, Juan Bosch and Horacio Ornes. With Figueres as sponsor, Bosch and Ornes agreed to form a coalition government in anticipation of the overthrow of dictator Rafael Trujillo. As the United States moved to rally the hemisphere against Fidel Castro, Trujillo had become expendable, because the United States needed to demonstrate that it opposed all dictators, not just those on the left.

For over a year, the CIA had been in contact also with dissidents inside the Dominican Republic who argued that assassination was the only certain way to remove Trujillo. The CIA station in Ciudad Trujillo (now Santo Domingo) had encouraged the dissidents and actually delivered to them three pistols and three carbines "attendant to their projected efforts to neutralize Trujillo." Because the Bay of Pigs failure created an uncertain situation, the United States tried to put the brakes on this operation and refused to pass along additional weapons to the dissidents which the Dominican station already had, specifically M-3 machine guns. The National Security Council, meeting on May 5, "noted the President's view that the United States should not initiate the overthrow of Trujillo before [knowing] what government would succeed him."

On May 30, Trujillo was ambushed and assassinated. The same "action group" with whom the CIA had been in contact and to whom it had delivered pistols and carbines carried out the attack. According to the 1975 report of the Church Committee, there was "no direct evidence" that CIA weapons had been used in the assassinations and the effect of the Bosch-Ornes pact upon the events that transpired remains a matter for speculation. Nonetheless, the CIA described its role in "changing" the government of the Dominican Republic "as a 'success' in that it assisted in moving the Dominican Republic from a totalitarian dictatorship to a Western-style democracy." Bosch himself was elected president of the Dominican Republic. Sacha Volman followed him there, establishing a new "research and publication center" and taking with him the CIA funding that used to go to Figueres in Costa Rica. Though one cannot prove that there was a coordinated link between the external and internal opposition groups, Meyer was in a position to know what both elements were doing. In March 1962, Meyer's IOD was merged with the Covert Action staff, and Meyer became chief of the new and enlarged unit.

In this review of Meyer's activities in Costa Rica and the Dominican Republic, there have been repeated references to Fidel Castro and the Cuban Revolution. In fact, most of the CIA's clandestine operations in Latin America during the 1960s occurred in the context of Cuban developments.

Elsewhere in the hemisphere, too, CIA actions had the objective, "No more Cubas." In British Guiana (which became independent Guyana in 1966), the CIA worked through its assets in the international trade union movement to topple the pro-Communist government of Prime Minister Cheddi Jagan. In the early 1960s, Jagan had made friendly overtures toward Castro and had chosen to make the labor unions a factor in his bid for absolute power. In 1963 and 1964, the American Federation of Labor (AFL) and its international allies, the Inter-American Regional Labor Organization (ORIT) and the International Confederation of Free Trade Unions (ICFTU), helped stage an eighty-day general strike that prevented Jagan's takeover of the unions and led to his eventual political defeat.

Tom Braden later revealed that when he was head of the IOD, he had passed money to American labor leaders to fight Communist labor unions in Italy and Germany. Columnist Drew Pearson wrote, "Jay Lovestone, sometimes called [AFL-CIO president George] Meany's minister of foreign affairs . . . takes orders from Cord Meyer [Braden's successor] of the CIA." Lovestone, who was appointed executive secretary of the AFL Free Trade Union Committee after World War II and a dedicated cold warrior, needed little prodding from Braden and Meyer in opposing Communist influence in the international labor movement. At about the time that Meyer took charge of expanded operations in international organizations as chief of the Covert Action staff, Lovestone helped create the American Institute of Free Labor Development (AIFLD) for the purpose of training labor leaders in Latin America in labor organizing techniques and tactics. The AIFLD was one of several

AFL-CIO entities that received covert funding from the CIA; Philip Agee alleged that its collaboration with CIA stations abroad was extremely close, amounting to a "country-team effort."

In the British Guiana case, Jagan accused the AIFLD of intervening in the general strike and denounced its executive director, Serafino Romualdi. Romualdi, the AFL's long-time "roving ambassador" in Latin America, did not deny the charge but showed only nonchalance: "I simply put at the disposal of the strike committee the services of six graduates of [AIFLD]. . . . who were working as interns with various local unions. They performed so well that one of them, David Persaud, later was elected President of the BGTUC [British Guiana Trade Union Congress].'" In reality, the operation had not been simple. The strike became very violent and had taken a toll of 160 lives and required huge sums of money to sustain. Jagan insisted that there were eleven, not six, AIFLD graduates active in the strike, and one critic claimed there were "more visitors to that tiny country in the name of 'labor solidarity' in 18 months than in the previous 18 years." Romualdi charged that Cuba and Russia had acted as "strikebreakers" by shipping food and fuel to Jagan, but, in the end, before British Guiana became independent, Jagan was out as premier.

Jagan's defeat paralleled another CIA initiative, at the other end of South America in Chile. The CIA's intervention in Chile began in 1962, with a $50,000 covert contribution to the Christian Democratic party; it lasted through 1970-73, when it made an $8 million expenditure to oppose the government of Salvador Allende. Chile, a nation with a democratic tradition and chronic economic ills, troubled the United States because its leftist political parties appeared to be capable of achieving electoral victory. During the period 1962-69, the United States provided Chile with more than a billion dollars in direct, overt economic assistance to improve economic and social conditions. During the same period, the CIA acted covertly to strengthen the Christian Democratic party as the most viable reformist movement. It expended during a fifteen-year period of discreet cooperation...was based on a shared commitment to a common purpose. The NSA leadership wanted to cooperate with democratic and representative university student groups abroad and to oppose the attempt of the Communists to dominate the international student community. The Agency shared that objective and was prepared to help them achieve what they had already decided to do. "II The students had been denied open support by the State Department and Congress because "they were considered too far to the left in the general climate of McCarthyism and anti-intellectualism of the 1950s. They had then turned to the CIA and accepted its secret funding. Under the arrangement, "CIA funds would support only the international division of the National Student Association; only the NSA President and the International Affairs Vice President would be witting of the CIA connection. Each year, after the election of new student leaders, the CIAheld a secret briefing for the new officers, and elicited from them a secrecy agreement."

Despite the seeming "blank check" relationship between the CIA and the NSA, the Agency in fact made "operational use" of individual students. Students attending world youth congresses were asked to report on "Soviet and Third World personalities" and to observe "Soviet security practices." In 1957, a U.S. student delegate to the Sixth World Youth Festival in Moscow "was instructed to report on Soviet counterintelligence measures and to purchase a piece of Soviet-manufactured equipment. Besides these actions pertaining to the international sphere, the CIA intruded upon the functioning of NSA itself by influencing the selection of officers, spotting sympathetic leaders and promoting their candidacies. It was this latter aspect that created the greatest furor.

Immediately after the publication of the *Ramparts* article about the NSA, the New York Times and the Washington Post published lists of private American organizations and foundations that had received CIA secret funding. The presence of educational and private voluntary organizations, labor unions, elements of the media, and religious groups on the list aroused grave concerns about the effects of CIA operations upon the "independence and to insist upon human rights compliance and unload associations with dictators without developing viable alternatives. However, such policy decisions could be firmly pursued through open diplomacy (without returning to the days of Cord Meyer and the covert funding of the non-Communist left, as much to deceive the Congress and the American people as to protect secrets). Carter's failure to force Anastasio Somoza to leave Nicaragua in January 1979 was a policy error and had no relationship to the status of Clandestine Services.

That Clandestine Services had declined, there was little doubt. Even the Carter administration tried "to resurrect covert action" in 1980 '41 after events brought President Carter around to George Kennan's thinking of thirty years earlier. The idea of a contingency force was updated, as stated by Stansfield Turner: "the talent necessary for covert action is available in the CIA and it must be preserved." Carter extended covert support "to opponents of the Sandinistas," including "newsprint and funds to keep the [opposition] newspaper La Prensa alive,"50 and he responded to the Soviet invasion of Afghanistan in December 1979 with covert arms shipments to Afghan rebels. U.S. intelligence was not caught unawares by the Soviet invasion of Afghanistan, as Carter's critics charged, but Carter, shocked by Soviet recklessness, resorted to covert action to "punish the Soviets," since going to war "wasn't feasible."" The. tragic clandestine rescue mission that was aborted in the Iranian desert in April 1980 was a failure, but it was no more a failure than the Bay of Pigs in the heyday of Allen Dulles.

If Carter's "failures" were also "intelligence failures," the problem was in the function of clandestine intelligence collection (HUMINT). In reforming Clandestine Services, no one had made clear the distinction between foreign intelligence or espionage and covert action. When Ranelagh affirmed that the CIA under Carter and Turner had "lost the quality of being special,"51 he overlooked the fact that the FI people had lost out a long time before (to say nothing of the DDI analysts). Turner's purge of two hundred covert operators did not ruin the CIA, and Carter's problems in foreign affairs were more complex than his obvious disdain for covert action.

STEAMSHOVEL PRESS

VIRTUAL GOVERNMENT
BY ALEX CONSTANTINE
AVAILABLE FROM FERAL HOUSE.

I. MOCKINGBIRDGATE

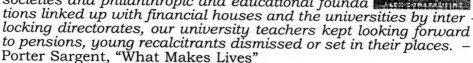

So the muckrakers were suppressed, the news papers were reduced, brought into safe hands, writers were controlled, books privately censored, publishing houses bought into and influenced, peace societies and philanthropic and educational founda tions linked up with financial houses and the universities by inter-locking directorates, our university teachers kept looking forward to pensions, young recalcitrants dismissed or set in their places. – Porter Sargent, "What Makes Lives"

The seeding of public opinion, often explained (when the straining dams of secrecy leak) as a necessary reaction to Communism, has since served to conceal the criminalization of the intelligence agencies. The CIA's early forays into mind control experimentation on unconsenting subjects, for example, were justified by an ersatz cover story that POWs of the Korean War had been "brainwashed" by their captors. In fact, the Army investigation was unable to document a single case of "brainwashing' among the prisoners released by the North Koreans. The word was coined by Edward Hunter, a veteran OSS propagandist recruited by Dulles, the Nazi-collaborating oligarch who, in fact, conceived of MOCKINGBIRD as a mass mind control operation.

The Korean War itself was urged along by propaganda oozing from the front pages of the country's leading newspapers. A detailed study of the disinformation assault, I. F. Stone's *Hidden History of the Korean War*, first appeared in 1952. The book sold well overseas, but in the States, as explained in a note from the publisher in later editions, it "met with an almost complete press blackout and boycott. The book has almost entirely *disappeared*, even from public libraries, and it rare turns up in the second-hand book market."

The muckracking era was yesterday's coffee grounds—corporate franchising of the print media saw to it. "When it began," lamented George Seldes in *1000 Americans*, a survey of American corporate power published in 1947, muckraking journalism had advocates in "A people who had the general welfare at heart, but as the probes went deeper and further, and seemed to spare none of the hidden powers, the politicians as well as other spokesmen for money, business and profiteering turned savagely upon the really free press and *destroyed* it... Trash may indeed be the opium of the people, but it was not the real aim of the magazines to stupefy the public, merely to suppress the facts, merely to pullify, to create a wasteland."

A Niagara of pro-American propaganda sponsored by the U.S. Information Agency (USIA), a CIA symbiont, shaped domestic and foreign political sensibilities beginning in the early 1950s. In this period, a niagara of books with USIA funding were disseminated by Praeger, Inc., the Franklin Press and other publishing houses bearing, of course, no indication of their actual origin.

By the mid-Reagan era, the USIA would spend nearly a billion dollars per anum to export propagandizing magazines, books (an average of three million a year) and exhibitions. The Agency sponsored ten magazines and commercial bulletins in twenty languages, including *Topic* (South Africa) and a radio teletype network that disseminated propaganda to 159 outlets overseas. Some 200 films acquired from private domestic studios were distributed, and a television program entitled *Worldnet*.

The CIA came to dominate the Monopoly board of the corporate press, and drew a card from the stack marked with that monocled millionaire in the top hat (bearing a curious resemblance to Allen Dulles) calling for a strategy of psychological warfare, the art of calculated deceit, often with catastrophic results.

Cord Meyer, Jr., the ranking Mockingbird in Europe, then a *Newsweek* correspondent, swung widely throughout Europe inciting student and union protests. "This localized psychological warfare is ultimately, of course, warfare against the Russians," Davis emphasized, "who are presumed to be the source of every leftist political sentiment in Italy, France, the entire theater of Meyer's operations. In Eastern Europe his aim [was] to foment rebellion. (*Steamshovel* Debris: Click here for a *Portland Free Press* report on Gloria Steinem's early connection to this operation.)

GLORIA STEINEM AND THE CIA
BY DANIEL BRANDT

Excerpted from *Portland Free Press* March/April 1997

If you don't know who John McCoy was, suffice it to say that he was chairman of Rockefeller's Chase Manhattan Bank and was a key figure in U.S. cold war strategy. Other names mentioned below, C.D. Jackson and Cord Meyer, were top figures in U.S. intelligence. Since there are only several paragraphs that mention Steinem - on two pages from the text and one from the footnotes - I will quote them in full. The source is Kai Bird, *The Chairman: John J. McCloy and the Making of the American Establishment* (New York: Simon & Schuster, 1992), pp. 483-84, 727. Note that Bird's documentation includes a letter from Steinem to Jackson while she was getting money from the CIA:

"In the summer of 1959, just before McCloy took his family for an extended trip to Europe, C.D. Jackson wrote to remind McCloy that later that sunnner a World Youth Festival was scheduled to take place in Vienna. Jackson asked McCloy to contribute an article, perhaps on the "benign and constructive aspects" of the U.S. occupation of Germany. The piece would appear in a daily newspaper to be published in Vienna in conjunction with the festival. McCloy agreed, and the article was published (in five languages) in a newspaper distributed by a twenty-five-year-old Smith graduate named Gloria Steinem.

"McCloy's connection to Steinem went beyond contributing an article to the propaganda operation of which she was an editor in Vienna. Late in 1958, he and Jackson had discussed how the United States should respond to the expected Soviet propaganda blitz in Vienna. Previous gatherings of this kind had always been held in Moscow, East Berlin, or other cities in Eastern Europe. These events were major propaganda circuses, and the CIA was determined, in the words of Cord Meyer, a career CIA officer, 'to compete more effectively with this obviously successftil Communist apparatus.'

"Washington expected some twenty thousand students and young scholars from all over the world to converge on Vienna that summer for the three weel festival. Consequently, the CIA wanted an organized student presence in Vienna in order to counter Soviet propaganda.

"C.D. Jackson recognized the Vienna Youth Festival as 'an extremely important event in the Great Game.' He explained, 'This is the first time commies have held one of these shindigs on our side of the iron curtain; and what goes on, how it goes on, and what the follow-up will be is, I think, extremely important.'

"By the time Jackson first approached McCloy, in the autumn of 1958, he and Cord Meyer, head of the CIA's International Organizations division (IO), had a plan. The Agency would provide discreet funding to an 'informal group of activists' who would constitute themselves as an alternative American delegation to the festival. The CIA would not only pay their way but also assist them to distribute books and publish a newspaper in Vienna. Among other individuals, Jackson and Meyer hired Gloria Steinem to work with them. Steinem had recently returned from a two-year stint in India, where she had been a Chester

Bowles Asian Fellow.

"'I came home in 1958,' Steinem later explained, 'full of idealism and activism, to discover that very little was being done. ... Private money receded at the mention of a Communist youth festival.' Convinced that a contingent of liberal but anticommunist American students should go to Vienna, she heard through her contacts at the National Student Association that there might be funding available to finance American participation in the festival. Working through C.D. Jackson and Cord Meyer, Steinem then set up an organization in Cambridge, Massachusetts called the Independent Service for Information on the Vienna Youth Festival. She obtained tax-exempt status, and Jackson helped her raise contributions from various American corporations, including the American Express Company. But most of the money came from the CIA, to be managed by Jackson in a 'special account.' The entire operation cost in the range of $85,000, a not inconsiderable sum in those years. (Steinem's organization, later renamed the Independent Research Service, continued to receive support from the CIA through 1962, when it financed an American delegation to the Helsinki Youth Festival.) Steinem ended up working closely with Samuel S. Walker, Jr., vice-president of the CIA-funded Free Europe Committee. Because

the Austrians did not want to be associated with the Free Europe Committee, the Agency set up a commercial front called the Publications Development Corporation (PDC). Walker was made president of this dummy corporation, funded in part by 'a confidential one-year contract' worth $273,000 from the Free Europe Committee. His job was to supervise the book-and-newspaper operation at the Youth Festival. . .

In 1956, "the CIA learns that the Soviets will indeed kill 60,000 MOCKINGBIRD-roused Hungarians with armored ranks.'" Nevertheless, Radio Free Europe urged the people of Hungary to resist the Kremlin, the conclusion of an investigative committee of the UN: Many Hungarians "had the feeling that Radio Free Europe promised help." They believed military aid from the West would arrive to back an uprising. On November 5, a year later, a dry, unsteady voice crackled through the static of a Hungarian radio station:

Attention: Radio Free Europe, hello. Attention. This is Roka speaking. The radio of revolutionary youth Continual bombing. Help. help. help Radio Free Europe forward our request. Forward our news. Help...

And on November 6, another broadcast:

We appeal to the conscience of the world. Why cannot you hear the call for help of our murdered women and children? Have you received our transmission?

Attention! Attention! Munich! Munich! Take immediate action. In the Dunapentele area we urgently need medicine, bandages, arms, food and ammunition.

The final transmission, 24 hours later:

Must we appeal once again? We have wounded ... who have given their blood for the sacred cause of liberty, but we have no bandages ... no medicine. The last piece of bread has been eaten.

Those who have died for liberty ... accuse you who are able to help and who have not helped. We have read an appeal to the UN and every honest man. Radio Free Europe, Munich! Radio Free Europe, Munich ...

Operation MOCKINGBIRD was an immense financial undertaking. Funds flowed from the CIAlargely through the Congress for Cultural Freedom (CCF), founded by Tom Braden, a "liberal" who would make his mark as a syndicated columnist and co-host of CNN's *Crossfire* opposite Ultracon Pat Buchanan. The CCF was founded in June, 1950 by prominent academics assembled in Berlin's U.S. zone at the Titania Palace Theater. The CCF, directed by Denis de Rougemont, was formed to "defend freedom and democracy against the new tyranny sweeping the world." About 20 periodicals were financed by the front, including *Encounter in the UK, The New Leader, Africa Report* and *El Mundo Nuevo* in Latin America.

STEAMSHOVEL PRESS

THE CONSPIRACIST

The following interview with *Steamshovel* editor Kenn Thomas appeared in *Immerse*, a techno/ambient/atmospherica/ industrial/noise/jazz/electronics/ forteana/graphics/film/print zine produced in the UK. The issue (003) also included an interview with *Saucer Smear*'s James "It was a Fugo balloon; no it was a Mogul balloon" Moseley and gives some attention to Philip "'twasn't nothin'" Klass. Visit *Immerse* at www.haywire.co.uk/immerse.

Steamshovel Press is the bible of conspiracy theory. Kenn Thomas is the editor of this quarterly collection of snapshots from the dark side of reality. From the JFK assassination and Watergate to Area 51 and the Octopus cabal, *Steamshovel* is the acknowledged authority.

A NEED TO KNOW

Kenn began his quest for the truth, or at least a plausible version of it, at the ripe old age of five. Although he certainly wasn't conscious of the fact, something happened which would shape his perceptions for years to come. "When I was five years old they shot JFK! It guaranteed that one of my strongest early memories always would be of conspiracy. In a conscious way, though, as a reader and student of Conspiracy, the best I can track it is back to comedian Lenny Bruce. My early abiding interest in Bruce's comedy led me to Paul Krassner's *The Realist* (Krassner ghosted Bruce's autobiography), and from that I learned about the work of Mae Brussell, the intellectual foremother of conspiracy research in the US." Such synchronicity still lends a guiding hand. "Recently, while looking at my copy of Bruce's 1957 samizdat booklet, *Stamp Help Out!*, I noticed reference to Wilhelm Reich, which I thought was rather far out. In 1957 Reich was embroiled in his final battle with the Con, and it killed him. Bruce eventually came to understand that his own life was ruined by a police conspiracy." Kenn's abiding interests in both hidden history and the works of the 'beat' generation of Ginsberg, Kerouac and Burroughs led to the first early attempts at formulating a fanzine of sorts. "Steamshovel began as a small newsletter circulated primarily to convince book publishers to send review copies of books. It had a secondary purpose of presenting an interview with Ram Dass I conducted that I was unable to get published elsewhere. This story is recounted in the introduction to the *Steamshovel* back issue anthology, *Popular*

Alienation.

"Like most writers, I resent the predicament of having to do work without guarantee that it will be published and paid for, so *Steamshovel* became my outlet for writing that I didn't already have pre-sold. At the time, I worked as the rock music critic for a daily newspaper and was getting a lot of things published in local and regional newspapers and magazines. I began to notice, however, that the more I wrote about things that interested me, the less I had to say in the mainstream forum."

GENESIS OF AN INQUIRING MIND

The early issues of *Steamshovel* included an interview with Imamu Amiri Baraka and it was Baraka's connection with the New York branch of the Fair Play For Cuba Committee, of which Lee Harvey Oswald was the sole member of the New Orleans chapter, which propelled *Steamshovel* in a more conspiracy driven direction. "By the time of the third issue of *Steamshovel*, Mae Brussell had died and Bob Banner, who published a quality conzine called *Critique*, abandoned his effort. Conspiracy culture seemed waning. This happened in the late 1980s: factional fighting beset Mae Brussell's admirers; Oliver Stone's *JFK* movie and that damned *X-Files* show were well into the future; even the impact of the Internet had not yet been felt fully. "In a panic, I published a call for papers on conspiracy topics for publication in the following issue. At the time also, I developed a friendship with someone who had access to printing equipment. With all the conspiracy-related articles and the free printing, *Steamshovel* number four became the first magazine-sized issue. Money from selling that issue paid for the subsequent issues and I started doing the legwork to get distribution. "The current issue of *Steamshovel* has an interview with the late great Tim Leary and reproduces a Catholic Charities report on Neal Cassady. So that 'beatnik' thing remains an important part of the magazine. There's even a newsclipping reproduction I took from a New Orleans paper in the 1960s: Do Newspaper Boys Grow Up To Be Beatniks? 'Beatnik' is a vague concept to begin with—it defines everybody from Woody Guthrie to John Lilly— (it's actually a red smear, as in 'Sputnik') and difficult to measure. The only thing the New Orleans paper could say was that you could hardly call Bob Hope one. This new *Steamshovel* also has a nine-page article on David Ferrie, Lee Harvey Oswald's albino pilot buddy, who lived a 'beatnik' lifestyle."

THE CONSPIRATORS' HIERARCHY

Along the way Kenn has been aided by many in the loose knit research community, most of whom have been published in *Steamshovel*'s pages. Many have become close colleagues, one such gentleman being the prolific author Jim Keith, an Immerse icon and penman of classics like *Secret & Suppressed, Casebook On Alternative 3, Black Helicopters Over America* and *OKBOMB*. "I met Jim Keith in the flesh first in Atlanta, Georgia at the Phenomicon conference. I knew of him previously from his zine *Dharma Combat*, which published many interesting writers from the marginals arena, including G. J. Krupey, Wayne Henderson and X. Sharks DeSpot, all of whom later wrote for *Steamshovel*. After the Heaven's Gate deaths, I pointed out to Keith that one of the dead, someone named Darwin Lee Phillips, previously played with a rock band called Dharma Combat. Keith remembered that he gave permission for the band to use the name. It's possible that Phillips found out about the Heaven's Gate group through its ad in *Steamshovel* #9. That makes *Steamshovel* as guilty as the Hale-Bopp comet for that Heaven's Gate disaster!" Another well known comrade in arms has been Jim Martin of the mail order Flatland Books. "I think I attracted Jim Martin's attention with an article on Reich in *Steamshovel* #2. Martin had a tremendous insight for seeing something of value in *Steamshovel* as it looked back then. If I had thought of his Flatland book service at the time, I would have felt (there was) less of a threat to the kind of marginals/conspiracy material I thought was disappearing and may not have developed

Steamshovel into a zine. He gave tremendous guidance on what to do and how to do it, from his experience as a printer and bookseller, and Flatland remains one of the best places to find this stuff."

ECONOMICS AND THE CON

Even with such assistance from the researchers themselves, *Steamshovel* is still plagued by the economics of magazine publication, something *Immerse* is only too aware of. "Both subscriptions and news stand sales rise with each issue and I have a hard time holding on to back issue stock, even with the *PopAlien* anthology. Unfortunately, *Steamshovel*'s chief distributor, Fine Print, just declared bankruptcy. The thousands of dollars it owes *Steamshovel* appear somewhere at the bottom of a list of 2200 creditors and *Steamshovel* may never see the money. That is currently slowing down production of the next issue considerably. Zine distributors are notoriously unreliable business partners. Even when they do what they're supposed to do, they have unfair returns policies and sales practices that I'm told are rooted in the Mafia. I always am forced to find a book project or hit the lecture trail just to raise money to produce the new issue. Zine economics are so bizarre that even success does not guarantee future success."

THE OCTOPUS

Steamshovel's editor has been involved in several book projects. The previously mentioned *Popular Alienation* collected together the contents of most of the back issues, albeit devoid of ad copy (so if you want to see the advertisement for the Heavens Gate suicide cult you'll have to chase down a copy of #9). Recent titles include *NASA, Nazis & JFK: The Torbitt Document* and *The Octopus: Secret Government And The Death Of Danny Casolaro*. The book on Casolaro's research, co-authored with Jim Keith, has ensured some recent publicity as has the phenomenal success of 'conspiracy as soap opera' television programmes like *The X Files* and *Dark Skies*. "The media profile has increased a lot recently due to the publication of *The Octopus*. I'm doing a lot of print and radio promotion for that. It covers the case of Danny Casolaro, who died under mysterious circumstances while he was investigating the Justice Department theft of the PROMIS computer software, the Inslaw case. "Casolaro was waiting for the book contract to come forward, with all that he knew, if he had kept a larger media profile, he may not have suffered his fate. *Crossfire*, a popular cable news program here, wanted to have me on in the wake of Heaven's Gate, but I was busy visiting David Hatcher Childress's clubhouse outside of Chicago, looking actually to meet up with *Nexus* publisher Duncan Roads who never showed. Jonathan Vankin, author of *60 Greatest Conspiracies*, did make that program, however, but they changed his title from the derisive 'conspiracy theorist' to 'internet researcher', the new bugaboo. "The major media always warps things into unrecognisable dimensions. The CBS program *60 Minutes* wasted an hour and a half of Vankin's time with an interview for a feature that only briefly flashed his website. In recent weeks I have talked to producers from two British documentary teams, one person from the Discovery channel, and someone else from an HBO special on the making of Mel Gibson's 'Conspiracy Theory' movie. I doubt if any of that will amount to substantial publicity for *Steamshovel*."

TORBITT

The new edition of the Torbitt document which Kenn has worked on has also recently been published, under the title *NASA, Nazis & JFK*. For the uninitiated, The Torbitt document was a manuscript written by a Texan lawyer under the pseudonym of William Torbitt and which claimed to illuminate the inside workings of the military-industrial cabal who may have murdered JFK. We asked for Kenn's comments on this seminal document. "The second printing of *NASA, Nazis & JFK*, which is the title for the edition of the Torbitt that I annotated and introduced for Adventures Unlimited Press includes an afterward by Len Bracken making the case that it might be Soviet disinformation. My annotations were designed to emphasise what the Torbitt has to say about the Paperclip Nazi role in the assassination, which is certainly not the main point of the document. "Martin Cannon and *Lobster* editor Robin Ramsay have both complained that there doesn't seem to be any independent verification for the existence of Defense Industrial Security Command (DISC), the police agency that the Torbitt holds out as culpable in the assassination. I have argued that veteran researcher Penn Jones wrote about DISC (although his source may have been Torbitt); that a lawsuit was filed in California over a call made by Oswald to a DISC agent in Raleigh, North Carolina; that the address of the agency's headquarters should be listed in the city directory of Columbus, Ohio from 1963; and that (famed JFK researcher, John) Judge connected the group to Kerr-McGee and the Karen Silkwood murder. Look it up in the current DC phone book and you'll find something called the Director of Industrial Security-Capital Region, which basically retains the DISC acronym. So it's real. I think the best thing about the Torbitt is the view it presents of transnational corporations and how intelligence services work for them and not the country they ostensibly represent." Kenn is working on two new projects as well as attempting to get the next issue of *Steamshovel* together. "I am currently annotating and writing substantive introductory notes to *Were We Controlled?* by Lincoln Lawrence, a classic on mind control technology to be published this summer by David Hatcher Childress' Adventures Unlimited Press. The other is a book on the Maury Island incident, the first UFO sighting of the modern lore. This book will be based on correspondence by one of those involved, Fred Crisman, who also is suspected of being one of the tramps in the railroad yard at Dealy Plaza on assassination day. "At one time, Crisman had Marshall Riconosciuto as a business partner, whose son is Michael Riconosciuto, the chief informant in the Casolaro case. So that promises to be a fascinating look at conspiracies spanning the generations. IllumiNet will publish that within the next six months, in time for the 50th anniversary of the incident."

E-Conspiracy

Steamshovel have followed the trend in establishing a site on the world wide web but Kenn is a little dubious about the often heard suggestion that electronic publishing will replace the printing press. "I have noticed a pattern common with many websites: an initial enthusiasm where changes and updates are made often and then a tremendous drop off. Like putting up a billboard and walking away. *Steamshovel* has a link to a site that shows the word 'Shit!' lit up in the windows of a college building from a photo taken on the night of the Kennedy assassination. That site has been up there unchanged for three years. The *Steamshovel* site includes a column called *The Latest Word* containing material that never appears in the magazine. I change it often, but not as often as I would like. It's difficult to make that work pay, so the energy goes into work that keeps the magazine alive. *Steamshovel* will never become all-electronic. If I get to the point where I can change *The Latest Word* column every week, I expect to issue a challenge to other conspiracy websites to do the same. The *Steamshovel* website, by the way, is at www.umsl.edu/~skthoma.

Flame Wars

Since the popularisation of the Internet, conspiracy and even more so specifically UFO related sites have become very common-place. Along with this has come the inevitable gossip and rumour regarding and between researchers, something which plagues the UFO community to a great extent (as often reported by Jim Moseley in his irreverent newsletter Saucer Smear - see interview in this issue of Immerse).

"The acrimony that exists between many researchers bugs me. It seems to me fundamental to give everyone the right to be wrong, to suspend judgement until you can come to some complete understanding of various points of view, and simply to accept that multiple points of view on a topic is as final as some things get. I don't like anonymous flame wars on the net - although I understand the need to vent - and so I just do a lot of lurking until I find a productive conversation into which I can inject some research or analysis.

"One problem is that the intelligence community does have its assets, infiltrators and provocateurs, so honest disagreements become charged with the suspicion that one or the other side is spreading disinformation. In many cases, the charges are true. I had one such person follow me to London and demand an audience with a BBC producer I had traveled with to an infra-red imaging lab to test a Reichian orgone box. The same person has supplied disinformation about Reich to the so-called 'skeptics' press, including CSICOP (Committee For The Scientific Investigation Of Claims Of tTe Paranormal), *Skeptical Inquirer* and Martin Gardner, for many years. There's an essay about this on the *Steamshovel* webpage called Toxic Disinformation."

PHIL KLASS HIS "LITTLE NOBODIES"

Kenn's disparaging views of the sceptical community extends to the crown king of Ufological debunking, publisher of the *Skeptics UFO Newsletter* and many books on the subject, Phil Klass. Klass was interviewed by Immerse, along with Jim Moseley, at the 1997 Fortean Times UnConvention and that interview appears elsewhere in this magazine. Comparing and contrasting Kenn's and Phil's viewpoints is an interesting exercise.

"The last time I saw Phil Klass quoted in the *New York Times*, he sniffed that those who have UFO experiences are 'little nobodies' craving attention. It's obviously a prejudiced and unscientific point of view, especially concerning a phenomenon that has affected all kinds of people over all of human history, no matter what one thinks of any particular case or set of cases. I do think it's interesting that as the *Fortean Times* becomes more mainstream, it begins to have more people like Phil Klass show up at its conferences. Without putting too fine a point on it, since I do still have immense respect for the Forteans, when I sat on a panel with Peter Brookesmith at the last UnCon (in 1996 Kenn lectured on the Casolaro/Maury Island axis, Wilhelm Reich's persecution by the US Government and took part in a panel discussion on the topic of UFOs and Governments) he argued that Belgium could not be part of the international-al UFO cover-up because, well, *because they're Belgian!* He was being clever, of course, but it's the kind of quip, like Klass and his 'little nobodies' remark, that shows the rush toward a dismissal of the topic rather than engagement with it."

EXTRADIMENSIONAL UFOLOGY

"A much more reasoned point of view about UFOs than that of Phil Klass recently was expressed to me by *Steamshovel* contributor Roy Lisker, who is a scientist and a mathematician and has reached no closed-minded conclusions about the phenomenon:"

"...suppose that it was possible that a sentient consciousness in our world could exist entirely on the surface of a two-dimensional plane. This mind would be unable to conceive of a third dimension, except as an unpic-turable mathematical construction. If it were possible for one of us to com-municate with this being, we might say something like: "Don't you realise that all you have to do is go 'up'?" Say we then took a stone and dropped it through his plane. He would interpret this event, a simple causal phe-nomenon in our world, as an uncaused, arbitrary event in the physics of his world. However, the true causes of the disturbances created by the stone passing through his world would be intrinsically unknowable to him as the limitations on his consciousness do not give him access to the third dimension in which we live.

"Likewise, it 'ought to be obvious' to us, that all we have to do in order to enter a fourth (spatial) dimension is to go up* (the direction of "up-asterisk"!). Up* might then be a dimension which is unknowable to our consciousness-in-the-world by virtue of the limitation or our sensory organs to a three dimensional continuum. If there was a fourth spatial dimension then, just as in the example with the dropping of the rock, an event from that dimension could 'pass through' our world without our being able to reconcile it with our physics. Its causes would be 'intrinsically unknowable'.

"Still, four or more dimensions pose no problems for a mathematician. In terms of their purely mathematical content, one can easily plot lines, describe shapes and axiomatize any space with any number of dimensions. In fact, many of today's mathematicians are only comfortable in Hilbert's Space, the vector of space of infinitely many dimensions. Four dimensional space, therefore, is not 'unthinkable' as a mathematical object; but a fourth dimension of physical space, if there is one, is unknowable to us, since no-one with a mind like ours can conceive any way of moving in the direction up*."

ALIEN SEX MAJIC

Along with the idea of extradimensional/ultraterrestrial entities, another plausible theory is the 'alien craft as black project and alien abduction as mind control'. Chief proponents of this theory are Martin Cannon, author of *The Controllers*, and Alex Constantine, author of *Psychic Dictatorship In The USA*.

"Reich said it best: 'everyone has part of the truth'. Cannon and Constantine have both presented convincing cases that many alien abduction scenarios serve as government psyops (psychological warfare operations), as has Jacques Vallee. John Judge makes a good case that Nazis developed flying saucers. Certainly not all unusual aerial phenomena fall into this category, though, and not every abduction case tracks back to a psyop.

"Cannon and I had a tiff when I tried to get him to do a sidebar to an interview I planned in *Steamshovel* with Cathy O'Brien, who claims to have been made into a sex slave by an MKULTRA program. Cannon believes that O'Brien and her partner, Mark Phillips, are frauds who use details about a real mind-control program called Operation Monarch to embellish a dog-and-pony show. I wanted Cannon to do something on the real Monarch; he didn't want me to give O'Brien/Phillips any space at all. So it concerns me when any researcher thinks he has the one 'real' answer. It tends to strangle dialogue."

THE WILD SIDE

And what of Kenn's feelings on the convoluted tales of US government/grey alien treaties and hybridisation schemes of 'Wild' Bill Cooper and others of like mind.

"Everyone has part of the truth. Cooper's take on the Kennedy assassination, for instance, that the driver shot JFK with a .45, has elements of truth. The driver does put on the brakes; you can see them come on the Zapruder film. There are photos of an agent picking up a .45 slug from the opposite silde of Elm Street after the motorcade has passed. In fact, disinfo schemes always contain elements of truth, which is not to say that Cooper is a disinformationalist. He certainly didn't create the circus atmosphere that surrounds much of the UFO community.

"It's really the nature of the Beast: an aerial and psychological phenomenon that affects millions; governments hiding the data they have collected on it to preserve their credibility (which they lose as well if, as they say, they do not collect data on it); a history that has built up a lore; entrepreneurs trying to exploit the commercial possibilities of all this excitement.

Every researcher/writer/lecturer is a natural product of that spectacle."

DISINFOTAINMENT

Such reasoned and thought provoking views on the UFO topic are indeed rare in this days of supposed alien autopsy videos, grey and abduction 'mania', and disinfotainment like the *X Files*.

"Television is the very essence of the Conspiracy, a mind-control device that transmits stimulation for the eyes and ears but leaves the brain wanting. So *X-Files*, *Dark Skies*, even programs like *Fortean TV*, can never become more than part of the culture of denial. All this stuff about Area 51, alien abductions, government conspiracies, Fortean phenoms—it's all just fodder for a silly TV show. Students of the conspiracy culture, publishers of magazines like *Steamshovel*, become the 'Lone Gunman' geeks on *X-Files*. Meanwhile, *X-Files* writer Chris Carter lectures for the CSICOP, which happened recently."

OKBOMB

The ongoing trial of Oklahoma bombing suspect Tim McVeigh is another media circus waiting to happen but thus far seems not to have received the epic international proportions of the OJ Simpson trial. With talk of a decidedly conspiratorial defence strategy by McVeigh's attorneys, it may soon become a media led case of 'conspiracy on trial'.

"Lois Fortier just testified and even the mainstream news reports noted that her story sounded very rehearsed. She's the wife of McVeigh chum Steve Fortier. Both of them at first insisted that McVeigh could not have had anything to do with the bombing but when the FBI threatened them with the death sentence, they changed their story and made up the current one. *Steamshovel* reported on this in issue #14.

"Hoppy Heidelberg, the person whose common sense questions caused him to be dismissed from the original OKBomb grand jury, has stated openly that police authorities will not call in certain witnesses because they may be informers or *provocateurs* attached to government undercover operations. Apparently McVeigh isn't even telling his lawyers about who he worked with. He's either taking it all like a good soldier or they never got that mind control implant out of his butt (as detailed in *Immerse* 001). I cannot see how a conviction will arise out of all this, and I called it right when the criminal trial jury acquitted OJ Simpson. Anyone following the case in the papers would do well to read Jim Keith's *OKBomb!* book from IllumiNet. It asks all the pertinent questions."

TWA 800

The other current mass media 'conspiracy' story has been the TWA Flight 800 splashdown. We asked Kenn what the current climate's like - Stinger, US Navy friendly fire, mechanical failure or, as some of the more extremists have alleged, UFO?

"The theories now also must account for these continued sightings of missile-like objects in nearby airspace by pilots and airline passengers, as well as the eyewitnesses to the missile event when the plane came down. Pronouncement by the National Transportation Safety Board that mechanical failure took down TWA800 will satisfy nobody, especially anyone familiar with Sherman Skolnick's exposure of that agency's cover-up of the 1973 Chicago Midway crash that killed E. Howard Hunt's wife Dorothy and other Watergaters. Skolnick discussed this with *Steamshovel* in issue #11. The NTSB is now floating its TWA800 'mechanical failure' conclusion in the press to see how the airlines respond."

HISTORY IS A LIE

The mainstream press titillate the masses with coverage of 'wacky' conspiracy theories, which are more often than not more plausible than the official version. The history books are unfortunately much the same, the victors write the history and the first victim is the truth. Conspiracy theory is shunned as 'nutters talking about aliens and faked moon landings'.

"The process of tenure and promotion often involves conspiracy, if I under-stand university department politics correctly. So academics have a vested interest in steering away from the study of the process. After tenure, you find people like John Mack (tenured at Harvard) and Courtney Brown (tenured poli sci professor at Emory University who claims to also work as a remote viewer) who come forward with things. Also, educational bureaucracies must insist that they know the 'truth'about things, even though they mostly just regurgitate government and corporate media reports, which by any measure is a tiny, distorted part of the spectrum of available information. Many postal workers in this country keep better historical files than many history professors, who often work from pre-fabbed textbooks."

—Leigh Neville with Dashwood II

Steamshovel Press is available from PO Box 23716, St. Louis, MO 63121 at the current subscription rate for four issues at 26US dollars or 7US dollars per copy. *Steamshovel* also sells *Popular Alienation, NASA,Nazis & JFK,* and *The Octopus.* Kenn can be contacted via email at <u>kennthomas@umsl.edu</u> or browse *Steamshovel's* website by going to <u>http://www.umsl.edu/~skthoma</u>

steamshovel press

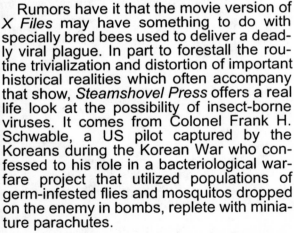

OF BUGS AND BOMBS
Introductory note by Kenn Thomas

Rumors have it that the movie version of *X Files* may have something to do with specially bred bees used to deliver a deadly viral plague. In part to forestall the routine trivialization and distortion of important historical realities which often accompany that show, *Steamshovel Press* offers a real life look at the possibility of insect-borne viruses. It comes from Colonel Frank H. Schwable, a US pilot captured by the Koreans during the Korean War who confessed to his role in a bacteriological warfare project that utilized populations of germ-infested flies and mosquitos dropped on the enemy in bombs, replete with miniature parachutes.

The story has another angle, however. It might have been coerced from Schwable under Korean brainwashing torture. Other airman captured during the Korean War claimed that similar "confessions" were forced from them.

After Korean complaints over the germ bug bombs, promised investigations by the International Red Cross and the World Health Organization never materialized. A 1952 scientific commission, which had as a member a witness to WWII Japanese germ warfare who spoke fluent Chinese, concluded that the charges were true. A preliminary investigation of Schwable after the war went nowhere. Secret post-WWII deals between the US and the infamous Shiro Ishii's Unit 731, the germ warfare program of imperial Japan, are documented by Jonathan Vankin in in *Steamshovel Press* #9.

Authors Jon Holliday and Bruce Cummings note in their history, *Korea The Unknown War* (Pantheon, 1988) that "The argument that probably carried the most weight [that Schwabel's charges were false] was that the USA could not have used a weapon as horrible as germ warfare, though nothing can be established by this assertion. The USA was engaged in germ-warfare research. It has employed Japanese and Nazi germ-warfare experts and was at the time rushing through work on the nerve gas Sarin, a chemical weapon that was banned by the Geneva convention. The evidence shows preparations for using germ warfare (which do not prove anything about whether it was used or not.)" Sarin gas, of course, is chemical weapon of choice for the Aum Shinrokyo sect.

Interestingly, after the Korean War US church groups began the Heifer Project, a program to rebuild the Korean insect population lost to the widespread use of DDT. It shipped over planeloads of honey bees.

U.S. WAGES GERM WARFARE IN KOREA STATEMENT OF PRISONER OF WAR, COLONEL FRANK H. SCHWABLE

Colonel Frank H. Schwable, 04429, former Chief of Staff of the United States First Marine Aircraft Wing, broadcasting in North Korea in February, 1953, the full details of the strategic plan and bacteriological warfare operations of American aircraft in Korea

The [North Korean] Hsinhua Agency has made public the following full text of the signed deposition made by Colonel Frank H. Schwable, Chief of staff of the U.S. First Marine Aircraft Wing, disclosing the strategic plan and aims of the American Command in waging germ warfare in Korea.

I am Colonel Frank H. Schwable, 04429, and was Chief of Staff of the First Marine Aircraft Wing until shot down and captured on July 8, 1952. My service with the Marine Corps began in 1929 and I was designated an aviator in 1931, seeing duty in many parts of the world. Just before I came to Korea, I completed a tour of duty in the Division of Aviation at Marine Corps Headquarters.

DIRECTIVE OF THE JOINT CHIEFS OF STAFF

I arrived in Korea on April 10, 1952, to take over my duties as Chief of Staff of the First Marine Aircraft Wing. All my instructions and decisions were subject to confirmation by the Assistant Commanding General, Lamson-Scribner. Just before I assumed full responsibility for the duties of Chief of Staff, General Lamson-Scribner called me into his office to talk over various problems of the Wing. During this conversation he said: "Has Binney given you all the background on the special missions run by VMF-513?" I asked him if he meant "suprop" (our code name for bacteriological bombs) and he confirmed this. I told him I had been given all the background by Colonel Binney.

Colonel Arthur A. Binney, the officer I relieved as Chief of Staff, had given me, as his duties required that he should, an outline of the general plan of bacteriological warfare in Korea and the details of the part played up to that time by the First Marine Aircraft Wing.

The general plan for bacteriological warfare in Korea was directed by the United States Joint Chiefs of Staff in October, 1951. In that month the Joint Chiefs of Staff sent a directive by hand to the Commanding General, Far East Command (at that time General Ridgway), directing the initiation of bacteriological warfare in Korea on an initially small, experimental stage but in expanding proportions.

This directive was passed to the Commanding General, Far East Air Force, General Weyland, in Tokyo. General Weyland then called into personal conference General Everest, Commanding General of the Fifth Air Force in Korea, and also the Commander of the Nineteenth Bomb Wing at Okinawa, which unit operates directly under FEAF.

The plan that I shall now outline was gone over, the broad aspects of the problem were agreed upon and the following information was brought back to Korea by General Everest, personally and verbally, since for security purposes it was decided not to have anything in writing on this matter in Korea and subject to possible capture.

OBJECTIVES

The basic objective was at that time to test, under field conditions, the various elements of bacteriological warfare, and to possibly expand the field tests, at a later date, into an element of the regular combat operations, depending on the results obtained and the situation in Korea.

The effectiveness of the different diseases available was to be tested, especially for their spreading or epidemic qualities under various circumstances, and to test whether each disease caused a serious disruption to enemy operations arid civilian routine or just minor inconveniences, or was contained completely, causing no difficulties.

Various types of armament or containers were to be tried out under field conditions and various types of aircraft were to be used to test their suitability as bacteriological bomb vehicles.

Terrain types to be tested included high areas, seacoast areas, open spaces, areas enclosed by mountains, isolated areas, areas relatively adjacent to one another, large and small towns and cities, congested it's and those relatively spread out. These tests were to be extended over an unstated period of time but sufficient to cover all extremes of temperature found in Korea.

All possible methods of delivery were to be tested as well as tactics developed to include initially night attack and then expanding into day attack by specialized Squadrons Various types of bombing were to be tried out, and various combinations of bombing, from single planes up to and including formations of planes, were to be tried out, with bacteriological bombs used in conjunction with conventional bombs. Enemy reactions were particularly to be tested or observed by any means available to ascertain what his counter-measures would be, what propaganda steps he would take, and to what extent his military operations would be affected by this type of warfare.

Security measures were to be thoroughly tested -both friendly and enemy. On the friendly ride, all possible steps were to be taken to confine knowledge of the use of this weapon and to control information on the subject. On the enemy side, every possible means was to be used to deceive the enemy and prevent his actual proof that the weapon was being used.

Finally, if the situation warranted, while continuing the experimental phase of bacteriological warfare according to the Joint Chiefs of Staff directive, it might be expanded to become a part of the military or tactical effort in Korea.

INITIAL STAGE

The B-29s from Okinawa began using bacteriological bombs in November, 1951, covering targets all over North Korea in what might be called random bombing. One night the target might be in Northeast Korea and the next night in Northwest Korea. Their bacteriological bomb operations were conducted in combination with normal night armed reconnaissance as a measure of economy and security.

Early in January 1952, General Schilt, then Com manding General of the First Marine Aircraft Wing, was called to Fifth Air Force Headquarters in Seoul, where General Everest told him of the directive issued by the Joint Chiefs of Staff, and ordered him to have VMF-513-Marine Night Fighter Squadron 513 of Marine Aircraft Group 33 of the First Marine Aircraft Wing-participate in the bacteriological warfare program. VMF-513 was based on K8, the Air Force base at Kunsan of the Third Bomb Wing, whose B-26s had already begun bacteriological operations. VMF-513 was to be serviced by the Third Bomb Wing.

While all marine aircraft (combat types) shore based in Korea operate directly under the Fifth Air Force, with the First Marine Aircraft Wing being kept informed of their activities, when a new or continuing program is being initiated, the Fifth Air Force normally has initially informed the Wing as a matter of courtesy.

Towards the end of January 1952, Marine night fighters of Squadron 513, operating as single planes on night armed reconnaissance, and carrying bacteriological bombs, shared targets with the B-26s covering the lower half of North Korea with the greatest emphasis on the western portion. Squadron 513 coordinated with the Third Bomb Wing on all these missions, using F7F aircraft (Tiger Cats) because of their twin engine safety.

K8 (Kunsan) offered the advantage of take-off directly over the water, in the event of engine failure, and both the safety and security of over-water flights to enemy territory.

For security reasons, no information on the types of bacteria being used was given to the First Marine Aircraft Wing.

In March 1952, General Schilt was again called to Fifth Air Force Headquarters and verbally directed by General Everest to prepare Marine Photographic Squadron I (VMJ-1 Squadron) of Marine Aircraft Group 33, to enter the program. VMJ-1 based on K3, Marine Aircraft Group 33's base at Pohang, Korea, was to use F2H-2P photographic reconnaissance aircraft (Banshees).

The missions would be intermittent and combined with normal photographic missions and would be scheduled by the Fifth Air Force in separate, top-secret orders.

The Banshees were brought into the program because of their specialized operations, equipment, facilities and isolated area of operations at K3. They could penetrate further into North Korea as far as enemy counteraction is concerned and worked in two-plane sections involving a minimum of crews and disturbance of normal missions. They could also try out bombing from high altitudes in horizontal flight in conjunction with photographic runs.

During March 1952, the Banshees of Marine Photographic Squadron 1 commenced bacteriological operations, continuing and expanding the bacteriological bombing of North Korean towns, always combining these operations with normal photographic missions. Only a minimum of bomb supplies were kept on hand to reduce storage problems, and the Fifth Air Force sent a team of two officers and several men to Y\3 (Pohang) to instruct the marine specialists in handling the bombs.

The Navy's part in the program was with the F9Fs (Panthers), ADs (Skyraiders) and standard F2Hs (Banshees), which as distinct from the photographi— configuration, used carriers off the east coast of Korea.

The Air Force had also expanded its own operations to include squadrons of different type aircraft, with different methods and tactics of employing bacteriological warfare.

This was the situation up to my arrival in Korea. Subsequent thereto, the following main events took place.

OPERATIONAL STAGE

During the latter part of May 1952, the new Commanding General of the First Marine Aircraft Wing, General Jerome, was called to Fifth Air Force Headquarters and given a directive for expanding bacteriological operations. The directive was given personally and verbally by the new Commanding General of the Fifth Air Force, General Barcus.

On the following day, May 25, General Jerome outlined the new stage of bacteriological operations to the Wing staff at a meeting in his office at which I was present in my capacity as Chief of Staff.

The other staff members of the First Marine Aircraft Wing present were: General Lamson-Scribner, Assistant Commanding General;, Colonel Stage, Interligence Officer (G2); Colonel Wendt, Operations Officer (G3) and Colonel Clark, Logistics Officer (G4). The directive from General Barcus, transmitted to and discussed by us that morning, was as follows:

A contamination bell was to be established across Korea in an effort to make the interdiction program effective in stopping enemy supplies from reaching the front lines. The Marines would take the left flank of this belt, to include the two cities of Sinanju and Kunuri and the area between and around them. The remainder of the belt would be handled by the Air Force in the centre and the Navy in the east or right flank.

Marine Squadron 513 would be diverted from its random targets to this concentrated target, operating from K8 (Kunsan) stiff serviced by the Third Bomb Wing, using F7Fs (Tiger Cats) because of their twin engine safety. The Squadron was short of these aircraft but more were promised.

The responsibility for contaminating the left flank and maintaining the contamination was assigned to the Commander of Squadron 513, and the schedule of operations left to the Squadron's discretion, subject to the limitations that:

The initial contamination of the area was to be completed as soon as possible and the area must then be recontaminated or replenished at periods not to exceed ten days.

Aircraft engaged on these missions would be given a standard night armed reconnaissance mission, usually in the Haeju Peninsula. On the way to the target, however, these planes would go via Sinanju or Kunuri, drop their bacteriological bombs and then complete their normal missions. This would add to the security and interfere least with normal missions.

Reports on this program of maintaining the contamination belt would go direct to the Fifth Air Force, reporting normal mission numbers so-and-so had been completed "via Sinanju" or "via Kunuri" and stating how many "superpropaganda" bombs had been dropped. Squadron 513 was directed to make a more accurate "truck count" at night than had been customary in order to determine or defect any significant change in the flow off traffic through its operating area.

General Barcus also directed that Marine Aircraft Group 12 of the First Marine Aircraft Wing was to prepare to enter the bacteriological program. First the ADs (Skyraiders) and then the F4Us (Corsairs) were to take part in the expanded program, initially, however, only as substitute for the F7Fs...

General Jerome further reported that the Fifth Air Force required Marine Photographic Squadron I to continue their current bacteriological operations, operating from K3 (Pohang). At the same time Marine Aircraft Group 33 at K3 was placed on a stand-by, last resort, basis. Owing to the distance of K3 from the target area, - large-scale participation in the, program by Marine Aircraft Group 33 was not desired. Because the F9Fs (Panthers) would only be used in an emergency, no special bomb supply would be established over and above that needed to supply the photographic reconnaissance aircraft. Bombs could be brought up from Ulsan in a few hours - if necessary. The plans and the ramifications thereof were discussed at General Jerome's conference and arrangements made to transmit the directive to the officers concerned with carrying out the new program.

It was decided that Colonel Wendt would initially transmit this information to the commanders concerned and the details could be discussed by the cognizant staff officers as soon as they were worked out.

FIRST MAW'S OPERATIONS

Marine Night Fighter Squadron 513 Next day then, May 26, Colonel Wendt held a conference with the Commanding Officer of Squadron 513 and, I believe, the K8 Air Base Commander and the Commanding Officer of the Third Bomb Wing, and discussed the various details.

The personnel of the Fifth Air Force were already cognizant of the plan, having been directly informed by Fifth, Air Force Headquarters.

Since the plan constituted for Squadron 513 merely a change of target and additional responsibility to maintain their own schedule of contamination of their area, there were no real problems to be solved.

During the first week of June, Squadron 513 started operations on the concentrated contamination belt, using cholera bombs. (The plan given to General Jerome indicated that at a later, unspecified date-depending on the results obtained, or lack of results-yellow fever and then typhus in that order would probably he tried out in the contamination belt.)

Squadron 513 operated in this manner throughout June and during the first week in July that I was with the Wing, without any incidents of an unusual nature.

An average of five aircraft a night normally covered the main supply routes along the western coast of Korea up to the Chong Chon River but with emphasis on the area from Phyngyang southward. They diverted as necessary to Sinanju or Kunuri and the area between in order to maintain the ten-day bacteriological replenishment cycle.

We estimated that if each airplane carried two bacteriological bombs, two good nights were ample to cover both Sinanju and Kunuri and a third night would cover the area around and between these cities.

About the middle of June, as best I remember, the Squadron received a modification to the plan from the U.S. Fifth Air Force via the Third Bomb Wing. This new directive included an area of about ten miles surrounding the two principal cities in the Squadron's schedule, with particular emphasis on towns or hamlets on the lines of supply and any by-pass roads.

MARINE AIRCRAFT GROUP 12

Colonel Wendt later held a conference at K6 (Pyongtaek) at which were present the Commanding Officer, Colonel Gaylor, the Executive Officer and the Operations Officer of Marine Aircraft Group 12. Colonel Wendt informed them that they were to make preparations to take part in the bacteriological operations and to work out security problems which would become serious if they got into daylight operations and had to bomb up at their own base K6. They were to inform the squadron commanders concerned but only the absolute barest number of a additional personnel, and were to have a list of a limited number of hand-picked pilots ready to be used on short notice. Colonel Wendt informed them that an Air Force team would soon be provided to assist with logistic problems, this team actually arriving the last week in June.

Before my capture on July 8, both the ADs (Skyraiders) and the F4Us (Corsairs) of Marine Aircraft Group 12 had participated in very small numbers, once or twice, in daylight bacteriological operations as a part of regular scheduled, normal day missions, bombing up at K8 (Kunsan), rendezvousing with the rest of the formation on the way to the target. These missions were directed at small towns in Western Korea along the main road leading south from Kunuri and were a part of the normal interdiction program.

MARINE AIRCRAFT GROUP 33

Colonel Wendt passed the plan for the Wing's participation in bacteriological operations to Colonel Condon, Commanding Officer of Marine Aircraft Group 33, on approximately May 27-28.

Since the Panthers (F9Fs) at the Group's base at Pohang would only be used as last resort aircraft, it was left to Colonel Condon's discretion as to just what personnel he would pass the information on to but it was to be an absolute minimum.

During the time I was with the Wing, none of these aircraft had been scheduled for bacteriological missions, though the photographic reconnaissance planes of the Group's VMJ-1 Squadron continued their missions from that base.

SCHEDULING AND SECURITY

Security was by far the most pressing problem affecting the First Marine Aircraft Wing, since the operational phase of bacteriological warfare, as well as other types of combat operations, is controlled by the Fifth Air Force.

Absolutely nothing could appear in writing on the subject. The word "bacteria" was not to be mentioned in any circumstances in Korea, except initially to identify "superpropaganda" or "suprop."

Apart from the routine replenishment operations of Squadron 513, which required no scheduling, bacteriological missions were scheduled by separate, top-secret, mission orders (or "FRAG" orders). These stated only to include "superpropaganda" or "suprop" on mission number so-and-so of the routine secret "FRAG" order for the day's operations. -Mission reports went back the same way by separate, top-secret dispatch, stating the number of "suprop" bombs dropped on a specifically numbered mission.

Other than this, Squadron 513 reported their bacteriological missions by adding "via Kunuri" or "via Sinanju" to their normal mission reports.

Every means was taken to deceive the enemy and to deny knowledge of these operations to friendly personnel, the latter being most important since 300 to 400 men of the Wing are rotated back to the United States each month.

Orders were issued that bacteriological bombs were only to be dropped in conjunction with ordinary bombs or napalm, to give the attack the appearance of a normal attack against enemy supply lines. For added security over enemy territory, a napalm bomb was to remain on the aircraft until after the release of the bacteriological bombs so that if the aircraft crashed it would almost certainly burn and destroy the evidence.

All officers were prohibited from discussing the subject except officially and behind closed doors. Every briefing was to emphasize that this was not only a military secret, but a matter of national policy.

I personally have never heard the subject mentioned or even referred to outside of the office, and I ate all of my meals in the Commanding General's small private mess, where many classified matters were discussed.

ASSESSMENT OF RESULTS

In the Wing, our consensus of opinion was that results of these bacteriological operations could not be accurately assessed. Routine methods of assessment are by (presumably) spies, by questioning prisoners of war, by watching the nightly truck count very carefully to observe deviations from the normal, and by observing public announcements of Korean and Chinese authorities upon which very heavy dependence was placed, since it was felt that no large epidemic could occur without news leaking out to the outside world and that these authorities would, therefore, announce it themselves. Information from the above sources is correlated at the Commander-in-Chief, Far East level in Tokyo, but the over-all assessment of results is not passed down to the Wing level, hence the Wing was not completely aware of the results.

When I took over from Colonel Binney I asked him for results or reactions up to date and he specifically said: "Not worth a damn."

No one that I know of has indicated that the results are anywhere near commensurate with the effort, danger and dishonesty involved, although the Korean and

Chinese authorities have made quite a public report of early bacteriological bomb efforts. The sum total of results known to me are that they are disappointing and no good.

PERSONAL REACTIONS

I do not say the following in defence of anyone, myself included, I merely report as an absolutely direct observation that every officer when first informed that the United States is using bacteriological warfare in Korea is both shocked and ashamed.

I believe, without exception, we come to Korea as officers loyal to our people and government and believing what we have always been told about bacteriological warfare that it is being developed only for use in retaliation in a third world war.

For these officers to come to Korea and find that their own government has so completely deceived them by still proclaiming to the world that it is not using bacteriological warfare, makes them question mentally all the other things that the government proclaims about warfare in general and in Korea.

None of us believes that bacteriological warfare has any place in war since of all the weapons devised bacteriological bombs alone have as their primary objective casualties among masses of civilians-and that is utterly wrong in anybody's conscience. The spreading of disease is unpredictable and there may be no limits to a fully developed epidemic. Additionally, there is the awfully sneaky, unfair sort of feeling of dealing with a weapon used surreptitiously against an unarmed and unwarned people.

I remember specifically asking Colonel Wendt what were Colonel Gaylor's reactions when he was first informed and he reported to me that Colonel Gaylor was both horrified and stupefied. Everyone felt like that when they first heard of it, and their reactions are what might well be expected from a fair-minded, self-respecting nation of people.

Tactically, this type of weapon is totally unwarranted-it is not even a Marine Corps weapon-morally it is damnation itself; administratively and logistically as planned for use, it is hopeless; and from the point of view of self-respect and loyalty, it is shameful.

F. H. Schwable, 04429 Colonel, U.S.M.C. 6 December, 1952

STEAMSHOVEL PRESS

Trevor James Constable

TREVOR JAMES CONSTABLE ON CURTIS LEMAY

The following letter was sent to Michael Theroux at *Borderlands* magazine in response to comments by Trevor James Constable that appeared previously in the magazine. Constable wrote *The Cosmic Pulse of Life* and many other books that built upon his interpretation of the work of Wilhelm Reich. He also was an associate of Curtis LeMay, an important World War II figure who also ran as George Wallace's vice-presidential candidate in 1968. Constable once told interviewer Tom Brown that "I knew Wallace would be assassinated and Curtis LeMay would be president...We had a chance to have a completely honest gentleman as president." Here, Constable expounds upon his relationship with LeMay in a letter that never made it into *Borderlands*. Borderlands is a remarkable alternative science journal that can be found in the *Link Tank* below.

Dear Borderlands

I enjoyed the current issue a great deal, especially Trevor James

Constable's reflections on the fate of weather engineering after he passes, which hopefully will not happen until much later than he seems to anticipate. He can certainly take some credit for the continued interest in Reich's atmospheric engineering work, although in his own work it went through some mighty interesting changes. Constable makes his point well, though, that the environmental needs remain constant, or actually get worse as time moves along, thus ensuring continued interest in various forms of climate control.

Borderlands should discuss with Constable in more detail his relation - ship with Curtis LeMay, touched upon in the book he mentions, Loom of the Future *(Garberville, 1994). Constable did a kind of cloud-busting work with LeMay, who hardly qualifies as the unarmored hero against the anticiviliza - tion. Lemay was responsible for the fire-bombing of Tokyo in pre-Hiroshima World War II, and ran as George Wallace's vice-presidential candidate in 1968. Lemay also warned Barry Goldwater off investigating the possible existence of Roswell grey alien bodies at Wright Patterson Air Force Base. According to one story, Lemay was smoking a stogey in the observation bleachers at the JFK autopsy at Bethesda. Could Constable add anything to this lore?*

Kenn Thomas Steamshovel Press

FROM LETTERHEAD OF:
RAYMOND F. TOLIVER, COL. USAF (RET.) TREVOR J. CONSTABLE AUTHORS AND HISTORIANS

Kenn "Steamshovel" Thomas wants more detail on my relationship with the late General Curtis LeMay. Kenn's statement that I "did a kind of cloudbusting work with LeMay" is a somewhat inaccurate description of the work we did. our activities did not involve cloudbusting or cloud-busters in any way whatsoever.

The General became involved with me during my Operation Clincher in the 1990 Southern California smog season. Complete detail of the Clincher operation was provided in the Journal of Borderland Research after its successful conclusion. Suffice it to say here that Clincher adminis-tered the worst knock to Southern California smog that it had ever received in a single season in history, right across the statistical spectrum, EXACTLY AS FILED IN ADVANCE WITH N.O.A.A. Nobody else has ever given such advance notice, and objectively fulfilled such an undertaking in providing clean air, anywhere.

Clincher shook the smog bureaucracy and all the crooked politicians, neurotic lawyers and greedy businessmen to whom "fighting" smog is financially or organiza-tionally beneficial, and to whom its eradication is the worst nightmare. Fourteen operating bases and the crucial personal intervention of General Curtis LeMay were required to bring this off. Each base was equipped with one or more "Spider" etheric vortex generators. No cloudbusters were employed.

Curtis LeMay

To organize Clincher and secure operating sites over a four-county area, I had to call in all my markers. I managed to get locations everywhere except Riverside. That region became my bete noir because of its numerous smog emergencies in pre-vious seasons. Smog shifts into Riverside and concentrates there from areas farther west.as each day advances past the noon hour. Assistance was denied me in Riverside from the Chamber of Commerce on down. Things like this happen when you have a new idea, capable of frightening little men. This was a dismal and desperate experience, for it put the success of Clincher in jeopardy.

The late Arthur Libby Neff had a highly effective Spider at his home in Pasadena, where it was making unprecedented inroads on smog. He suggested that we take my problem to General Curtis LeMay, who lived in Riverside. "You can't miss with him" said Art Neff, "he's got all your aviation books and he knows who you are." Colonel Raymond.F. Toliver USAF Ret., my co-author on military books for over 30 years, had been one of General LeMay's briefing officers at the Pentagon. He confirmed that the General knew that I was his literary partner, and would listen to me without prejudice.

A meeting was arranged at the General's Riverside home. Today, Kenn Thomas sees Curtis LeMay only as one "who hardly qualifies as the unarmored hero against the anticivilization." When I went to see the General I was not interested in such esoteric aspects of LeMay as Kenn mentions, but only in getting vital assistance. I knew that LeMay was not just an outstanding military leader, but, in the words of Barry Goldwater, was a "can-do" guy, somebody who went right at a project and got it done before ordinary guys got off their tails. The General and I exchanged pleasantries about numerous mutual friends in aviation, including Germany's General Adolf Galland, whose official biography I had just completed, and to which General LeMay had kindly contributed a dust jacket blurb, via Art Neff.

CONSTABLE AND LEMAY TOGETHER.

The General listened skeptically but carefully to what I told him about the smog reduction project. A gleam came into his eyes when I described the total lack of cooperation by Riverside political and business leaders. Leaving an introductory videotape with him I departed, with an invitation to return in two days.

As an aviation historian and author, I well knew about the fire-bombing of Tokyo. I well knew also about the bombing of Pearl Harbor, and the rape of Manila, and the Bataan Death March. Military people must do what their governments require. As long as war is not abolished, for which abolition MacArthur was the world's most effective advocate, one is blessed to have straight-ahead, honest leadership and competence like that of General LeMay. Their raison d'etre since antiquity has been to win their countries' wars. Solid soldiers and patriots like LeMay would be anathema to today's dishonest engineers of world political control, and wars without victories.

Central to my personal assessments of such people as I encounter on earth, is my conviction that the Laws of Karma ensure that all debts are paid and weighed in the Cosmic scale. Human evaluations of people and events are of little karmic force or effect, and nobody — but nobody — "gets away" with anything. Thus it is not within my purview to hold the firebombing of Tokyo against Curtis LeMay. I have also limned the lives of numerous German fighter pilots of World War II on the same basis, finding all of them to be exceptional men, regardless of what their duties in war required them to do. Life is too short to expend it in a search for perfection.

I actively supported Wallace/LeMay in 1968, because I distrust establishment politicos, such distrust becoming total by 1997. Wallace and LeMay were convulsing all the electoral projections. Most importantly, I knew Curtis LeMay was the first straight-shooter to run on.a presidential ticket in the U.S. in decades. I love honest men. I was also in no doubt that George Wallace, were he to win, would be assassinated by America's unelected rulers. That would make Curtis LeMay president.

People who might still blanch from such an honest straight-shooter running America, should take a good look at contemporary Washington, jumping with political thuggery and rotten with corruption. Give me President Curtis LeMay any day.

General LeMay was waiting for me on his front lawn when I returned to his home. He looked at me beadily. There was no igood morning'. On the contrary, he waved an admonishing finger at me, as though annoyed. He went right to the point. "You never convinced me one bit with that videotape," he said. "Not one bit." There was an awkward

pause. "But I want one of those damned smog things of yours in my backyard," he blurted. When I pulled out a Mark II Spider from my car, he helped me install it in his patio. The former Chief of Staff of the USAF and founder of the Strategic Air Command, was good with tools, a natural tinkerer. When the Spider was set up, I had him pass the palm of his left hand across the apex of one of the projector

Constable and LeMay Together

cones. He immediately reacted to the subtle emission, passing his hand incredulously across the truncated apex of the cone, time after time. His mouth fell open. "My God," he said. He tried the same procedure on the twin cone. This time there was a more forceful expletive.

STEAMSHOVEL PRESS

The DISC Debate

Bob Harris contributed the following correspondence on the topic of the existence of Defense Industrial Security Command. The Torbitt Document names DISC as the police agency behind the Kennedy assassination. For background on this debate, see the *Steamshovel* book, *NASA, Nazis & JFK*.

Bob Harris is a stand-up comedian, Jeopardy champion, and longtime writer for *National Lampoon* who has also given serious lectures on covert politics at over 250 colleges nationwide. His commentaries now air daily on CBS News radio in Los Angeles, and his columns appear weekly in a dozen alternative newsweeklies and monthly in Z magazine. *His online archive is at* www.goodthink.com/harris.html.

Re DISC: yes, apparently it exists, but evidently not in DC under another name. When I mentioned it once in passing to a close friend who works pushing papers for a defense contractor and has a pretty high clearance, he casually said, "oh, you mean Disco." Disco? "Yeah, Disco, those are the people who keep all the files on anyone with a security clearance." (The "o" stands for "organization.")

My friend thought that *everyone* knew what Disco was. Probably everyone he works with does. If he's right, certainly anyone who processed clearances would, and that would be thousands of people. I've since asked two other folks I know who have clearances; one confirmed, one claimed (truthfully, I think) ignorance.

The address given in the Torbitt Document (1064 W. Broad St. in Columbus, Ohio, if memory serves), could have been correct at the time, but I was there once and it's still a federal building, except I seem to recall it was a GSA storage facility or something like that. I suppose it could have some secret offices, but that sounds a little too James Bondian for my tastes. My friend thinks it's now in Alabama, possibly at the big Huntsville NASA facility. He also seems to think Disco was always a NASA thing.

Apparently, Disco was/is a classified aspect of what (I think) was called the Industrial Security Act of 1957, which mandated that all contractors doing classified work maintain files and run internal anti-communist surveillance. You'll find what I'm trying to remember in Peter Dale Scott's book *Deep Politics And The Death of JFK.* As you probably know, Scott proposes the possibility that Oswald became an internal security dangle, both at JCS in Dallas and Reily in New Orleans, possibly even at the TSBD, where where another employee, Joe Molina, was under some sort of investigation.

This would sure explain all those Reilly workers who got jobs at NASA.

Unless I'm mistaken, Linda Hunt notes in *Secret Agenda* the Lodge Act of 1950, which made it easier for defense contractors to hire Paperclip exiles than America citizens. Many of the hired exiles went, of course, into anti-communist security. This might Oswald's milieu of Soviet exiles in the DFW area as a Disco thing, not a CIA thing.

That Albert Jenner, who Scott notes was legal counsel to General Dynamics, was put in charge of the conspiracy segment of the WR screams out confirmation of this hypothesis. This is in the WC testimony, but highly overlooked (except by Scott and on my CD/ROM): Oswald's first attempt to get a job in DFW was a phone call to Max Clark, a former anti-communist security officer at General Dynamics. This is utterly wrong is Oswald was a real commie, but makes perfect sense if he's a free-lance Disco dangle. Not that Jenner mentioned that in the WR. I also suspect there was a Disco or similar connection to the Texas Employment Commission's contact with Oswald, which would explain the way the folks there got the hell out of dodge after Dealey Plaza.

Wandering into the deep end, of course DISC/Disco imaginably also fits w/King and RFK shootings as the source for intel access both to Ray's Canadian aliases and Thane Cesar via his previous employment at (I think) Lockheed... notice I said imaginably.

Now if you'll excuse me, Scully, Mulder, and Jolly West are at the door. If I don't know you tomorrow, please don't be offended.

More On Maury Island

Ron Halbritter first examined the Maury Island incident in Steamshovel Press #12, *uncovering the connection of the famous UFO incident to JFK assas - sination figure Guy Bannister. Ron Halbritter has written at length on Maury Island in major magazines, and has been featured on the television show* Sightings *discussing the topic.* Steamshovel *currently plans a volume on the subject for release early next year by IllumiNet Press.*

THE TRUTH BEHIND MEN IN BLACK
BY JENNY RANDLES (St. Martin) AND
ALIEN AGENDA BY JIM MARRS
(HarperCollins) reviewed by Ron Halbritter

Woe, woe, woe is me. Two books that include the Maury Island incident and two respected writers crash and burn. The big problem is that they appear to believe what other people have written without taking the basic steps of confirming the copied data.

On page 31 of her MIB book, Jenny Randles says that Harold Dahl, fearing damage from the UFO with mechanical trouble above him, "fled for the safety of some caves."

Jenny, where did these caves come from? There are no caves on Maury island and there doesn,t seem to be any references to the caves in statements by Harold Dahl, Fred Crisman, Kenneth Arnold, Captain Emil Smith or by the reporters Paul Lance and Ted Morello. Note the SIGHTINGS television episode f February 12, 1997, where the Reverend Bob Le Roy is sitting on the gunnel of a boat with the Maury Island location behind him . You can see the beach, trees and some steep bluffs, but no caves. (Bob Le Roy,s brother, Barney Le Roy was a witness to the Maury Island UFO and can identify the correct location to within 50 feet.)

On page 37 and 38 Jenny Randles, refers to the much quoted Harold T. Wilkins investigation of 1951. Wilkins describes his attempt in *Flying Saucers On The Attack* , page 62.

"I wrote an air mail letter from Bexleyheath, Kent, England, to Chrisman, at Tacoma, on January 23, 1951... was returned, arriving back at my English address in Kent, on April 7, 1951. I had endorsed the front of my air letter asking that it be forwarded to Mr. Chrisman,s private address, if he were no longer in the US Coastguard Service. Someone at Tacoma had written on the letter: "Not Coast Guard". ... and it was returned to me undelivered. Yet, it is certain that someone in the Coast Guard Service knew where Mr. Chrisman had gone and declined to forward the letter to him.

Wilkins wrote a single letter to the wrong NAME (it,s Crisman, not Chrisman) and sent to the wrong address. Crisman was not ever associated with the Coast Guard and "Not Coast Guard" seems an appropriate response. No one in the Coast Guard knew Crisman nor had an obligation to track him down to deliver a letter. Dahl and Crisman were "patrolling for logs", a time-honored method for Pacific Northwest fishermen to meet their bills when the fishing is bad. Loose logs in the bay are not only a hazard to navigation, but are worth cash at the lumber companies. Ray Palmer changed "patrolling for logs" to "Harbor Patrol" and Wilkins assumed "Harbor Patrol" meant the US Coast Guard. I wonder what would happen if I wrote, "Jenny Randles, c/o RAF, England."

Much has been made of the "disappearance" of Harold Dahl, and Fred Crisman because the truth is not exciting enough to be good journalism. In fact, Dahl had to make payments on his 83' ex-minesweeper, and with the loss of his boom of logs during the UFO event had his boat repossessed by the finance company. Dahl moved twenty miles south to Tenino, Washington, where he started a used furniture/second hand store and lived peacefully until his death in 1982. Crisman "disappeared" by using his G.I. Bill and attending the University of Oregon to become a school teacher.

Behind Fox Mulder,s desk in *The X-Files*, hangs a poster that states, "I want to Believe!" and so it is when one picks up *Alien Agenda*. I want to believe, not in aliens, but in Jim Marrs. I want to believe that he has done the research and combed his facts as carefully as he did in *Crossfire, The Plot That Killed Kennedy.* I want to believe that this is an author I can trust, someone I can quote as an authority.

Jenny Randles

Unfortunately, that isn,t the case. One example, is the Maury Island incident. Marrs spends 20 pages (79-99) discussing the Maury Island case, quoting at length from Paris Flammonde,s book *UFO EXIST!* and throughout it appears that Marrs didn,t notice that Paris Flammonde didn,t do any original research; Flammonde simply quoted from the Kenneth Arnold / Ray Palmer book, *Coming of the Saucers*. Doesn,t the legal community call that hearsay?

Marrs also uses as a reference *UFO,s the Final Answer* by David and Therese Marie Barclay. Readers will recall that Kenneth Arnold first observed "flying saucers" while searching for marine C-46 that had crashed in the cascade mountains with 35 marines aboard. Eight months after the C-46 crash, while investigating the Maury Island case, two Army Intelligence officers were killed when their B-25 crashed. The Barclay,s research was so poorly done that on page 109 of their book they placed the missing marines aboard Davidson and Brown,s B-25. Mr. Marrs, this not a reliable source.

And how did Jim Marrs, famous for his investigation into the Kennedy assassination overlook the curious business that Guy Bannister, the FBI agent who investigated Kenneth Arnold, was the same Guy Bannister that District Attorney Jim Garrison two decades later would accuse of participating in the Kennedy conspiracy.

And that is just the beginning, for decades, there have been privately circulating a manuscript called The Easy Papers. The manuscript claims to be a service record of Fred Crisman, as a CIA "internal disruptor". Shame on Jim Marrs for giving credence to this piece of nonsense. Those who have actually studied the document realize it was written in the very distinct style of Fred Crisman himself. The contents of The Easy Papers are at best simply silly. It begins, as all CIA reports must, with the hyperbole, *"Lord Help us if Crisman finds out about this report"*.

The body of the report consists of a Fred Crisman resume, with an explantions that all those jobs he got fired from were actually CIA assignments and he claims he was getting paid to *"disrupt"*.

In real life, between 1953 and 1960 Crisman had, and lost teaching positions at Elgin, Oregon; Huntingdon, Oregon; Tacoma, Washington; Buckley, Washington; Tacoma, Washington, Longview, Washington; Salem, Oregon and finally from 1960 to 1963 at Rainier, Oregon.

IRON MOUNTAIN, 1967

REPORT FROM
IRON MOUNTAIN

SUPPRESSED

LEONARD C. LEWIN

Following is the *U.S. News & World Report* on *The Report from Iron Mountain* from November 20, 1967. The *Iron Mountain Report* continues to have some currency among conspiracy researchers. Hoaxed or not, the unintentially humorous situation its publication set off should not be lost on readers. Pentagon bureaucrats found it so plausible that, according to the caption underneath a DC skyline photo that accompanied this article, "In Washington, a "manhunt" began for the unidentified author." "Hoaxed" political analysis reached a new peak recently with the publication of *The Real Report on the Last Chance to Save Capitalism in Italy*. Those with an interest in *Iron Mountain* would do well to check out the *Real Report*, reviewed near the bottom of the main *Steamshovel* page with a link to its publisher, Flatland Books.

HOAX OR HORROR? A BOOK THAT SHOOK WHITE HOUSE

There can be no peace, but endless war may be good for the U. S. anyway-that is the conclusion reported in a volume causing a severe case of jitters in official Washington. Reason: The book purports to be based on a secret, Government-financed study by top experts. Some say it is grimly serious. Others call it leg-pulling satire. Whatever the truth, it is something of a sensation in high places.

"Report From Iron Mountain" was published October 16 by the Dial Press of New York City. It has an introduction by Leonard C. Lewin, a New York free-lance writer.

Mr. Lewin wrote that the manuscript was made available to him in 1966 by a member of the 15-man "Special Study Group" which produced the work.

That person is referred to as "John Doe" and is described as a profes - sor of social science from "a large Middle Western University."

The manuscript identifies "Iron Mountain" as the assembly point for the study group, near Hudson, NY.

The Library of Congress, on November 10, told "U.S. News & World Report" that "Iron Mountain" has not been registered. To do so would require divulging at least the nationality of the author.

Did a select group of prominent Americans meet in secret sessions between 1963 and 1966 and produce a report that advised the U. S. Government it could never afford an era of peace?

Yes-according to the mysterious new book, "Report From Iron Mountain on the Possibility and Desirability of Peace." No-came a resounding chorus from worried Government officials, who, nonetheless, were double-checking with one another-just to make sure. The response of experts and political observers ranged from "nutty" to "clever satire" to "sinister."

IS WAR NECESSARY? Central theme of the book, which purports to reflect the unanimous view of 15 of the nation's top scholars and economists, is this: War and preparations for it are indispensable to world stability. Lasting peace is probably unattainable. And peace, even if it could be achieved, might not be in the best interests of society.

All this set off a blazing debate in early November, cries of "hoax"-and a "manhunt" for the author.

Sources close to the White House revealed that the Administration is alarmed. These sources say cables have gone to U. S. embassies, with stern instructions: Play down public discussion of "Iron Mountain"; emphasize that the book has no relation whatsoever to Government policy.

LBJ's REACTION. But nagging doubts lingered. One informed source confirmed that the "Special Study Group," as the book called it, was set up by a top official in the Kennedy Administration. The source added that the report was drafted and eventually submitted to President Johnson, who was said to have "hit the roof"-and then ordered that the report be bottled up for all time.

As the turmoil mounted, so did the speculation about those who participated in writing "Iron Mountain."

John Kenneth Galbraith, former Ambassador to India, was quoted by "The Harvard Crimson" as having parried the question of authorship.

Mr. Galbraith, who reviewed "Iron Mountain" under a pseudonym, was reported to have said: "I seem to be, on all matters, a natural object of suspicion." And he added: "Dean Rusk, Walt Bestow, even Robert Bowie could as easily have written the book as 1. Yes, Rusk could."

Several sources turned toward Harvard in general as the site of authorship. One even went so far as to suggest that the book is an effort by Kennedy forces to discredit Lyndon Johnson.

A BIG SPOOF? Whatever else it was, "Iron Mountain" raised fears at high levels that it would be a mother lode for Communist propagandists. There was also a feeling that if the book is just an elaborate spoof, it is not likely to find understanding or sympathy in world capitals.

In the academic community, many held the view that "Iron Mountain" was a hilarious hoax-a kind of dead-pan parody of the studies emanating from the nation's "think tanks."

One history professor at a large Midwestern university, telephoned by "U.S. News & World Report," came on the line with these words: "I didn't do it." But he added: "Whoever did is laughing his sides off. He's saying, in effect, 'Look, if you read and take seriously some of the bilge in these exalted studies, you might as well read and take seriously my little exercise.' "

In all the furor, a literary analogy cropped up. Not since George Orwell's "1984" appeared some 18 years ago has there been such a controversial satire.

"WAR IS PEACE." Mr. Orwell's characters spoke a language called "newspeak." They lived by the all-powerful state's slogan: "War is Peace."

In "Report From Iron Mountain," the language is the flat, metallic jargon dear to the U. S. bureaucrat. The message: War is, "in itself, the principal basis of organization on which all modern societies are constructed."

STEAMSHOVEL PRESS

JFK on TFX

Anyone looking through the old tales of hookers and mobsters in Seymour Hersh's new JFK book, *Dark Side of Camelot* will come to some interesting new information. Hersh reports that members of the security operation for General Dynamics broke into the apartment of Judith Exner Campbell in August 1962. According to Hersh, they used whatever they found there to black mail JFK into making a controversial award of the TFX (Tactical Experimental Fighter) plane development to General Dynamics. (The TFX later evolved into the F-111) Hersh claims all this became known because the FBI spied on the General Dynamics spies.

Such private covert ops as a tool of corporate control grew from practices like those of former Senator George Smathers, interviewed by the ABC television program based on Hersh's book. In the 1950s, Smather's law firm hired guards from a subsidiary of the security services apparatus of his friend George Wackenhut. The guards worked at the nuclear-bomb site in Nevada and Cape Canaveral, despite federal prohibition against such an arrangement between government and private police. The private group Wackenhut still supplies security to the US-owned Area 51. *Steamshovel* examines this issue in the book *NASA, Nazis and JFK* (click *Steamshovel* book cover above), and also makes available *The Torbitt Document Supplement*, with a longer article on Smathers.

Additionally, *Steamshovel* presents here JFK's public statements as president on the TFX. It includes references to various dimensions of the controversy surrounding the contract with General Dynamics, the topic of Kennedy's last speech on November 22, including early financial commitment to it from Australia, home of Pine Gap, the down-under Area 51.

THE

DARK SIDE

OF

CAMELOT

SEYMOUR M.

HERSH

News Conference, 3/21/63

Q. Mr. President, the TFX contract is causing a lot of controversy on Capitol Hill. Senator Symington told the Senate that the investigation was affecting military morale and ought to be wound up quickly. How do you feel about it?

THE PRESIDENT: I see nothing wrong with the Congress looking at these matters. My judgment is that the decision reached by Secretary McNamara was the right one, sound one, and any fair and objective hearing will bring that out. Mr.

McNamara chose the plane he chose because he felt it most efficient, because he thought it would do the job and because he thought it would save the Government hundreds of millions of dollars. Everything I have read about the TFX and seen about it confirms my impression that Mr. McNamara was right. We have a very good, effective Secretary of Defense with a great deal of courage, who is willing to make hard decisions, and who doesn't mind when they are made that a good many people don't like it. This contract involves a large amount of money and naturally some people would prefer it to go another place than the place which the Secretary chose. I think the Secre tary did the right thing and I think this investigation will bring that out, and I have no objection to anyone looking at the contract as long as they feel that a useful function is served.

Q. Do you think the hearing that has been held has been fair and objective?

THE PRESIDENT: I would think that-I'm confident that we all know a lot more about the TFX than we did before, and that's a good thing. And my judgment is that the more this hearing goes on, the more convinced people are finally that Secretary McNamara is a very effective Secretary of Defense and that we're lucky to have him. ...

Q. Mr. President, the TFX fighter plane controversy has drawn more attention to Senator Case's criticism of those politicians who in recent campaigns have urged the public to elect candidates on the grounds that they can bring more big defense contracts into those particular States, the implication being that they could use political influence to do this. Now, do you feel that this sort of a proposition to the public builds confidence that these big defense contracts are being let fairly?

THE PRESIDENT: I think the contracts are being let fairly. But of course, there's great competition, and it's no wonder because thousands of people, jobs are involved. The fact of the matter is defense contracts have been concentrated in two or three States really, in space contracts, because those States have had the historical experience and also because they have a concentrated engineering and educational infrastructure which puts them in a successful position. For example, a good percentage of the contracts traditionally in space have gone to the State of California, and in defense, because the great defense plants-for all the reasons, really, since the end of World War 11. So Senators and Congressmen who are concerned about unemployment among their citizens, who are concerned about the flow of tax dollars, will continue to press. But the fact of the matter is that we have a Secretary of Defense who's making very honest judgments in these matters, and I know from personal experience that some Senators and Congressmen who recently visited Secretary McNamara, asking to present plans from being turned down, who happen to be members of my own party, and indeed, even more closely related, have been rejected by the Secretary of Defense.

Q. If I may follow that up, Senator Case has proposed that a watchdog com - mittee be created to look into these—

THE PRESIDENT: To watch the Congressmen and Senators? Well, that will be fine, if they feel they should be watched! ...

Q. Mr. President, in regard to the TFX contract, would you describe your per sonal role, specifically? Did you make any suggestions as to who should get the contract?

THE PRESIDENT: No, I did not. No. This was completely the Defense Department.

Q. Do you share the view of some officials in the Pentagon that members of the McClellan committee, particularly those up for reelection next year, may have been politically motivated in attacking the award to General Dynamics?

THE PRESIDENT: As I said, when a contract goes to one State, then the company may involve or the Senators may involve or the Congressmen want it to go to another. I would not get into that question, because I do not think that is the important point. I assume that the McClellan committee, on which I once served, will render a fair judgment. Number 2, I am confident of the TFX contract because I am confident of Secretary McNamara. Therefore, as I've said, this hearing can go on as long as they feel it serves a useful result, and whatever the motivations may be-and I wouldn't attempt to explore them-I have confidence in the committee and the members involved.

News Conference, April 3, 1963

Q. Is it valid, sir, for the Government to give a defense contract to a firm in order to keep that firm as part of the production arsenal of this country? And, two, did that happen in the case of the TFX award to General Dynamics?

THE PRESIDENT: No, to the last part. In the first case, if it is a hypothetical case, I would say it would depend on the circumstances, how great the need is. Is it for particular kinds of tools which we might need in the case of an emergency? I can think of cases where it would be valid. It has nothing to do with the TFX.

News Conference, 5/8/63

Q. Sir, the fact that Admiral Anderson was not retained as Chief of Navy Operations has been written about in such a way as to imply that he did not meas - ure up to your expectations as a head of the Navy, that he might have bucked reor - ganization plans, that he opposed Defense Secretary McNamara on the TFX, and other things which you probably are familiar with Is it true that he was not retained as a sort of warning to others in the Navy to get in line with the Secretary and your - self?

THE PRESIDENT: No, that isn't the reason As a matter of fact, Admiral Anderson is going to continue to serve the United States Government. I am very gratified that he has. I talked with him today and he has agreed to accept-to continue to serve the United States Government in a position of high responsibility. So quite obviously, the reasons-if I did not have the highest confidence in him I would not want him to continue.

Q. Could you tell us what post, Sir, he will serve in?

THE PRESIDENT: No, I—he continues as, of course, head of the Navy through August and therefore at an appropriate time this summer we will make an announcement. But he has agreed to continue to serve and I am delighted because I think he will be a great addition to the Government in this new position which requires a good deal of skill, which requires a good deal of dedication, and to which I would appoint someone for whom I had only a high regard.

News Conference, 8/20/63

Q. Mr. President, do you see anything in the relationship of the Secretary of the Navy Korth to the TFX contract which would suggest a conflict of interest?

THE PRESIDENT: No, I don't. I have the highest regard for Mr. Korth, Mr. Gilpatric, Mr. McNamara, and it seems to me the matter has been looked into for many months and I think they have emerged in a very good position.

News Conference, 10/31/63

Q. Mr. President, Navy Secretary Korth had some correspondence which indi - cated he worked very hard for the Continental National Bank of Fort Worth while he was in Government, as well as for the Navy, and that during this same period of time that he negotiated, or took part in the decision on a contract involving that bank's-one of that bank's best customers, the General Dynamics firm. I wonder if this fulfills the requirements of your Code of Ethics in Government, and if, in a gen - eral way, you think that it is within the law and proper?

THE PRESIDENT: In the case of the contract-the TFX contract-as you know, that matter was referred to the Department of Justice to see whether there was a conflict of interest and the judgment was that there was not. That is number one. Number two, the amount of the loan to the company. That bank was one of a number of banks which participated in a line of credit and it was relatively a small amount of money, as bank loans go. So in answer to your question, I have no evidence that Mr. Korth acted in any way improperly in the TFX matter. It has nothing to do with any opinion I may have about whether Mr. Korth might have written more letters and been busier than he should have been in one way or another. The fact of the matter is, I have no evidence that Mr. Korth benefited improperly during his term of office in the Navy. And I have no evidence, and you have not, as I understand it-the press has not produced any, nor the McClellan committee-which would indicate that in any way he acted improperly in the TFX. I always have believed that innuendoes should be justified before they are made, either by me, in the Congress, or even in the press.

Remarks at a Rally in Fort Worth in
Front of the Texas Hotel, November 22, 1963

Mr. Vice President, Jim Wright, Governor, Senator Yarborough, Mr. Buck, ladies and gentlemen:

There are no faint hearts in Fort Worth, and I appreciate your being here this morning. Mrs. Kennedy is organizing herself. It takes longer, but, of course, she looks better than we do when she does it. But we appreciate your welcome.

This city has been a great western city, the defense of the West, cattle, oil, and all the rest. It has believed in strength in this city, and strength in this State, and strength in this country.

What we are trying to do in this country and what we are trying to do around the world, I believe, is quite simple: and that is to build a military structure which will defend the vital interests of the United States. And in that great cause, Fort Worth, as it did in World War II, as it did in developing the best bomber system in the world, the B-58, and as it will now do in developing the best fighter system in the world, the TFX, Fort Worth will play its proper part. And that is why we have placed so much emphasis in the last 3 years in building a defense system second to none, until now the United States is stronger than it has ever been in its history. And secondly, we believe that the new environment, space, the new sea, is also an area where the United States should be second to none.

And this State of Texas and the United States is now engaged in the most concentrated effort in history to provide leadership in this area as it must here on earth. And this is our second great effort. And in December-next month-the United States will fire the largest booster in the history of the world, putting us ahead of the Soviet Union in that area for the first time in our history.

And thirdly, for the United States to fulfill its obligations around the world requires that the United States move forward economically, that the people of this country participate in rising prosperity. And it is a fact in 1962, and the first 6 months of 1963, the economy of the United States grew not only faster than nearly every Western country, which had not been true in the fifties, but also grew faster than the Soviet Union itself. That is the kind of strength the United States needs, economically, in space, militarily.

And in the final analysis, that strength depends upon the willingness of the citizens of the United States to assume the burdens of leadership.

I know one place where they are, here in this rain, in Fort Worth, in Texas, in the United States. We are going forward. Thank you.

NOTE: The President spoke at 8:45 a.m. (c.s.t.) to a group assembled in a park - ing lot across the street from the Texas Hotel where the Chamber of Commerce breakfast was about to begin. In his opening words he referred to Vice President Lyndon B. Johnson, Representative Jim Wright, Governor John B. Connally, and Senator Ralph W. Yarborough, all of Texas, and to Raymond Buck, president of the Fort Worth Chamber of Commerce.

Remarks at the Breakfast of the Ft. Worth Chamber Of Commerce. 11/22/63

Mr. Buck, Mr. Vice President, Governor Connally, Senator Yarborough, Jim Wright, members of the congressional delegation, Mr. Speaker, Mr. Attorney General, ladies and gentlemen:

Two years ago, I introduced myself in Paris by saying that I was the man who had accompanied Mrs. Kennedy to Paris. I am getting somewhat that same sensation as I travel around Texas. Nobody wonders what Lyndon and I wear.

I am glad to be here in Jim Wright's city. About 35 years ago, a Congressman from California who had just been elected received a letter from an irate constituent which said: "During the campaign you promised to have the Sierra Madre Mountains reforested. You have been in office one month and you haven't done so." Well, no one in Fort Worth has been that unreasonable, but in some ways he has had the Sierra Madre Mountains reforested, and here in Fort Worth he has contributed to its growth.

He speaks for Fort Worth and he speaks for the country, and I don't know any city that is better represented in the Congress of the United States than Fort Worth. And if there are any Democrats here this morning, I am sure you wouldn't hold that against him.

Three years ago last September I came here, with the Vice President, and spoke at Burke Burnett Park, and I called, in that speech, for a national security policy and a national security system which was second to none-a position which said not first, but, if, when and how, but first. That city responded to that call as it has through its history. And we have been putting that pledge into practice ever since.

And I want to say a word about that pledge here in Fort Worth, which understands national defense and its importance to the security of the United States. During the days of the Indian War, this city was a fort. During the days of World War I, even before the United States got into the war, Royal Canadian Air Force pilots were training here. During the days of World War II, the great Liberator bombers, in which my brother flew with his co-pilot from this city, were produced here.

The first nonstop flight around the world took off and returned here, in a plane built in factories here. The first truly intercontinental bomber, the B-36, was produced here. The B-58, which is the finest weapons system in the world today, which has demonstrated most recently in flying from Tokyo to London, with an average speed of nearly 1,000 miles per hour, is a Fort Worth product.

The Iroquois helicopter from Fort Worth is a mainstay in our fight against the guerrillas in South Viet-Nam. The transportation of crews between our missile sites is done in planes produced here in Fort Worth. So wherever the confrontation may occur, and in the last 3 years it has occurred on at least three occasions, in Laos, Berlin, and Cuba, and it will again-wherever it occurs, the products of Fort Worth and the men of Fort Worth provide us with a sense of security.

And in the not too distant future a new Fort Worth product-and I am glad that there was a table separating Mr. Hicks and myself-a new Fort Worth product, the TFX Tactical Fighter Experimental-nobody knows what those words mean, but that is what they mean, Tactical Fighter Experimental-will serve the forces of freedom and will be the number one airplane in the world today.

There has been a good deal of discussion of the long and hard fought competition to win the TFX contract, but very little discussion about what this plane will do. It will be the first operational aircraft ever produced that can literally spread its wings through the air. It will thus give us a single plane capable of carrying out missions of speed as well as distance, able to fly very far in one form or very fast in another. It can take off from rugged, short airstrips, enormously increasing the Air Force's ability to participate in limited wars. The same basic plane will serve the Navy's carriers, saving the taxpayers at least $1 billion in costs if they built separate planes for the Navy and the Air Force.

The Government of Australia, by purchasing $125 million of TFX planes before they are even off the drawing boards, has already testified to the merit of this plane, and at the same time it is confident in the ability of Fort Worth to meet its schedule. In all these ways, the success of our national defense depends upon this city in the western United States, 10,000 miles from Viet-Nam, 5,000 or 6,ooo miles from Berlin, thousands of miles from trouble spots in Latin America and Africa or the Middle East. And yet Fort Worth and what it does and what it produces participates in all these great historic events. Texas, as a whole, and Fort Worth bear particular responsibility for this national defense effort, for military procurement in this State totals nearly $1 1/4 billion, fifth highest among all the States of the Union. There are more military personnel on active duty in this State than any in the Nation, save one-and it is not Massachusetts-any in the Nation save one, with a combined military-civilian defense payroll of well over a billion dollars. I don't recite these for any partisan purpose. They are the result of American determination to be second to none, and as a result of the effort which this country has made in the last 3 years we are second to none.

In the past 3 years we have increased the defense budget of the United States by over 20 percent; increased the program of acquisition for Polaris submarines from 24 to 41; increased our Minuteman missile purchase program by more than 75 percent; doubled the number of strategic bombers and missiles on alert; doubled the number of nuclear weapons available in the strategic alert forces; increased the tactical nuclear forces deployed in Western Europe by over 60 percent; added five combat ready divisions to the Army of the United States, and five tactical fighter wings to the Air Force of the United States; increased our strategic airlift capability by 75 percent; and increased our special counter-insurgency forces which are engaged now in South Viet-Nam by 600 percent. I hope those who want a stronger America and place it on some signs will also place those figures next to it.

This is not an easy effort. This requires sacrifice by the people of the United States. But this is a very dangerous and uncertain world. As I said earlier, on three occasions in the last 3 years the United States has had a direct confrontation. No one can say when it will come again. No one expects that our life will be easy, certainly not in this decade, and perhaps not in this century. But we should realize what a burden and responsibility the people of the United States have borne for so many years. Here, a country which lived in isolation, divided and protected by the Atlantic and the Pacific, uninterested in the struggles of the world around it, here in the short space of 18 years after the Second World War, we put ourselves, by our own will and by necessity, into defense of alliances with countries all around the globe. Without the United States, South Viet-Nam would collapse overnight. Without the United States, the SEATO alliance would collapse overnight. Without the United States the CENTO alliance would collapse overnight. Without the United States there would be no NATO. And gradually Europe would drift into neutralism and indifference. Without the efforts of the United States in the Alliance for Progress, the Communist advance onto the mainland of South America would long ago have taken place.

So this country, which desires only to be free, which desires to be secure, which desired to live at peace for 18 years under three different administrations, has borne more than its share of the burden, has stood watch for more than its number of years. I don't think we are fatigued or tired. We would like to live as we once lived. But history will not permit it. The Communist balance of power is still strong. The balance of power is still on the side of freedom. We are still the keystone in the arch of freedom, and we will continue to do as we have done in our past, our duty, and the people of Texas will be in the lead.

So I am glad to come to this State which has played such a significant role in so many efforts in this century, and to say that here in Fort Worth you people will be playing a major role in the maintenance of the security of the United States for the next 10 years. I am confident, as I look to the future, that our chances for security, our chances for peace, are better than they have been in the past. And the reason is because we are stronger. And with that strength is a determination to not only maintain the peace, but also the vital interests of the United States. To that great cause, Texas and the United States are committed. Thank you.

NOTE: The President spoke at 9 a.m. (c.s.t.) in the Texas Hotel in Fort Worth. In his opening words he referred to Raymond Buck, president of the Fort Worth Chamber of Commerce, Vice President Lyndon B. Johnson, and to Governor John B. Connally, Senator Ralph W. Yarborough, Repre. sentative Jim Wright, Byron Tunnell, Speaker of the State House of Representatives, and Waggoner Carr, State Attorney General, all of Texas. He later referred to Marion Hicks, a vice president of Fort Worth General Dynamics and vice president of the Fort Worth Chamber of Commerce.

After the breakfast at the Texas Hotel in Fort Worth the President flew to Love Field in Dallas. There he acknowledged greetings for a brief period and then entered an open car. The motorcade traveled along a zo-mile route through down - town Dallas on its way to the Trade Mart, where the President planned to speak at a luncheon. At approximately 12:30 P-m - (c.s.t.) he was struck by two bullets fired by an assassin.

The President was pronounced dead at 1 p.m. at the Parkland Hospital in Dallas.

Steamshovel still hasn't gotten over the passing of its heroes and comrades Timothy Leary, William S. Burroughs and Allen Ginsberg, all within a year's span. While it continues to mull over an appropriate memorial for these great creative minds and godfathers of the info-age, *Steamshovel* presents here a new historical, conspiracy-oriented analysis of Beat history. This essay was written by Adam Gorightly shortly before the death wave that took the greatest minds of their generation. It focusses on Neal Cassady, safe in heaven dead long before.

THE VISIONS OF NEAL & THE BEATS
BY ADAM GORIGHTLY

A new Kerouac book! The image of Cassady in San Quentin below is from Al Aronowitz's Beat Papers, Column 23. Visit www.bigmagic.com/pages/blackj/column23.html for more. (c. Harry Redl)

Mystics and seers down through the ages have reacted to their environments in various manners. Most have been viewed as outcasts, social misfits swimming against the consensus tide of popular convention. Some have been burned alive, or nailed to the cross; others excommunicated, their writings fed to bonfires of the religiously fanatic. Some chose the contemplative life, isolating themselves from the confusion of the cities, high atop mountain monasteries in deep meditative retreat. But in this modern age, it seems, there is no escape from the mounting acceleration that appears to be sweeping us ever faster toward the millennium. Thus has been born a new category of mysticism: Guerrilla Khundalini. The urban sprawl invades our open spaces and it's cacophony assails the human mind, as mysticism and a crumbling culture collide, giving birth to the holy mad man, or as Kerouac deemed this holy goof: Ignu.

The visionary of our apocalyptic age is bound to be a tormented soul, subject to an occasional psychotic split. These modern age 'mystics' are merely a reflection of their times; products of contemporary set and setting. So the likes of a Neal Cassady, Allen Ginsberg or William Burroughs are not true mystics in the real sense of the word. They are — in essence — distorted visionaries, desolate angels; their mystic vision impaired by the lunacy of the age. This ostensibly leads to their excessive or peculiar behavior, as some would perceive the manifold machinations of the Beats, and related movements. Another limiting factor is the parasitic star syndrome, where the modern mystic/guru is mass marketed ala *On The Road*, *The Electric Acid Kool-Aid Test* or the tune "Cassidy" by the Grateful Dead. In this paradigm Jesus would have been a co-opted major movie star in cool shades. Rock stars and Beat icons have joined the ranks in the cathedrals of idol worship; the sacraments and names have changed, but the rituals remain much the same. The burning of incense and candles and the imbibing of strange wines. Back in my wayward youth we'd 'turn on' a black light to 'illuminate' that famous Hendrix-smoking-a-doobie poster with "Stone Free" blaring at top volume, as along came Mary to consecrate our red-eye chants comparing Jimi to God. In retrospect, these remembrances seem just as much ritual as any church service I've ever attended. Furthermore, *The Legend of Dulouz* speaks to me on a much larger scale than all the Bibles dreamt of in your philosophy, Bob Larson.

* * *

During the summer of 1948, poet Allen Ginsberg experienced a series of "visions" triggered in part by the absence of his beat circle of friends, who had, at this time, dispersed themselves like a beatific virus in varying directions across the globe. "I gave up, I shut down the machinery, I stopped thinking, I stopped living," as he later described his psychological make-up during this period. Ginsberg's state of mental dissolution — or ego loss — immediately brings to mind the writings of Carlos Castaneda, and his mentor don Juan, who instructed his apprentice that in order to lift the veil of ordinary reality one must 'stop the world.' In his own unique fashion this is what Ginsberg unintentionally attained, as he — for the first time — had no immediate circle of friends in whom to confide; "...no New Vision and No Supreme Reality and nothing but the world in front of me, and not knowing what to do with that." Psychologically discombobulated, Ginsberg immersed himself in various religious and metaphysical tracts such as Saint Teresa of Avila, Saint John of the Cross, and William Blake. One afternoon, while reading Blake's "Ah, Sunflower" Ginsberg experienced the first in a series of transcendent visions that over the next decade dominated his every waking thought. It was there in his solitary apartment that he heard "a voice of rock...like the voice of the Ancient of Days." Ginsberg realized immediately that this voice was none other than the spirit of Blake speaking directly to him. In the early evening dusk, Ginsberg gazed upon the booming metropolis outside his lonesome window, as suddenly the view he'd witnessed hundreds of times before was instantly transformed. He saw God. "I suddenly realized that this was it!...This was the moment I was born for." Over the following weeks, the voice of the immortal bard returned to Ginsberg again and again, triggering an endless stream of mystical visions, both euphoric and paranoiac.

Some might suspect that Ginsberg was in the throes of a psychotic break, as he wandered for weeks in a mystical trance, under the guidance of Blake's immortal voice. At other times these visions turned horrific, as Ginsberg suddenly saw beyond the veils that cover human faces, deep into the hidden soul of suffering humanity.

When at last the visions surceased, Ginsberg was left with a deep conviction, as he vowed to himself: "Never deny the voice—no, never forget it, don't get lost mentally wandering in other spirit worlds or American or job worlds or advertising worlds or earth worlds." Be true to thyself, and the voice inside your heart, was the universal message Ginsberg brought back from his vision-quest. As has been stated since time immemorial, there is a fine line that separates the mad man from the genius. There are none better who illustrate this point than Ginsberg and his fellow Beats.

* * *

When I suggest that the likes of a Kerouac, Ginsberg, Burroughs and Cassady are modern day mystics, I mean in the sense of the holy mad man; the solipsistic saint. A common and undeniable thread running through these mystical experiences is the deliberate application of artificial stimuli to induce sacred and terrifying visions. Lost in Illumination—suffering the cumulative ills of societal dysfunction—their symptoms, a reflection of the times. Their cold turkey was the dark night of the soul. The Illumination so bright, it momentarily blinded them. But as the first mainline flash wore off, it was replaced by the essence of their vision, in all it's magnificent and terrifying glory.

In primitive cultures—where shamanism has been practiced for millennia—visions of this magnitude are prepared for through years of ritual and rigorous training. In this manner the eternal mysteries take years to unravel, through numerous esoteric rites and levels of initiation. It could then be said that such artificial sacraments as peyote, LSD-25 and ayahuasca are a nickel bag of mixed blessings. This instant freeze dried Illumination purchased on the street for a couple bucks can sometimes perpetuate a disorienting environment, an assault—or derangement—to the senses; a confusion of spheres. Or a term Newspeakian Joan d'Arc has coined that could be applied to this form of balls-to-the-wall Transcendentalism, the aforementioned Guerrilla Khundalini. With instant vision comes instant karma, as well: Virtual Heaven & Hell. Perhaps this is the reason why the Cassadys and Burroughs of the world flirted so openly with the criminal element; maybe this is why they chased with reckless abandon chemical dragons through the figurative flames—into the bottomless pit and across the Abyss—only to be resurrected time and again; to rise victorious from the ashes of their self-inflicted suffering. Without going through 'Hell', one can never truly appreciate the bounties of Heaven; Nirvana. Without surrendering to the carnal desires, one can never fully comprehend the spirit world which exists beyond the limitations of corporeal flesh. (No one knows what really went down when William Burroughs shot his common-law wife, Joan Vollmer—dead in the head—while allegedly playing William Tell with her in Mexico. Nonetheless this nefarious episode has been a personal Hell that

Burroughs has had to live with for the past 40 years.)

Some will be outraged, no doubt, when I compare the likes of Burroughs to Thomas Aquinas and other like saints. Hedonism, nihilism & existentialism are not oft considered saintly attributes, though what I think Ginsberg, Burroughs, Kerouac and Cassady all shared in common with the saints of old is a dedication to a principle and way of life (on the Beaten path, though it might have been) devoting themselves to the search for enlightenment, albeit through a queer assortment of means. A longhaired Jesus once prophesied: "My father's house has many mansions" which could denote varying levels of consciousness, esoteric knowledge and myriad metaphysical systems employed to realize these heightened neurological states, as employed by the Beats and subsequent countercultural currents.

Don't get me wrong: I don't find anything particularly glamorous about the junkie lifestyle. But Burrough's approach to hard-core drug addiction was so unlike the junkies of his day, that it set him light years apart, particularly in relation to the generations of doomed who've followed blindly after. His was a search for the true and underlining meaning of addiction, need and control. Burroughs' re/search became a larger model and metaphor for his entire philosophy . Burroughs once stated his personal belief that, as long as he was learning from his addiction, it held some importance for him, no matter how dark and lost he was in this self taught education on the edge. When finally he freed himself from the shackles of opium bondage, homosexual urges replaced his junk cravings, taking him even further down the dark path of self discovery, a journey which he documented in Queer, his second literary endeavor, the followup to his first novel, Junkie. Where these two books were the basis of his self-taught existential education, *Naked Lunch* became his Master's Thesis. In 1953, Burroughs journeyed into the Amazon in search of an hallucinatory agent he'd heard extraordinary tales of; the shamanic vine, Yagé. Purportedly — along with the transcendental jungle visions ascribed to it — Yage (also known as Ayahuasca) was said to possess other mysterious qualities. One such being the possible facilitation and/or increase of telepathic abilities, as exhibited by its vomit spewing users. This prospect intrigued Burroughs, as over the years he'd begun to develop certain telepathic powers, establishing mental contact most notably with his late common law wife and speed fiend, Joan Vollmer. Upon occasion she and Bill would perform paranormal parlor tricks of a telepathic nature for the amusement of curious bohemian onlookers with benzedrine inhalers on their breath.

The brujos of the Amazon — who Burroughs eventually located, and from them partook of this sacramental vine — believed that their ayahuasca-produced visions were the communications of disembodied souls from the spirit world. If one looks into the wide array literature on this subject, many are the mind-bending accounts of those who've imbibed from the brujo's gooey spoon. According to Burroughs — no novice to drug experimentation — Yage, as he said at the time, "...is the most powerful drug I have ever experienced. That is, it produces the most complete derangement of the senses...It is like nothing else. This is not the chemical lift of C, the sexless, horrible sane stasis of junk, the vegetable nightmare of peyote, or the humorous silliness of weed. This is insane overwhelming rape of the senses." The more conservative minded among us might wonder: Why would anyone want to rape their senses? But this, in essence, was the credo of the Beats. One of the major influences on the Beat Movement was the French Decadent, Rimbaud, who wrote:

"A poet makes himself a visionary through a long, boundless, and systematized disorganization of all the senses. All forms of love, of suffering, of madness; he searches himself, he exhausts within himself all poisons, and preserves their quintessences. Unspeakable torment, where he will need the greatest faith, a superhuman strength, where he becomes all men the great invalid, the great criminal, the great accursed — and the Supreme

Scientist! For he attains the unknown! Because he has cultivated his soul, already rich, more than anyone! He attains the unknown, and if, demented, he finally loses the understanding of his visions, he will at least have seen them! So what if he is destroyed in his ecstatic flight through things unheard of, unnameable: other horrible workers will come; they will begin at the horizons where the first one has fallen!" Arthur Rimbaud (May 15, 1871)

It may appear to the short-sighted that I'm an apologist for the excesses of the Beats. Well, maybe so. Over the years I've derived unfathomed value from their cumulative words and deeds. I believe they touched a raw nerve in the psyche of the post World War II generation, envisioning a new spirit that came partially to fruition with the sixties psychedelic counter-culture, then afterwards with seventies Punk sensibility, and still currently reverberating in our collective craniums as a species, in some dormant shape or form. Anyone who believes Rush Limbaugh's vision of America is the true destiny of our nation is either deluded, or in on the grand Masonic scam. Kerouac saw it like was, and had the conviction and honesty to bare his soul with blood from vein to pen on holy parchment. Dig:

"...Japhy (Gary Snyder) was considered an eccentric around campus, which is the usual thing for campuses and college people to think whenever a real man appears on scene—colleges being nothing but grooming schools for the middleclass non-entity which usually finds it's perfect expression on the outskirts of the campus in rows of well-to-do houses with lawns and television sets in each livingroom with everybody looking at the same thing and thinking the same thing at the same time while the Japhies of the world go prowling in the wilderness to hear the voice crying in the wilderness, to find the ecstasy of the stars..." (*The Dharma Bums*, pg. 32-33.)

In another section from *The Dharma Bums*, Kerouac accurately prophesied (through the voice of character Japhy Ryder) a 'rucksack revolution'. This mid-fifties revelation foresaw an advent generation of long haired backpacking hitchhikers, seeking something more than what conventional society of the time had to offer:

"I've been reading Whitman, know what he says, Cheer up slaves, and horrify foreign despots, he means that's the attitude for the Bard, the Zen Lunacy bard of old desert paths, see the whole thing is a world full of rucksack wanderers, Dharma Bums refusing to subscribe to the general demand that they consume production and therefore have to work for the privilege of consuming, all that crap they didn't want anyway such as refrigerators, TV sets, cars, at least new fancy cars, certain hair oils and deodorants and general junk you always see a week later in the garbage anyway, all of them imprisoned in a system of work, produce, consume, work, produce, consume, I see a vision of a great rucksack revolution thousands or even millions of young Americans wandering around with rucksacks, going up to the mountains to pray, making children laugh and old men glad, making young girls happy and old girls happier, all of 'em Zen Lunatics who go about writing poems that happen to appear in their heads for no reason..." (*The Dharma Bums*, pg. 77-78)

On another note, there are those who would suggest that the Beat Movement was part of a grand conspiracy; and the Beats themselves unwitting pawns in this game. In one of his many broadsheets self-published over the years, Kerry Thornley once posited this theory, without actually elaborating on exactly what this conspiracy entailed. Perhaps what Thornley was alluding to is the same theme found in Todd Brendan Fahey's *Wisdom's Maw*, which suggests that Ken Kesey as well as the Beats were part of an elaborate scheme concocted by the American Intelligence Community to infiltrate and supply the sixties counterculture with mind altering drugs, ostensibly to test their reactions, and—long range—to influence widespread social control. Theoretically, this was all conducted under the covert auspices of such infamous CIA mind control projects as Artichoke and MK-ULTRA. Such countercultural icons as Kesey and

Leary—Fahey suggests—were chosen by the CIA and Military Intelligence as facilitators of this grand experiment, whose powerful side effects are still lingering to this day in the collective craniums of it's unwitting participants.

Kerouac—toward the tail-end of this life—was also of the impression that the sixties counterculture had been co-opted by sinister forces. Soddened by liquor, and dismayed by what he felt was the unpatriotic posture assumed by these long haired freaks (who, adding insult to injury, had credited his books for their hippie dippie philosophy) Kerouac feared a Communist Conspiracy was behind the tumultuous events of that era. One also gets the impression in later comments that he believed the Jews played a part in these behind the scenes manipulations. Kerouac—one of the more open-minded and tolerant souls of his generation—by the end of the sixties had turned into a slurring, often incoherent, commie bashing rummy, whose literary output dwindled as his intake of hard liquor increased. The last thing Kerouac wrote before his death was a screed directed at the hippies and the anti-war movement entitled, "After Me, the Deluge."

In a poem dedicated to his passing, Gregory Corso compared Kerouac's destruction by alcohol to the disastrous effects that Fire Water had exacted upon the Native American culture. This in retrospect is a fitting metaphor. The same forces that nearly drove the America Indian to extinction, were in fact the same powers that delivered Kerouac to an early grave. He drank for the same reasons the Indians did; to bury the pain, and to escape from the tragedy of a self-destructive civilization teetering on the edge of ruin.

Ginsberg, on the other hand, passionately embraced the sixties counterculture, growing long his hair and beard, donning lovebeads, and participating in love-ins, acid tests and anti-war demonstrations. At the outset of the decade, he participated in Tim Leary's psilocybin research at Harvard. On the momentous night of November 26, 1960, Ginsberg received a vision from on high instructing the mad poet that he would be The Messiah to herald in a psychedelic revolution. Under Leary's supportive guidance—and 36 milligrams of psilocybin—Ginsberg wandered downstairs naked, determined to alert the world's leaders that a new epoch was at hand: Instead of nuclear mushroom clouds, mushrooms of an entirely different nature would intervene, bringing love and illumination to a world on the brink of nuclear annihilation. Ginsberg got on the phone and started placing calls to the Kremlin and White House, identifying himself to the telephone operator as God (he spelled it out for her, G-O-D). Unsuccessful in his attempts to reach Kennedy or Kruschev, Ginsberg got ahold of Kerouac and informed The King o' the Beats that: "I am high and naked and I am King of the Universe. Get on a plane. It is time!" It was the wish of both Leary and Ginsberg that the world's leaders get togetherin a United Nations type setting, and drop psilocybin all at one time. This, they agreed, would cause "...Everyone to plug in at once and announce the Coming Union of All Consciousness."

This wasn't the first time Ginsberg had attained a mystical state under the influence of mind altering drugs. But in the company of Dr. Leary a great plan started to form—in Ginsberg's mushrooming mind—of a psychedelic revolution, with the likes of Leary and himself leading the charge, spearheading a mass movement that would transform the planet, sending spores around the world. Leary, later on, turned on Kerouac and Burroughs, as well, though each had mixed emotions regarding their respective experiences. Ken Kesey, with his own huge stash of Owsley manufactured LSD, shared the same chemical illumination with Neal Cassady. Whether or not Leary and Kesey were witting members of the aforementioned MK-ULTRA mind control programs, we may never positively ascertain, though their respective participations in LSD proliferation were monumental in promoting the sixties psychedelic scene.

Ginsberg first became acquainted with LSD in 1959, through government sponsored research at the Menlo Research Institute in Palo Alto. Kesey and Jerry Garcia were also early volunteers for these mind-bending experiments, which many connect directly to MK-ULTRA. This before the term psychedelic was in the popular lexicon. At this time psychedelics were referred to as 'psychomimetic' drugs; drugs that reportedly brought about temporary psychosis. Kesey and the other adventurous souls who volunteered their brains for science received 75 dollars a day. Due to a bad trip courtesy of the Menlo Research Institute, Ginsberg composed a poem under the influence of LSD, aptly titled, "Lysergic Acid" of which the following is an excerpt: It is a multiple million eyed monster it is hidden in all it's elephants and selves it hummeth in the electric typewriter it is electricity connected to itself, if it hath wires it is a vast Spiderweb... I, as well, have beheld this multiple million eyed monster, hidden — as it is — in all elephants and selves. Like Ginsberg, acid brought about this nightmarish vision, on the full-size Technicolor viewing screen behind my closed eyelids. Whether or not this monstrous, Bosch-like archetype is inherent exclusively to practitioners of Guerrilla Khundalini, I can not authoritatively address. Nevertheless, I find it interesting that Ginsberg's description of this demonic entity — viewed under the influence of lysergic acid diethylamide — matches almost perfectly my own temporary psychedelic psychosis, producing what would appear to be a shared thematic experience linking the drug experimentation of the Beat subculture with my own generation of Guerrilla Khundalini adepts, forming — one might conjecture — a metaphysical conspiracy that bridges generations; that of a religion of elitists waving no particular banner (except maybe, a "freak flag"), dedicated to the principle of discovering "GOD" on their own terms, without benefit of a mediating agency, or dogmatic agenda. Robert Anton Wilson summed it up best in his intro to *Cosmic Trigger* when categorizing this new age of holy mad men:

"We are all evolving into the use of new neurological circuits, which will make us superhuman in comparison to our present average state. The activation of these new circuits creates a great deal of temporary weirdness until we learn to use them properly..."

This concept of 'evolving...new neurological circuits' (or whatever you want to call it) is not something entirely novel to the human experience. This neurological expansion of consciousness — which opens the figurative "door of perception" — has long been ajar, allowing only an initiated few to glimpse through it's cosmic crack. The Beats just pushed the door open further, placing their New Vision more prominently before the masses, albeit projected through the distorted lens of The Media. What followed a decade later totally blew "the door" off it's hinges, with the subsequent psychedelic/neurological revolution fostered by the likes of such sixties luminaries as Kesey, Leary, R.A. Wilson, and more recently, The Brothers McKenna.

While some might find my personal multiple-million-eyed-monster-made-manifest-by-LSD experience — this so-called "bridge between generations" — a bit tenuous, a more obvious and enduring case could be made for Cassady, who steered his karmic wheel across two cultural phenomenons, starting on the road with Kerouac in the late forties/early fifties in his role as the infant terrible of the Beats, and then later in the mid-sixties with Kesey and the Pranksters, as the elder statesman of lunatic psychedelia. These respective pilgrimages set the tone for what was to follow, first with the Beat Movement, then afterwards with the sixties counterculture. Both of these movements exhibited religious attributes and inward yearnings that led to mass societal movements, though admittedly short-lived in a wide spread sense.

Delving even deeper into this line of reasoning, another obvious link connecting countercultural movements was the tragic figure of Bill Cannastra, who actualized the punk ethic a quarter of a century before it's pierced nipple metamorph. An intimate of Kerouac's, Cannastra — known for dancing naked to Bach fugues on shattered glass — was another model of life teetering on the edge; a practitioner of self abuse and suicidal tendencies. A law school dropout, he spearheaded a core group of "subter-raneans" as Kerouac would later dub them. This New York school of soci-etal misfits often gathered for drunken all night debaucheries at Cannastra's infamous downtown loft, gutted as it was of any semblance of rational decor, littered with broken records, stained mattresses, and slashed car seats. In this manner, the "Church of Bill" served as an early blueprint of the Punk ethic. As a character in John Clellon Holmes' *Go*, rhap-sodized,"Don't you know that people who can't believe in anything else always believe in Bill?"

In nothing less than the dramatic fashion Cannastra conducted his life, with equal theatrics it ended. In 1950 The Church of Bill officially closed it's doors for good when it's unholy architect attempted to climb out of a sub-way window as it was leaving a New York train station and was immedi-ately, and ceremoniously decapitated. Thus brought the physical manifes-tation of the Church of Bill to a grand and grisly finale.

* * *

Situating himself in the company of intellectual bohemians, Neal Cassady's sparkling intellect burned with primal intensity, dedicated as he was to living in the Now. Unfortunately — in a world of everyday responsi-bilities — some suffered needlessly due to Neal's psychotic spur of the moment recklessness. What with his unbridled libido and voracious appetite for speed, both chemical and automotive, he left in his wake a slew of ruined relationships and demolished cars, with dirty bandage wrappings dangling from his thumb. But I think it was this primal energy that so enraptured the imaginations of Kerouac, Ginsberg, et al. As Ken Kesey once upon a moment of clarity stated, "I saw that Cassady did everything a novel does, except that he did it better because he was living it and not writing about it."

When he first crossed Cassady's off-centered path, Kesey was consid-ered one of the up and coming talents on the American literary scene. Having experienced critical acclaim and success with *One Flew Over The Cuckoo's Nest*, Kesey's second novel *Sometimes a Great Notion*, was released soon after. Many found it unusual then, that — after these two early tri-umphs — his next work of fiction was decades in the making. It was as if he'd put a hold to his literary career to follow the lead of Cassady, by turn-ing his life into a novel, which is exactly what it became with the release of Tom Wolfe's *Electric Kool-Aid Acid Test*, detailing the zany antics of Kesey and his Merry Pranksters, with Sir Speed Limit — as Cassady was called in later years — at the helm of Intrepid.

The Pranksters themselves felt as if they were tuned into certain para-normal frequencies, picking up on the very same etheric energies that Cassady had so finely dialed in. Often times, when they had misplaced a certain object, at just the point in time when they needed it most, the item in question — whatever it may have been, a roach clip or wrench — would mysteriously appear, as if they had willed it into being with their collective and chemically influenced thought-waves. As a group, they also developed an uncanny ability to find things in the dark, as if their cumulative inges-tion of acid had precipitated a new facility within their tuned-in heads. As Mountain Girl said of these off-the-wall abilities,"We were blind, but we had eyes in our feet. It set our heads swimming."

Literally overnight a monumental paradigm shift had swept away old worlds for new, blossoming rainbows of possibilities. LSD had lifted the veil, enabling a new way of seeing, to use the vernacular of Carlos Castaneda. For the Pranksters, Cassady was a role model of how to relate to the beautiful madness of a post-LSD world. From him, the Merry Pranksters took their lead. Quoth the cosmic clown, Wavy Gravy, "Neal was so far ahead of his time, that he'd point for those of us just struggling to be with the moment."

Neal's psychic powers manifested themselves in multifarious manners; some in the form of paranormal parlor tricks, similar to those performed by

Bill Burroughs in Mexico. One such showbiz like routine of Neal's was where he'd rattle off the serial number of a dollar bill whenever anyone pulled one from their pockets. Often times he'd get the entire number correct, all ten digits. Other precognitive feats Neal consistently performed were in the form of predicting when a person would enter a room, what their gender and physical appearance would be, and what type of mission they were on. On long lonely stretches of road Neal often performed a similar feat, predicting correctly time and again the make of the next vehicle that would pass them by in the night, and any particulars regarding the vehicle, such as a missing headlight, or body damage. Another peculiar mechanization of the 'Fastestmanalive!' (as Neal was also knighted) was his legendary tossing of the hammer, a four pound sledge that he wielded with all the skill and authority of the mighty Thor. Many felt that Neal's incessant hammer tossing was some sort of holy chore, like a zen monk chanting, or a saint's meditation. But once again, these were different mystics, using different methods to initiate enlightenment. Ken Kesey — in all his unconventional wisdom — believed that whenever the sure handed Cassady dropped his hammer, it was due to bad vibrations in the room, and that Cassady had purposely dropped the hammer to break up those negative vibes. To Kesey, there were no 'accidents' as far as Cassady was concerned. Cassady drove like a maniac all his life, though never once was he ever involved in a traffic accident. Many ascribed this good fortune to his remarkable relationship with time, able to live on the edge but in the same instance foresee coming changes in fractions of seconds.

One of the more remarkable statements from *On The Road* is when the Dean Moriarty/Cassady character animatedly proclaims, "We all know time!" The meaning of this pronouncement can be interpreted in a variety of ways, but my take on it is one of the observer perceiving time in terms of a Quantum Physics model; of several realities existing side by side, concurrent in time and space.

In all of Neal's frenzied and spasmodic actions, intimates were well aware of his innate and mind-blowing ability to carry on several conversations — with two or more people — simultaneously, gear-shifting his focus from one conversation level to the next with rapid fire precision, driving high speed through a telepathic traffic of souls switching lanes in stream of consciousness, oftentimes anticipating where each respective conversation was rolling well before arriving at it's destination, in an amphetamine fueled brainstorm of neurologic activity, spark-plug synapses firing at breakneck speed, steering through the highways and byways of the full tilt, locomotive high octane mind of 'Sir Speed Limit'.

When Neal was a young lad, his older half brother Jimmy often bullied him. It was Jimmy's habit to throw Neal onto a bed that pulled out from beneath a cupboard, then deposit bed and brother back into the wall. Unable to defend himself against his older brother's merciless thumpings — and afraid to shout out for help because it would cause Jimmy to attack him even more aggressively — Neal discovered a transformative method of turning his fear into a visionary experience, and in fact rather grew to enjoy the sensation he self-induced while trapped in the claustrophobic darkness. This sensation was akin to sensory deprivation effects produced in an isolation tank, as sometimes Neal would be locked in the pitch blackness of the wall for upwards to an hour. Trapped in this narrow passage with less than a foot of clearance, a disorientation of the senses would begin, like an "off balanced wheel whirling" in his skull, as Neal experienced a sensation that time was moving at triple speed, in "a loose fan-like vibration as it rotated into an ever-tightening flutter." The result was "strangely pleasant, yet disturbing enough to frighten, quickening the brain's action which resisted any rigorous attempt to throw it off and return to normal-headedness." Neal would recapture this feeling of psychic dislocation in later years under the influence of LSD and pot.

Sir Speed Limit's supranormal relationship with time would eventually exhibit itself most notably behind the wheel of a car, which he used as a physical extension for his free-wheeling Psyche, so in tune was the man with the combustive music of the road and rolling machines. All who rode with Neal would agree that something special was going on there, with his mind/body&soul in perpetual motion, communing with the automotive and holyboy road. As Mountain Girl once explained,"Neal felt when he was at the wheel of a car that his eyes were registering events ahead of the car at a certain rate and he was perceiving them at a certain rate and it takes a certain number of microseconds for the impulses to travel from the eyes to the brain and get processed and get down to the hand to turn the wheel. He was very sensitive to those tiny fragments of time. He was intimate with time."

It didn't take long for Kerouac to recognize Cassady's special talents. Through Cassady he was able to see the possibilities of a whole generation in the wide open balls to the wall revelatory search discovered on the road, stretching vast lonesome highways of the night, stealing gas and getting laid in the mad rush of his reeling senses, high on speed, blowing gage and ejaculatory wads from sea to frothy sea. From California to New York to New Orleans, then Texas and on to Mexico where Jack fell delirious with dysentery, as wayward Neal abandoned his old buddy for the call of the road, repeating his personal manic mantra of "Go-go-go!!" and vanishing in a cloud of dust, leaving behind lonesome Jack cold-sweating in his Mexican sickbed, beat.

One night, prior to his bout with dysentery (and Neal's sudden departure from Mexico) Kerouac beheld a spectral vision in the mexican jungle. Just before dawn, as Neal slept soundly by the roadside, a white horse trotted by, directly toward Neal, passing right beside where his sleep-filled head rested in slumber. The horse whinnied softly and continued on down that old road, into the city beyond. Thus Kerouac beheld a pale horse, the symbol of destruction, and the ending of time as we know it, symbolically representing an epoch that was already in it's death throes by the time the marketing geniuses of Madison Avenue got around to tagging a name to the best minds of Ginsberg's generation: Beatniks. (Like, cool, daddy-o.) So the writing was on the wall for both these kindred souls of the open road, instructing them that even though their impact would be felt for generations to come, their physical manifestations on the earth would be short-lived, with Neal coming to absolute ruin a decade and a half later in the same Mexican landscape of the mind, where — making good on a bet to count all the railroad ties between San Miguel and Celaya — he met his fate. Stoned on seconal and booze, Neal collapsed, dying of exposure to the elements. As apocryphal legend has it, his last words were, "64,928."

Kerouac — devastated by Cassady's passing — died a couple years later, due to severe extinction of the liver. Too many years of hitting the sauce had taken their toll on the once mighty King o' the Beats.

Selected Bibliography

Burroughs, William. *Naked Lunch*. Olympia Press, 1959.

ibid. *Junkie: Confessions of an Unredeemed Drug Addict*. Ace Books, 1953

ibid. *Queer*. Viking, 1985

ibid. with Allen Ginsberg. *The Yage Letters*. City Lights. 1963

Fahey, Todd Brendan. *Wisdom's Maw*. Far Gone Books, 1996.

Ginsberg, Allen. *Howl and Other Poems*. City Lights, 1956

Kerouac, Jack. *On The Road*. Viking Press, 1955, 1957.

ibid. *The Dharma Bums*. Viking Press, 1958.

Leary, Timothy. *Flashbacks: An Autobiography*. J.P. Tarcher, 1983.

Plummer, William . *The Holy Goof:A Biography of Neal Cassady*. Paragon House, 1990.

Stevens, Jay. *Storming Heaven: LSD and the American Dream*. Perrennial Library, 1988.

Watson, Steven . *The Birth of the Beat Generation: Visionaries, Rebels, and Hipsters, 1944-1960*. Pantheon, 1995.

Wolfe, Tom . *The Electric Kool-Aid Acid Test*. Farrar, Straus and Giroux, 1968.

STEAMSHOVEL PRESS

Aerial view of Tortuguero Lagoon

LONG SPARK RUNNING: NASA's *COQUI* EXPERIMENTS

By Scott Corrales

Skeptics of the UFO phenomenon enjoy pointing out that gullible ufomaniacs are constantly mistaking innocent barium test rockets launched into the upper atmosphere with interplanetary craft. These routine launches are usually reported in newspapers and early-morning radio shows to alert the unwary of the celestial display to follow in the evening.

Puerto Rico has been the stage for a number of such tests — identified under the harmless moniker of "Coqui", named after the island's unique arboreal frog — since 1992. But there is increasing evidence that the seemingly anodyne tests harbor a far more sinister purpose.

SKYROCKETS IN FLIGHT

In the spring and summer 1992, NASA launched the first Coqui sounding rocket, ostensibly to study the ionosphere. The eight-rocket series, launched at half-hourly intervals, was made up of Nike-Tomahawk and Black Brant and IX and VC rockets, was aimed at studying the ionosphere in conjunction with the Arecibo Observatory. A makeshift launch

Roosevelt Roads Naval Base, Ceiba, PR.

pad operated by the Goddard Space Flight Center's Wallops Island Fight Facility was erected at Laguna Tortuguero, the island's only freshwater lagoon, some 20 miles to the west of San Juan. The eight launches were declared successful by NASA officials, although the chemical payloads of the rockets were never recovered. The altitudes reached by the projectiles ranged from 80 miles to 268 miles, making the launches visible in locations as varied as the Turks and Caicos Islands, Antigua, Saint Croix, and Guadeloupe.

The purpose behind the rocket launches was the creation of a number of manmade disturbances in the ionosphere in order to discover its reactions to natural perturbations. The ionosphere, as defined by NASA press releases, is the level of ionized oxygen and nitrogen which reflects almost the entirety of solar radiation that impacts our planet. This absorption of radiation causes a significant degree of thermal excitement which makes the ionosphere a mirror-like reflector of radio waves, causing them to bounce within the surface contained between the planet's surface and the ionosphere itself. Experiments with barium rockets started as far back as 1960, when scientists first contemplated the creation of ion cloud experiments, thus giving rise to the discharging of barium in the upper atmosphere by means of rockets or satellites.

The Coqui experiments generated an even more curious "fallout": on May 25, 1992, Miguel A. Gonzales of Aguadilla saw a huge, egg-shaped ball of orange light descend upon thousands of prayerful spectators who were worshipping the alleged Marian apparitions in the community of Sabana Grande. The ball hovered over the worshippers before gradually dimming into a puff of smoke. UFO watchers reported a number of sightings on that day in the vicinity, where the religious gathering was held. State officials dismissed it all by saying that it was connected to the launching of the Coqui atmospheric test rocket that very same night.

THE PLOT THICKENS

Seven years later, and without the benefit of any hearings on the matter, NASA announced that the Coqu¡ experiments (now known as Coqu¡ II) would resume at the old Laguna Tortuguero launch center, which had in the intervening years become popular site for model aviators and amateur rocketeers. It was announced that the series of launches would begin in January

Old San Juan, PR.

1998. No public or environmental impact declarations had been released nor had the authorization of the local government been requested. It was not long before voices challenging the Coqu¡ project made themselves heard — resentment had been festering since 1992, when the Coqui I launches had led to the indiscriminate clear-cutting of trees in the Tortuguero area.

The contrarian opinions held that the gases and substances employed during the 1992 launches — barium, bromotrifluoride methane, gaseous nitrogen and argon and a host of related chemicals — and the rocket propellants (hydrogen chloride and aluminum oxide) had caused considerable harm to the environment as well as to people using the beaches from one end of northern Puerto Rico to the other. When physicians reported a rise in unexplained cutaneous eruptions among the population, it was argued that their patients had probably been exposed to jellyfish in the water or to other dermatological ailments.

Responding to these charges, the Project Coqui personnel argued that the gases employed during the tests were colorless, non-toxic and non-flammable, and therefore posed no risk whatsoever to neither humans nor the environment. Apparently, no mention was made of the fact that bromotrifluoride is an ozone-depleting substance, and that the outbreaks of gas were taking place particularly at levels which affected the ozone layer.

In mid-December 1997, Vega Baja mayor Luis Melendez Cano demanded that Dr. Maximo Cerame Vivas, the noted Puerto Rican scientist in charge of the new series of launches, furnish the required impact statements before being able to proceed with the launches from the Tortuguero Site, which is located within his municipality. The authorities apparently circumvented this request by providing Mayor Melendez with copies of the old Coqui I environmental statements with handwritten comments on the margins, arguing that the project was essentially the same. The old environmental statement further stated that Vega

Baja was not a densely populated area: the intervening years have seen the growth of a number of new housing subdivisions as the area turned into a major bedroom community of the San Juan metropolitan area.

Deeply troubled by the fact that Coqui II was significantly different from its predecessor, mainly due to the fact that the 1992 launches were conducted during the summer while the 1998 launches would be conducted during the winter, when the wind patterns are completely different, a new letter from Melendez insisted: "We acknowledge receipt of the EIS for the Coqui I project, which has apparently been resubmitted as part of this new effort. Nevertheless, we are troubled by the refusal to submit a new EIS for an event which must have considerable differences in spite of the apparent similarity. We hope that you will advise us on your reasons for negotiating and securing approval for this project without providing a new environmental impact statement." The town's municipal assembly unanimously resolved to support the mayor in this initiative. A spokesman observed that it was impossible to blindly agree with something that is not understood. Why was there so much secrecy concerning an allegedly harmless project?

Bilingual sign on US Navy Property, San Juan, PR

A MILITARY SOLUTION TO THE MYSTERY?

Speculation is rife concerning the real purpose of Project Coqui. Many have tried to link it with futuristic "cyberwar" operations currently under development by the Department of Defense. This vast array of unfriendly uses of the upper atmosphere includes the creation of "upper atmospheric turbulence", induced by chemicals transported via launchers as well as by radiation emitted from land-based installations such as the Arecibo Radiotelescope, which has conducted ionospheric heating tests since the early '70s and whose atmospheric ionization package was upgraded in 1994 at a cost of several million dollars, and shadier facilities such as the oft-mentioned HAARP facility in Alaska. The offensive use of such capacities would be centered on the complete and utter disruption of enemy command, control and communications by means of distorted radio waves or blinding pulses of light which would affect delicate systems. These electronic assaults could be explained away as meteorological phenomena, thus guaranteeing the attacker complete deniability during a peacetime application.

Though alarming, the above is really nothing new. In the late 1950's, both the former Soviet Union and the U.S. engaged in a series of nuclear atmospheric tests aimed at the production of charged particles in the ionosphere, ostensibly to study the disruption experienced by bomber and ICBM guidance systems. The possibility of "warping" regions of the atmosphere in order to deflect or vaporize ICBM's has also been considered. Scientists such as BernardEastlund have even spoken about the creation of a "shell" of charged particles which would drift around the planet, sizzling the electronics of any hapless object which enter the shell.

Despite the fact that Coqui is widely hailed as a NASA project, the connection with the military is clear. The rocket boosters and their chemical payload originated at the Roosevelt Roads Naval Base on the island's eastern coast, which once housed the Antilles Defense Command (transferred to Key West, Florida, in 1981) and the Atlantic Fleet Target Range. Roosevelt Roads is the world's largest naval facility, since it includes not only the thirty-thousand acre expanse of the base itself but the adjacent island of Vieques and the ocean surface between both islands. It is important to bear in mind the important role played by Puerto Rico in naval strategic planning: a number of major war games, such as Readex, Solid Shield, Ocean Venture '81, UNITAS, Readex 2-82 and Universal Trek 1-83, involving thousands of soldiers from many countries, dozens of surface ships and hundreds of airplanes, have taken place in the smallest of the Greater Antilles and its outlying islands.

In 1992, the U.S. Air Force was behind the launching of a Spirit II launcher which was used to lift a two-thousand pound auroral research telescope whose measurements were to be employed as part of the Strategic Defense Initiative's research into atmospheric perturbations. The launch was made from the Poker Flat Rocket Range, which is the largest of its kind in the world and has been funded by NASA over the past years, demonstrating yet again the strong connection which exists between the space agency and the military in this field of research.

Scott Corrales is a writer and translator of UFO and paranormal subjects dealing with Latin America and Spain. His work has appeared in magazines in the U.S., U.K., Japan, Spain and Italy. Corrales is also the author of Chupacabras and Other Mysteries, and his forthcoming Flashpoint: High Strangeness in Puerto Rico is being published in the U.K. by Amarna Ltd. He lives in Pennsylvania.

STEAMSHOVEL PRESS

Lobster is a journal of international parapolitics and conspiracy history of long standing in England. Robin Ramsay publishes it twice a year at 214 Westbourne Avenue, Hull, HU5 3JB, UK. Below is the second offering of a column begun by Ramsay in last issue of **Steamshovel.** The current **Lobster** contains absolutely indispensable information about military mind control technology by Armen Victorian, plus material on the Owen Oyston and Shayler affairs, a letter from Kenn Thomas on the **Nexus**-Libya connection, and reconsiderations of the 1970s and the uselessness of spies by editor Ramsay.

Letter from the UK

By Robin Ramsay

Down Mexico Way

At the beginning of November the British TV series on Channel Four, *Equinox*, did a report on the so-called 'earth lights' mysteries, the balls of light seen in the sky, associated with movements in the earth crust and thought to pre-figure earthquakes. Equinox took a team of scientists to Mexico to camp on a major fault-line and wait for said lights. None were forthcoming; but in the course of their inquiries the Equinox team came across the massive UFO flap which has been happening in Mexico in recent years. They interviewed the producer of the Mexican equivalent of the TV programme *60 Minutes*, who told them that in the midst of the 'flap' he had appealed on air for viewers to send inany videotape they had taken of the strange lights in the sky. He received 6,000 video-tapes!

Jesus loves me

The Guardian (London) 2 October 1996 reported that a self-styled Catholic priest was jailed for 10 years for sexually assaulting two teenage boys. Frederick Linale called himself the British Archbishop of the Old Roman Catholic Church, and met his first victim through an advertisement in the Church Times. Kennedy assassination buffs will remember another distinguished alumnus of the Old Catholic Church - David Ferrie, the character memorably, if inaccurately, portrayed by Joe Pesci in Stone's *JFK*. Over a decade ago, in Britain, the Old Catholic Church was also used as cover for predating on boys by the notorious Roger Gleave, self-styled Bishop of the Medway. It must be all that Catholic kitsch - or something.

Splendour in the grass

Issue 13 of the excellent *Flatland* reported some recent comments by the astronomer Carl Sagan on the crop circles phenomenon. Sagan, like many other 'sceptics', attributes the British crop circles to a couple of middle-aged self-confesses hoaxers, Doug and Dave, who emerged from obscurity a couple of years ago to demonstrate how, with planks of wood strapped to their feet, they had made the circles. How the British media loved this story! All those idiots sitting out on the hillsides all summer waiting for aliens to make the circles! Doug and Dave got oceans of coverage, the watchers of crop circles got enough ridicule to last a life-time and the mass media in Britain declared the story dead. None of the journalists bothered to check where Dave and Doug had been on any of the evenings when circles had been observed - and video-taped - forming. This was one of those stories that was just too good to check.

Meanwhile, away from the guffawing tabloid hacks, the circles continued to form, in every-increasing complexity. Aerial photographs of some of the 1996 circles are reproduced in a double-page spread in October/November's *Nexus* magazine. Whatever the story of the crop circles amounts it is absolutely certain that these extraordinary images would be impossible to reproduce on the ground without - at the very minimum - a large team, overhead direction and control, from a helicopter, with radio communication with the ground: and even then with extreme difficulty. One or two of them would be hard to *draw*, let alone create on a com-field. There is still a genuine mystery here, aliens or no.

The smell of power

Some years ago it was revealed - I have forgotten where and by whom - that LBJ, while President, was in the habit of making his aides and cabinet members share the toilet with him while he was taking a dump. (The austere, buttoned-down Robert McNamara was the victim I remember. He *deserved* it, I remember thinking.) I had thought this was unique to LBJ until I read a collection of anecdotes, *Maxwell Stories* by Sam Jaffa (Robson Books, London 1992), about the late Robert Maxwell, the British-Czech media tycoon who died in mysterious circumstances aboard his yacht in 1991. Jenni Frazer, a journalist with the London *Jewish Chronicle* described interviewing Maxwell in 1986.

'We went into his private offices at the top of Maxwell House, Maxwell was in the bathroom. He was on the toilet and had left the door open. We couldn't ses him but we could hear him. It was disgusting. But I believe it was psychlogically important to him. He was letting us know that he didn't have to behave nicely because it wasn't necessary to impress us.' (p. 129) The psycho-analytically-minded of you can ponder on that for a while.

The British Watergate

The theory of liberal democratic societies like Britain and the United States, goes roughly this: there are interests in society which are aligned to political parties. The parties then contest elections and the winner takes over the state. ("The state" in this instance means "government bureaucracies.") In this theory the state/government is neutral and plays no part in the political process. In the United States this theory was exploded by the assassinations of the 1960s and the subsequent revelations of CIA and FBI covert operations. Whatever the theory says, in the United States the state, especially the secret state, is very definitely a player in the political 'game'. The name Colin Wallace won't mean much to readers outside the UK, but in his way he has been as important in undermining this childish theory in Britain as the assassinations and subsequent revelations were in the United States.

Wallace was an Information Officer, a civilian employee of the British Army, working in Northern Ireland when the civil war broke out there in 1969. Wallace was the only native member of the Army's Information Services there and quickly became indispensable in dealing with the world's media, and in explaining the complex sectarian politics to the English Army officers sent in, first to try and keep the sides apart and later to fight the IRA. In due course the Army dusted-off its counter-insurgency manual and in 1971 set up a psychological warfare unit, called Information Policy, under cover of the Army press office to wage psy-war on the 'terrorists' and their perceived supporters. Wallace, the man on the ground who knew the local landscape, became the key man in the secret psy-war unit. Information Policy was not an intelligence-gathering Organisation, and received its intelligence from other British outfits in Northern Ireland, notably MI5, the Security Service.

In 1974 the Conservative government of Edward Heath narrowly lost the General Election to the Labour Party led by Harold Wilson - a defeat in part caused by the Conservative government's inability to deal with a national strike by the National Union of Mineworkers which led to power-rationing and the whole of British industry being forced to work only three days a week. (During which three days, incidentally, it managed to produce almost as much as it had while working five or six. This point was swiftly forgotten, of course.) In MI5 and other sections of the British state, the theory developed that this strike, the Mineworkers' Union and, ultimately, the Labour Party itself, were being influenced by the dear old KGB.

A great machination on the night began in Britain, Citizens militias - we called them 'private armies' - began forming under elderly retired military and intelligence personnel to fight 'the Communist threat'. The conservative media began churning out stories of the threat to democracy: The *Times* even ran a series of articles discussing how and under what conditions a coup might be run by the British Army 'to defend democracy'. Prime Minister Wilson and all those around him were repeatedly burgled, phone-tapped and surveilled-, disinformation campaigns, including one by the CIA centred round the Czech defector Joseph Frolik, began. It was *the* great crisis of British post-war history, it ran through the Labour governments of 1974-79 and climaxed with the election of Margaret Thatcher, a rather dim but enthusiastic believer of the communist conspiracy theory.

In Northern Ireland in 1974 the intelligence arriving from M15 at Information Policy unit began to change. No longer was the intelligence about, and the projects directed against, the IRA or the Protestant paramilitary groups. Colin Wallace began receiving 'intelligence' - almost entirely fictitious - about members of the Labour Government and the politicians of the Conservative and Liberal Parties perceived to be too 'pink': allegations of Soviet influence, sexual and financial hanky-panky, even drug-taking. Wallace was tasked to use this 'intelligence' to create black propaganda projects. Hitherto an enthusiastic part-time soldier and conservative servant of the state, Wallace began to get cold feet and ultimately declined to work on this political disinformation project without specific political clearance from on-high. No such clearance was forthcoming, and in refusing to carry out the project Wallace joined MI5's shit list.

He was quickly set-up in Northern Ireland and caught giving classified material to a journalist - something he'd been routinely doing as part of his job for several years - as transferred out of Northern Ireland and eventually lost his job in 1976. MI5 nobbled the Civil Service Appeal Board hearing which dealt with his appeal against dismissed. (This was acknowledged by the government in 1990 and Wallace was paid $50,000 compensation.)

Prime Minister Harold Wilson, after resigning in 1976, began trying to find out who had been behind the campaign of disinformation and burglaries his Cabinet had suffered between 1974 and '76. He briefed a couple of journalists with his suspicions who wrote a series of (for Britain) sensational stories and then produced a book, in 1978. But the journalists had found nothing of substance to back-up Wilson's beliefs about an official campaign by the spooks against him, and Wilson - and his claims - were greeted with mass derision by the British establishment, most of the media and, it has to be said, most of his erstwhile political colleagues. Such things, old boy, just didn't happen in Britain. On being told in 1974 by a private detective that the headquarters of Britain's trade unions was bugged, the General Secretary of Labour Party, Ron Hayward, memorably remarked, 'We don't have Watergate politics in Britain.'

But Colin Wallace, by then working as an Information Officer in local government, knew what Wilson was talking about: he'd seen the MI5 files in 1974 when the disinformation campaign had been getting underway. He wrote to the retired Prime Minister but never got a reply: Wilson had been scared off by the chorus of disbelief which greeted his allegations. But the spooks had been alarmed by Wilson's tentative moves against them and they knew they had a loose cannon - Colin Wallace. So, in 1980 when Jonathan Lewis, a friend of Wallace's died in what looked like an accident - he fell in a river and banged his head - the spooks used this death to discredit Wallace, and framed him for Lewis's murder.

He was charged with and acquitted of Lewis' murder but got ten years for his manslaughter. (Second degree murder in the US?) In prison, the formerly loyal Queen and Country man Wallace was now seriously pissed-off and began writing-up his memories of the various covert and illegal activities he had witnessed or been a party to in Northern Ireland, and started contacting journalists, helped by another British Army officer, Fred Holroyd, who had also been blowing the whistle on covert operations in Northern Ireland. For a while the conviction for manslaughter, a campaign of negative briefing and disinformation by the Ministry of Defence to its media allies, the sheer complexity and novelty of Wallace's story, and the laziness of most journalists, did the trick, and Wallace was only taken seriously by a handful of journalists - including this writer - on the media fringe. But then, a few months after he was released from prison in 1986, after serving six years, the renegade MI5 officer, Peter Wright, appeared on the scene with his memoir, *Spycatcher*, and in which he wrote, albeit briefly, of clandestine operations against the Labour government of Harold Wilson in the 1970s, and the media tide turned. Three years of revelations followed of precisely the 'Watergate politics' that were not supposed to exist in Britain.

On October 9, 1996 after sixteen years of sustained legal activity by Wallace, his conviction for manslaughter was finally quashed at the Court of Appeal.

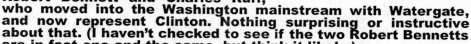

MONICAGATE, WATERGATE, JFK
BY PETER DALE SCOTT

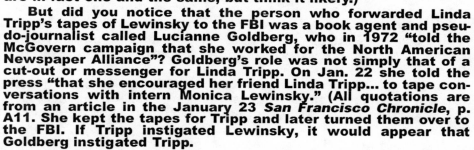

In *Deep Politics and the Death of JFK* I write that study of any one of our deep political crises will tell you more about the rest. Apparently this prediction holds true for Monicagate as well.

I am not talking about the recurrence of Washington lawyers like Robert Bennett and Charles Ruff, who moved into the Washington mainstream with Watergate, and now represent Clinton. Nothing surprising or instructive about that. (I haven't checked to see if the two Robert Bennetts are in fact one and the same, but think it likely.)

But did you notice that the person who forwarded Linda Tripp's tapes of Lewinsky to the FBI was a book agent and pseudo-journalist called Lucianne Goldberg, who in 1972 "told the McGovern campaign that she worked for the North American Newspaper Alliance"? Goldberg's role was not simply that of a cut-out or messenger for Linda Tripp. On Jan. 22 she told the press "that she encouraged her friend Linda Tripp... to tape conversations with intern Monica Lewinsky." (All quotations are from an article in the January 23 *San Francisco Chronicle*, p. A11. She kept the tapes for Tripp and later turned them over to the FBI. If Tripp instigated Lewinsky, it would appear that Goldberg instigated Tripp.

Both Tripp and Goldberg are apparently Republicans. Tripp was one of only two holdovers from the Bush White House. Goldberg was exposed in 1973 as "a spy for Nixon while she traveled with the press corps" covering McGovern's 1972 campaign. It was at this time that she said she worked for NANA (North American Newspaper Alliance), and supplied an address for NANA which "is the same as her current residence" in Manhattan. Watergate investigators "said the Nixon campaign paid her $1,000 a week."

Not mentioned in today's story is the relevant fact in 1972, as today, Lucianne Goldberg was snooping for sex. She told the late Anthony Lukas (*Nightmare*, p. 161) that the Nixon people "were looking for really dirty stuff...who was sleeping with whom, what the Secret Servicem men were doing with the stewardesses, who was smoking pot on the plane — that sort of thing."

SEX SCANDAL FIGURE HAD ROLE IN NIXON CAMPAIGN
BY GENE GIBBONS

WASHINGTON - A Manhattan book agent helping to fan the flames of the sex scandal that threatens to engulf Bill Clinton's presidency spied on Democrat George McGovern for the Nixon re-election campaign in 1972.

Lucianne Goldberg's involvement surfaced Thursday after she said she had recordings of former White House intern Monica

Lewinsky telling of an illicit affair with Clinton and of him urging her to cover it up by lying under oath to lawyers in the Paula Jones sexual harassment case.

The tapes were surreptitiously recorded by Lewinsky co-worker Linda Tripp, whom Goldberg said has been a friend since 1993.

Reached by telephone at her home in New York, Goldberg told Reuters Tripp made the tapes "at my suggestion because she needed to be protected."

"I'm a friend of Linda's. My only subjectiveness is that I like Linda, and Linda asked me to help her," Goldberg said.

The allegations on the tapes, which the president has denied, have plunged Clinton into the gravest crisis of his presidency. Legal experts said that if the charges are true, it could trigger a push for impeachment.

Goldberg said she had only listened to two of the 20 tapes of telephone conversations between Tripp and Lewinsky. "I believe these women ... It's true. You can't listen to these tapes and not know it's true," she told Reuters.

Ironically, Goldberg played a bit part in the impeachment drama that ultimately drove Richard Nixon from the presidency in 1974.

In 1972, a Nixon campaign strategist tapped Goldberg to work as a spy on George McGovern's campaign plane, where she posed as a magazine writer covering the Democratic presidential candidate.

Her role in the Nixon campaign came to light a year later during the Watergate investigation, which revealed that Nixon's re-election campaign conducted an extensive political dirty tricks operation to damage Nixon's Democratic rivals and derail McGovern's bid for the White House.

"I was working for Murray Chotiner," Goldberg told Reuters, referring to a Nixon political operative known for his slashing campaign tactics.

Asked if she was part of the Nixon dirty tricks operation, Goldberg said: "Well, they called it dirty tricks at the time, but I was not part of any dirty tricks thing."

On the current scandal, Goldberg said Tripp had given her the tapes and that she turned them over to Whitewater independent counsel Kenneth Starr.

"I was subpoenaed. That's how he got them. He sent the FBI around and they gave me the subpoena and my lawyer gave them the tapes and I don't have them any more," Goldberg said.

Starr has expanded his investigation to look into the sex scandal, which potentially involves several serious felonies, including suborning perjury and obstruction of justice.

Serious students of the JFK Assassination have long been interested in NANA, which supplied Priscilla Johnson (better known now as Priscilla McMillan) with the job (or, to some, cover) by which she voyaged to Moscow and there interviewed Lee Harvey Oswald on the urging of U.S. Consul Snyder.

After the assassination, Johnson developed a close relationship with Marina Oswald, in connection with a book contract originally arranged by C.D. Jackson of *Life Magazine* at the urging of Allen Dulles.

NANA was created by a senior veteran of OSS, Ernest Cuneo, and continued to have intelligence connections. In 1963, before the assassination, it had come under Congressional scrutiny for publishing Chinese Nationalist propaganda, for which it had been paid large sums without registering as a foreign agent. At this same time its President, Ernest Cuneo, was a member of the Citizens' Committee for a Free Cuba, a group calling in 1963 for a more militant anti-Castro policy, and meeting with dissident Cuban exiles.

I am not here suggesting anything about the guilt or innocence of Clinton, only that at least one of the people making his life difficult has a background suggestive of past intrigues. I hope that someone reading this can check Lucianne Goldberg's current address, and see if in fact (as she alleged) it was also the address of NANA. Feel free to forward this.

MYSTERIOUS DEATH OF MARY CAITRIN MAHONEY

Hidden behind all the attention drawn to activities in the life of Monica Lewinsky lies the unsolved murder of another former White House intern, Mary Caitrin Mahoney. On July 7 of last year, the bodies of the 25 year old Mahoney and two others, Emory Allen Evans (also age 25) and Aaron David Goodrich (age 18) were found at the Starbucks Coffee shop where Mahoney worked as a night manager. Evans and Goodrich also worked at the Starbucks, located in the relatively low crime area of Burleith, north of Georgetown in DC.

The store was not robbed. One local radio stationed reported that all three were shot in the head but that one body was riddled with bullets. Ms. Mahoney had recently fired an employee she suspected of taking money from the till. Nevertheless, some researchers added this murder to the statistically anomalous list of deaths associated with the Clinton administration. It happened in the days following Matt Drudge's initial leaks of Michael Isikoff's report on alleged Clinton sexual dalliances, which eventually led to the Lewinsky scandal. Also at the time, another former employer of Ms. Mahoney, Labor secretary <u>Alexis Herman</u> <u>was under scrutiny for an alledged pay-off</u> involving a satellite telephone system.

After a controversial delay, <u>police ran DNA tests on the sneakers of the</u> <u>onee suspect</u> in the Mahoney murder, the disgruntled employee, but could not connect them to the crime. In December, <u>three men were</u> <u>arrested for a related murder</u>—that of an informant assisting police in the Starbucks case.

D.C. POLICE-DELAYED SEIZING POSSIBLE STARBUCKS EVIDENCE

Shoes Had No Link to Slayings, Authorities Say

Washington 9/30/97 – D.C. police acknowledged yesterday That homicide detectives failed to Seize a pair of shoes that belonged to a potential suspect and that had a dark stain immediately after the Triple slaying at the Starbucks coffee Shop in July. But officials said the Shoes were seized later and held no evidence related to the shootings.

The shoes belonged to a former employee of the Starbucks on Wisconsin Avenue in Northwest Washington's Burleith neighborhood. He was questioned shortly after the shop's assistant manager and two other employees were found shot to death July 7 during what police have said may have been a robbery attempt.

A source familiar with the investigation into the Starbucks killings said that a day or so after the interview, an evidence technician mentioned that he had seen a stain that could have been blood on the former employee's shoes. Black-and-white photographs also showed the stain.

It was unclear whether the detectives failed to notice the stain or had dismissed It as not being relevant, the source said.

After the technician made his report, investigators obtained a warrant to seize the footwear, a pair of white gym shoes, from the man's home. Subsequent tests performed by the FBI showed that the stain was not blood.

Sgt. Joe Gentile, a police spokesman, said the potential delay in testing did not affect the evidence. Although it is department policy not to discuss evidence in investigations, he said, officials felt it necessary to clarify some matters about the case in light of broadcast media reports.

"Did we take the footwear at the time? No, we did not," Gentile said. "We got a warrant to seize the footwear and sent it to a lab for analysis...The last word I got was there was no blood. There is no evidence at this time to link the footwear to Starbucks."

He said any bloodstains could not have been removed between the time of the interview and the time the shoes were taken by investigators.

The former employee was not arrested in the case.

That the shoes were not taken during the first interview with detectives was first reported yesterday by WTOP radio (1500 AM, 94.3 FM).

The report comes as the D.C. police homicide division is under intense scrutiny by police officials as a result of the squad's failure to close most of the cases it investigates-and allegations of abuse of overtime pay.

D.C. Police Chief Larry D. Soulsby, himself under pressure to improve the departments performance, recently replaced all the homicide division supervisors and announced he is looking nationwide for a new commander for the unit.

The Starbucks slayings are among the most prominent of the homicides in the city that have gone unsolved. No suspects have been identified by police.

Starbucks Coffee Co., of Seattle, has offered a reward of up to $100,000 for information leading to the arrest and conviction of the killer of Mary Caitrin Mahoney, Aaron David Goodrich and Emory Allen Evans.

STARBUCKS MURDER INFORMANT KILLED

Washington, 12/06/97 — Three men were arrested Friday for allegedly killing an informant who was helping police solve the July slaying of three employees at a Georgetown Starbucks coffee shop. Police describe the informant (Saturday) as a cocaine user, and say he was attacked by several men who robbed and fatally beat him Thursday night.

Clintonkill theories partly inspired Hilary Rodham Clinton's observation that a "vast right-wing conspiracy" lies behind the Lewinsky manipulations. Indeed, researchers did link the Mahoney murder to the deaths of Kathy Ferguson and Bill Sheldon, figures in the Paula Jones case obscured in the news by the murder of Nicole Brown Simpson. As with Vince Foster, those deaths were ruled suicide. The murder accusations referred to by the first lady, however, involve Kevin Ives and Don Henry. Ives and Henry supposedly died after they stumbled upon the guns-and-drugs operation at the Mena, Arkansas air strip. A visibly corrupt medical examiner in Arkansas, named Fahmy Malak, supported by Clinton, ruled that the two young men died after smoking pot and falling asleep on railroad tracks. Conspiracy researchers know the Mena operation, of course, as an Ollie North/Bush-Reagan project that Clinton failed to investigate before marching on to the presidency.

US LABOR SECRETARY HERMAN DENIES CORRUPTION CHARGES
BY JIM WOLF

Washington - Labor Secretary Alexis Herman Thursday denied corruption charges against her that could lead to the appointment of an independent counsel. ``I want you to know that these allegations are not true,'' she told reporters before leaving on a trip to New York with President Clinton. She said she would not let the charges, which she did not detail, distract her from her job.

Clinton told reporters he did not believe charges that Herman sold her influence and made a show of looking supportive throughout the day trip to New York, even sheltering the beleaguered Cabinet secretary under his umbrella at one point.

In an ABC television interview aired Wednesday night, a businessman said that he had once delivered an envelope containing an unspecified sum of cash to Herman's home when she was working as a Clinton White House aide.

The Cameroon-born businessman, Laurent Yene, currently of no known address, said the cash was a 10 percent cut of consulting fees given to him by a client seeking a federal license for a satellite-telephone system.

Herman noted the Justice Department, under the Independent Counsel Act, was obligated to look into any specific and credible allegation that a Cabinet member may have committed a crime.

``I accept that as a part of this job,'' she said. She said her lawyer Neil Eggleston told the Justice Department she would cooperate fully.

Herman and Clinton attended a business conference in New York on expanding economic opportunity to minorities and women, and Herman drew a standing ovation after her remarks.

The two discussed policy matters and the day's events on their trip back from New York on Air Force One, said White House spokesman Mike McCurry.

Aspects of Yene's dealings with Herman first surfaced in April 1997, before Clinton chose her as labor secretary. At the time she was director of the White House Office of Public Liaison, dealing with many special interest groups.

Yene was a part-owner of a consulting business with Vanessa Weaver, a longtime Herman friend who bought the firm from Herman when she took the White House job.

One of Weaver's lawyers, Jeffrey Fried, said Weaver sued Yene in July 1997, charging him with misappropriating funds, including cash withdrawals from their business, and making false charges about Weaver and her business.

Another of Weaver's lawyers, Lawrence Barcella, said Yene had for six months been ``ducking'' service of the lawsuit against him. Asked how Yene might be reached, Barcella laughed and said: ``Good luck.'' Efforts to reach him were unsuccessful.

The Justice Department's public integrity section is conducting the preliminary investigation to decide if an independent counsel should be named. Under the law, the attorney general has 90 days, once such a probe has begun, to decide whether to ask a special federal court to appoint a counsel to conduct a full investigation.

The law permits the Justice Department to extend the preliminary investigation for 60 days if necessary.

Clinton said ``I don't believe that for a minute,'' when asked on Thursday by a reporter if Herman might have taken cash to pedal influence in his administration.

McCurry said in a statement Wednesday that Clinton ``continues to have full faith and confidence in Secretary of Labor Alexis Herman.''

TailGate, NaughtyGate, MonicaGate Clinton Scandal & Conspiracy [a/k/a ZipperGate]: http://www.shastalake.com/gate/index.html

"Klinton Body Count": http://www.marsweb.com/~watcher/klinton.html

---

TWO WITNESSES IN PAULA JONES CASE SHOT
Nicole Simpson murdered day after Paula Jones witness committed "suicide."

Two potential witnesses in the Paula Jones case were found shot in the head in 1994, although both deaths were ruled suicides. Their names were Kathy Ferguson and Bill Sheldon. Kathy Ferguson (died in May 1994) was the ex-wife of Arkansas state trooper Danny Ferguson, the man that escorted Paula Jones to Clinton s suite. Bill Sheldon was Kathy Ferguson s boyfriend who "allegedly" shot himself in June 1994, a day before Nicole Simpson and Ron Goldman were brutally murdered. Obviously the news media covered the more sensational of the two stories which would dominate the entire news media for the next year and a half. Only a handful of people know of the mysterious deaths of Kathy Ferguson and Bill Sheldon. In other words it is possible that O.J. Simpson may in fact be innocent of murdering his ex-wife Nicole and her friend Ron Goldman. They may have been victims of "Murder Incorporated" at the behest of President Clinton. The motive for killing Nicole would have been to create the most sensational news story imaginable the day after a key witness in the Paula Jones civil suit Bill Sheldon — was murdered. It was a diversionary tactic. Nicole Simpson s murder touched all of the hot buttons in the American psyche: racism, abused women, celebrities gone bad. Many called it the crime of the century. In addition, I recall that attorney Johnny Cochran questioned two former mobsters during the Simpson trial but the entire exchange was censored from the public. There has been little said or written about these two mobsters since. Could they have been the true killers? – Dave Sharp

---

Mena remains a vast right-wing conspiracy that many are anxious to investigate, not just Jerry Falwell, a peripheral blow-hard whose name recognition Ms. Clinton exploited. Lesser known names, like that of Richard Mellon Scaife, were examined by the "Communications Stream of Conspiracy Commerce" report issued by the White House last January. Fallout of the Lewinsky affair included the observation that Scaife's family tree includes William Mellon Hitchcock, who bankrolled Timothy Leary's Millbrook commune.

WHITE HOUSE CITES
STEAMSHOVEL PRESS

Steamshovel Press editor Kenn Thomas' article for the Washington *Post*, "Clinton Era Conspiracies" is among the first articles appearing in the 322-page White House Report entitled "Communications Stream of Conspiracy Commerce." The report made headlines in January when details emerged in *Wall Street Journal* (1) and the Washington *Post* (2) of its conspiratorial conclusions. The report suggests that right-wing ideologues report rumors get picked up by the British press—it singled out columnist Ambrose Evans-Pritchard—and transformed into hard news and reported in the mainstream US media, a magical "media food chain," without which apparently nothing bad would have ever been written about the Clinton administration. According to the *Post*, such a view "has long been expressed by Clinton strategist James Carville and other Clinton advisers" but the report "lays down the suspicion laden theories in cold-print, under the imprimatur of the White House."

Steamshovel once offered "Clinton Era Conspiracies" as a subscription premium. It deconstructed the give-and-take process of dealing with the Washington *Post* in *Steamshovel Press* #11 ("Things Are Gonna Slide: *Post*-partum Suppression"). *Steamshovel* concluded that it had minimized the inevitable watering down of info-underground reporting in a mainstream DC paper. It concluded, however, that the *Post* had stripped the article of important details and its presentation made it look like glib satire. The unedited essay now appears in the *Steamshovel* back-issue anthology, *Popular Alienation* (pp. 263-268). It certainly does not have its genesis in a right-wing think-tank, as the "Conspiracy Commerce" report might suggest.

Information from the *Steamshovel* article "INSLAW Octopus in Whitewater Currents," outlining the interest of the Clinton administration in the Danny Casolaro story, also found its way into the White House report second-hand, through an article by someone named Bixman who relied heavily on it.

The size and scope of "Communications Stream of Conspiracy Commerce" was obsfucated by *The Nation* magazine when it reported that "Mark Fabiani, then of the White House Counsel's office, aided by some lowly staffers at the Democratic National Committee, decided to illustrate the ["media food chain"] phenomenon and came up with 328 pages of supporting material. He added a two-and-a-half-page cover memo with the extremely infelicitous title...and began handing it to reporters..." (3) The report does primarily consist of photocopied newsclips and Internet download/print outs. It practically looks like the garden variety con zine of the 1990s. Pages of analysis accompany the photocopies, though, and ideology clearly informs the *Nation*'s misrepresentation. But if White House counsel received its usual chunk of taxpayer money for the work, the xeroxing and net searching certainly left plenty of change for power lunch conspiracy chats. Interestingly, the White House does not make "Communications Stream of Conspiracy Commerce" available as a government document. It can only be had through the DNC, although *Steamshovel* will supply it to readers at cost.

As with much of what it reports, *Steamshovel* affirmed part of the White House "Communications Stream" conspiracy theory in issue #14, which appeared in Fall 1995. In "The Conspiracy Conspiracy", author Jack Burden discusses at length Floyd G. Brown, the public relations hack responsible for

George Bush's "Willie Horton" ads, who is the first subject of deconstruction in the "Communications Stream" report. Burden writes:

"A huge amount of what you've read about Whitewater has not, contrary to what you may think, been dug up by the reporters whose bylines appear on the stories about the affair. The financial labyrinth of it all is too boring and time-consuming for your average journalist (or, for that matter, your average reader). [*Steamshovel* debris: Although it makes no direct connection with Brown, the "Communications Stream" report traces the money to Richard Mellon Scaife, who "uses the $800 million Mellon fortune...to propagate extremist views" and was described by *Wall Street Journal* as a "conservative philanthropist." "Communications Stream" analyzes *Wall Street Journal* as a mouthpiece for Brown.] Most of the Whitewater press emanates from an organization called Citizens United, headed by a the 33 year old Brown, who looks like Rush Limbaugh's younger, more desperate brother.

"Brown describes himself simply as a concerned conservative and claims no affiliation with the Republican party. He admits to having a financial base of some $3 million, supposedly raised by direct mail solicitations. His organization works round the clock to unmask what he sees as the Clinton Menace, devoting most of its expensive energy to Whitewater. Brown and co. issue daily press releases and hourly fax updates on the topic. They have a Whitewater conspiracy press kit they send out to reporters that practically writes the story for them. If a reporter asks them to, they'll probably set the type and cook the coffee.

"Of course Brown and company are just doing this because they "want to see the truth come out." Mainstream Republicans are supposedly embarrassed and disgusted by Brown's sleazeball tactics and shameless taste for the smear.

"But check it out: The last time Republicans were "embarrassed" by Floyd G. Brown was in the 1988 election, when they were embarrassed all the way to the White House. It was Brown who produced the racist Willie Horton TV ad which practically won the election for George Bush singlehanded. When Bush was confronted with complaints that the ad combined racist stereotypes with outright lies, he too condemned it. The ad continued to run, however, because it was the "independent" work of Brown and so, supposedly, out of Bush's control. Thus Bush was able to benefit from a race-baiting appeal while giving lip service to its condemnation. Of course Brown, Bush and the rest of the "conservatives" involved in this incident were completely unacquainted with each other and just wanted to see the truth come out. Just ask Michael Dukakis.

"This is the way the game is played by the well-funded media manipulators of the right. Consequently, it's not surprising to see right-wingers like Limbaugh, Falwell and D'Amato promoting the Clinton conspiracy cartoon. What's disturbing is the way that people who should know better—members of the countercultural left -have been sucked into the scam."

What distinguishes Burden's point of view from that of the "Communications Stream" report is the notion of blowback—that rumor reports by Brown and others are picked up by British tabloids and then concretized as hard news when the US press picks them up from Britain. Burdens argues instead that:

"Part of the psy ops strategy here is the exploitation of popular interest in conspiracy. Though mainstream rationalism would have it that American politics always proceeds in an open, orderly, democratic fashion—that conspiracy can't happen here—contemporary Americans know better. They've learned better. The Kennedy assassination seems to shriek conspiracy...Watergate was unquestionably a case of the C word, as was Iran-Contra. Conspiracies, at very high levels of the US establishment, do occur. This history has, understandably, made Americans profoundly suspicious of the words and deeds of the high and mighty.

"It has also contributed to the emergence of a new genre of popular culture, one we might call *conspiracy noir.* This genre is large and growing, and includes everything from the fiction of Robert Anton Wilson and Umberto Eco to TV shows like the *X Files*, Hollywood movies like *JFK* and comics like *The Invisibles*. Combining existential dread, political cynicism, fascinating occult mumbo jumbo and the sense of significant things hovering just beyond the veil, this genre has immense appeal as both entertainment and cultural myth.

"In Euro-American politics of the right, there is a tradition of conspiracy theory, an extremely checkered one. Far-rightists can always tell you the names and phone numbers of the members of the Ruling Cabal. And though such analyses are shrill, naively personalistic and often racist, they do arise from political conditions, of oppression and corruption, that are actual, though typically misread by the rightists."

Process aside, Burden considers the particulars of malfeasance and corruption that have been percolating about Clinton as having been over-reported, especially compared to the Teflon shield that protected serious examination of Iran-contra and other scandals of the previous Republican administrations. Whitewater, for instance, is "the kind of financial scam that the upper classes consider their birthright, the sort of thing for which the Republicans and the *Wall Street Journal* ordinarily give out medals." Burden says of the Iran-Contra airfield in Mena, Arkansas, "the stories...have the ring of credibility, given what else we know about Oliver's army [Oliver North]. The claim that then-Governor Clinton knew about and approved the use of the airstrip by the North network is a bit flimsier, but let's assume it's true. Does this mean that Clinton is part of what the Christic Institute calls the `secret team'? Is he a national security neofascist of Ollie North proportions? And if he is, then why are North and his political cronies working so mightily to destroy Clinton?"

It could well be argued that American politics now seemingly consists of internecine warfare and false dialogue among equally reprehensible politicos on supposedly varied ends of the spectrum. The process by which covert information becomes rumor, becomes news report and then becomes canon for any real public political dialogue that remains can only be described subjectively in a report like "Communications Stream". The report in effect tells the White House that there's nothing wrong, only right-wing rumors bent out of proportion by British blowback.

Buried in the *Wall Street Journal* coverage of the "Communications Stream" report, however, is the story of Kevin Ives and Don Henry, two kids who may have been killed because they happened upon the drugs-and-guns operation in Mena. No rumor here: those kids are dead and Fahmy Malak, the Clinton-supported medical examiner who declared that they fell asleep on railroad tracks after smoking pot, was visibly corrupt. The US attorney in Little Rock, Paula Casey, has done nothing to investigate the deaths. Unlike the Paula Jones picadillo and the Whitewater brouhaha, the story has not been caught up the "communication stream of conspiracy commerce", even though it fits neatly into what has been suspected about Mena by conspiracy students for many years. If it never emerges from the small reportage in the obviously partisan *Wall Street Journal* and on *The Mena Connection*, a videotape with oral history documentation Little Rock local news footage that circulates in the info-underground, will the White House communication conspiracy theory be put to rest?

NOTES

(1) Morrison, Micah, "White House Heat on Whitewater Beat," *Wall Street Journal,* January 6, 1997

(2) Harris, John F. and Baker, Peter, "White House Asserts a Scandal Theory," Washington *Post*, January 10, 1997

(3) "Full-Court Press: A Stupidity Conspiracy," *The Nation*, February 10, 1997, p. 5

STEAMSHOVEL PRESS

"VAST RIGHT-WING CONSPIRACY"

"Scaife, a fourth-generation heir to the Mellon fortune, is a billionaire who has funded numerous anti-Clinton ventures ..."

So, who's this Richard Mellon Scaife? Who are these Mellons?

When the OSS was first founded, Dulles protege Bill Casey (CIA director after Bonesman George Bush) presided over the European theatre, where covert operations were financed by Wall Street "nobility" from Anglophile Skull and Bones families. For example, Junius Morgan (son of J. P.) was OSS "treasurer." Casey's job later passed to David Bruce of Chase Manhattan and Kuhn-Loeb, early member of the Council on Foreign Relations and, via British Intelligence's Sir William Wiseman, member also of the "Rhodes Society." Bruce's brother-in-law was PAUL MELLON, millionaire banker [son of Andrew Mellon, Hoover's Treasury Secretary and ambassador to Great Britain] and OSS station chief in London, liaison to British Intelligence.

"After the war, certain influential members of the Mellon family maintained close ties with the CIA. The Mellon family foundations have been used repeatedly as conduits for Agency funds. Furthermore, Richard Helms was a frequent weekend guest of the Mellon patriarchs in Pittsburgh during his tenure as CIA director (1966-1973)." —*Acid Dreams*, Martin A. Lee and Bruce Schlain

Another member of the CIA-allied Mellon family was WILLIAM MELLON HITCHCOCK, Timothy Leary's "Godfather" and "the Daddy Warbucks of the Counterculture." In the early 60s, Billy Mellon-Hitchock almost singlehandedly bankrolled mass-production and distribution of LSD (which, hardly by coincidence, was at the time the subject of testing by the CIA's secret MK-ULTRA program) — financing this effort through known CIA fronts like Castle Bank in the Bahamas [founded by Watergate burglar E. Howard Hunt's onetime boss, Paul Helliwell, paymaster for the Bay of Pigs invasion], the Meyer Lansky syndicate's bank of choice for its money-laundering. Its special clientele also included Miami mob ally Bebe Rebozo, President Richard M. Nixon, Nixon campaign contributor and Golden Triangle heroin druglord Robert Vesco, the CIA's George Bush, and certain anti-Castro Cubans ... —ibid., pp. 242-246; also Lyndon LaRouche's *Dope, Inc.*

The Hoover Institution near Stanford University, a right-wing "think-tank" which masterminded the campaigns to elect both Ronald Reagan and George Bush, has long been a favored recipient of funding from the SARAH MELLON SCAIFE Foundation.

Sitting on its board of directors in 1963, when the Hoover Institution was searching for a Republican candidate to succeed the newly assassinated John F. Kennedy, was none other than RICHARD MELLON SCAIFE.

By the 1980s, when the Hoover Institution was plotting the candidacy of George Bush, its directorate read like an OSS/CIA reunion. [By the way, there WAS such a reunion in London in 1981, where ex-OSS operatives like Margaret Thatcher and CIA boss Bill Casey toasted old times, and NEW times under Reagan-Bush.]

Its directors included Emil Mosbacher Jr, State Department chief of protocol under Nixon, whose brother Robert was then co-chairman of the Republican National Committee and the national chairman of "Bush for President"; William B. Macomber Jr, CIA, once special assistant to John Foster Dulles and Ambassador to Iran; Philip Habib, Reagan's special ambassador to the Middle East; A. Carol Kotchian, president of Lockheed (implicated in CIA scandals throughout the '80s); Donald Rumsfield, RAND and CIA, right-hand man to Richard Nixon and special NATO representative; Hewlett-Packard's David Packard, like his predecessor Thomas Watson of IBM (OSS) "consultant" employed by the NSA and CIA; and directors of two other conservative think tanks —largely staffed by CFR members and Anglophile OSS/CIA veterans like William F. Buckley. Jeane Kirkpatrick (husband in OSS) and General Alexander Haig— the American Enterprise Institute and the Heritage Foundation.

The conspiracy is quite vast and *Steamshovel* urges readers to click on the hyperlinks above for a more full picture of it.

Thanks to Loren Coleman and Das Goat for information in this report.

STEAMSHOVEL PRESS

THE YOUNG PERSON'S GUIDE TO VAST RIGHT-WING CONSPIRACY
By Stucco Holmes

In a January 27th TV interview, Hillary Clinton asserted that the current sex scandal charges against her husband were part of "a vast right-wing conspiracy" that has targeted Bill Clinton "since the day he announced for president." The remark was immediately picked up and replayed throughout the mainstream media, who love a sensational soundbite. However, the first lady was widely criticized—and crudely psychoanalyzed—for uttering the dreaded C word and aligning herself with "paranoid conspiracy theorists." John Whitehead, founder of the Rutherford Institute, the conservative foundation funding the civil suit of Paula Jones, challenged the claim, saying, in so many words, "Conspiracy? Where's the evidence?"

Of course, when it comes to gathering evidence, the first lady doesn't have a conservative foundation to finance her efforts. Indeed, it may be impossible to prove such a conspiracy beyond a reasonable doubt. But it doesn't take a special prosecutor with 30 million in taxpayer dollars to look at the public record and see that there are patterns of association among Clinton's opponents and big bucks behind them. An enormous number of allegations have been made about Clinton in the last few years. Many of these—e.g., weird, *X-Files*-like scenarios about murder and drug-running— seem absurd, have proven groundless and fit the classic pattern of the political smear. Moreover, such allegations have not arisen randomly or even casually; they have been injected into the media—often by dint of sheer repetition—time and again, by the same sources and publications. Both the sources and the publications inhabit the far rightward end of the political spectrum.

Special prosecutor Kenneth Starr has strong personal and professional connections, both to political enemies of the administration like the tobacco companies as well as to wealthy, ultraconservative Clinton-haters like

Richard Mellon Scaife and Jerry Falwell. Scaife and Falwell have been hawking, for several years now, the sort of wild allegations concerning Clinton described above. Moreover, Starr is obviously close to the Rutherford Institute, the aforementioned conservative foundation that has taken over funding of the Paula Jones case. And John Whitehead, the afore-mentioned founder of Rutherford, has publicly endorsed the claims, hawked by Falwell, Scaife and company, that Clinton is a murderer and a drug-runner, etc.

It's a free country, of course, but it seems reasonable to consider the significance of such a chain of associations, particularly when we find, at their center, someone like a special prosecutor charged with investigating the president.

At any rate, it's clear that the people aligned most strenuously against Clinton share a good deal more than just a conservative political outlook. Whether that's a vast conspiracy or just American-politics-as-usual, you can decide. Described below are some of the key players and patterns of asso-ciation.

Who Appointed Kenneth Starr?

Few seem to know or remember it, but Kenneth Starr is the second independent counsel to work on Whitewater. The first, Robert Fiske, was also a Republican (though a moderate where Starr is an arch-conservative) and he was appointed by Attorney General Janet Reno. Ordinarily, such a prosecutor would be selected by a special three-judge federal panel, but at the time of Fiske's appointment, Congress had allowed the statute govern-ing independent counsels to lapse. In 1994, Fiske concluded that the death of Clinton aide Vince Foster had been a suicide, much to the chagrin of Clinton scndalmongers, who still insist that Foster's is a "mysterious death." Fiske was proceeding with his work when, about six months into the job, the independent counsel statute was reinstated. At this point, the three-judge panel intervened to remove Fiske and appoint a second special pros-ecutor, namely, Starr. The head of the panel, Judge David Sentelle, cited potential conflicts of interest involving Fiske, conflicts supposedly relating to Fiske's appointment by Reno, an employee of the administration under investigation.

In addition to being head of the panel that appoints special counsels, Sentelle is a judge in the US Court of Appeals. He is often described as a "protege" of Senator Jesse Helms, the powerful, ultraconservative Republican senator from North Carolina. Shortly before removing Fiske and appointing Starr, Sentelle had lunch with Helms and his colleague Lauch Faircloth (junior senator from North Carolina and another conservative Republican). At the time, Sentelle was considering a petition from Faircloth to have Fiske removed because of the alleged conflicts of interest described above. Of course, Sentelle's own behavior here has the appearance of a conflict of interest. This, at least, was the view of five former heads of the American Bar Association, all of whom publicly criticized the actions and legal ethics of Sentelle.

Sentelle was appointed head of the three-judge panel in 1992 by Supreme Court Chief Justice William Rehnquist. Rehnquist removed Judge George MacKinnon, a moderate Republican who had headed the panel for several years previous. It was MacKinnon, for instance, who appointed Lawrence Walsh, the special prosecutor who investigated the Reagan administration's Iran-Contra scandal. This case involved a Republican spe-cial prosecutor investigating a Republican administration. Sentelle brought a different philosophy to the process, claiming that, if an independent counsel were to be truly independent, he must be, in effect, an ideological opponent of the administration under investigation.

Enter Kenneth Starr. Starr, former Solicitor General in the Bush administration, first came to prominence in the Reagan Justice Department, where he worked closely with Alfred Regnery (see below), among others. Starr has a strongly Republican resume and is affiliated with conservative organizations like the Federalist Society (as is George Conway, a lawyer for Paula Jones, and Sentelle himself). Starr has also done work for the conservative Landmark Legal Foundation, with which Linda Tripp's lawyer, James Moody, is affiliated. Both groups have received large amounts of funding from Richard Mellon Scaife.

Richard Mellon Scaife

In the background of much of this is Richard Mellon Scaife, multimillion-dollar heir to the Mellon banking fortune and a man who might be described as the ultraconservative's ultraconservative. He owns numerous newspapers and is a major funder of conservative foundations and causes, including the aforementioned Landmark Legal and Rutherford outfits, as well as the American Spectator magazine, which has featured attack pieces on Bill and Hilary Clinton since before the 1992 election. In her autobiography, *Washington Post* owner/publisher Katharine Graham writes that, during Watergate, Richard Nixon suggested that Scaife buy up the *Post*.

Many of the crazier-sounding allegations against Clinton (e.g., the various Vince Foster Murder scenarios, which even Ken Starr has dismissed) have been retailed in the Scaife-owned *Pittsburgh Tribune-Review*. Scaife's Western Journalism Center produced the *Clinton Chronicles*—a video which purports to detail the various murders and Illuminati-like conspiracies with which the Monster Clinton has allegedly been involved. This video has for several years been promoted and sold by conservative televangelist Jerry Falwell on his *Old Time Gospel* Hour. Scaife also bankrolls the Free Congress Foundation, which last fall ran a $260,000 TV ad campaign asking women if they had been sexually harrased by the president and encouraging any interested parties to phone in to a "sexual harrasment hotline". From 1973 to 1975, Scaife ran Forum World Features, a foreign news service which was in fact a front used to disseminate CIA propaganda around the world.

In addition to all this, Scaife funds a special Chair in Legal Studies at Pepperdine University. Recall the time last year when, for a couple of days, Starr was going to junk Whitewater and take a job as dean of a law school. The law school in question was Pepperdine and the deanship in question was the Scaife chair. Starr is now expected to assume the position at Pepperdine when he completes his work as special prosecutor.

Jerry Falwell and the Rev. Sung Myung Moon

Falwell's Christian Heritage Foundation was going out of business a couple of years ago when suddenly, at the last minute, it became the recipient of a large infusion of funds. The money came from the Women's Federation for World Peace, one of the myriad fronts for the Rev. Sung Myung Moon. Moon, of course, is much more than a religious cult leader. He's a billionaire and a fanatical anticommunist who for decades has had extremely close ties to the Korean CIA (which in turn has very close ties to the American CIA). Since the early 1980s, Moon has pumped enormous sums into American political circles; numerous right-wing groups and Republican campaigns have benefitted from his largesse.

Moon's extensive holdings include two highly influential right-wing publications in the US, Insight magazine and the *Washington Times* newspaper. These publications have also been in the forefront of Clinton scandalmongering. It was *Insight*, for instance, that created the firestorm last fall over allegedly questionable burials in Arlington cemetery, with an article that raised the "possibility" of such practices while naming no sources and providing no evidence. Paul Rodriguez, editor of Insight, has acknowledged that the story was only "allegations and suggestions." The General Accounting Office just completed an investigation of the allegations, concluding that there had been no trading of burial plots for political favors.

Linda Tripp

Former White House secretary Linda Tripp is of course the person who (secretly and illegally) taped Monica Lewinsky discussing her alleged affair with President Clinton. Tripp was a holdover from the Bush administration; since she had Civil Service employee status (and so was difficult to fire) she was kept on by the Clinton team, who received much encouragement to do so from various Bush administration officials. Before coming to the White House, Tripp worked for the Department of Defense, where she had a Military Intelligence security clearance.

Tripp has been in the forefront of several of the "scandals" surrounding Clinton. She is the source for the report that the office of her boss, Clinton aide Vince Foster, was emptied, in a suspicious fashion, shortly after Foster's death. This claim was received with great enthusiasm by Republican Senator Alphonse D'Amato's Senate Whitewater Committee and generated much heat but no light. Margaret Carlson of *Time* has speculated that Tripp may have been the source of the mysterious leaks about which Foster loudly complained shortly before his death. (For what it's worth, three official investigations—including one by Starr—have now ruled Foster's death a suicide.) Tripp was also the source for the disputed claim that White House employee Kathleen Willey was fondled by Clinton.

Shortly before the current scandal broke, Tripp appears to have been in close touch with lawyers in both the Jones case and Ken Starr's office. While working in the Clinton White House, Tripp became friendly with FBI agent Gary Aldrich who, after leaving the White House detail, wrote a book (see below) retailing scurrilous, discredited rumors about Clinton's sex life. Like Aldrich, Tripp has worked closely with Lucianne Goldberg, a literary agent with right-wing and intelligence community ties, ostensibly on writing a tell-all book about the Clinton White House.

Lucianne Goldberg and Regnery Publishing

It was Goldberg, a New York literary agent who works with conservative authors, who encouraged Linda Tripp to illegally tape her conversations with Monica Lewinsky. Goldberg then turned the tapes over to Starr. She was quoted on CNN saying that she felt such tapes were necessary to her, well, project: "If you're going to strike at the king, you have to go ahead and kill him." Goldberg is no stranger to political dirty tricks. During the 1972 presidential election, she posed as a reporter in order to spy on Democratic candidate George McGovern for the Nixon campaign. According to Goldberg's own account, she was looking for "dirty stuff," i.e., information on sexual practices, etc., which could be used to smear or blackmail Democrats. She is reported to have been paid $1,000 per week by the Nixon campaign. During her stint as a spy for Nixon, Goldberg's cover was working for the North American Newspaper Alliance (NANA), an organization that has since been shown to have been a CIA front.

Goldberg has worked with several authors who have been published by Alfred Regnery, an avowedly rightist publisher. Among the books recently published by Regnery are two which attack Clinton: *Unlimited Access*, by former FBI agent (and friend of Linda Tripp) Gary Aldrich, and *The Secret Life of Bill Clinton*, by British Tory journalist (and advisor to Paula

Jones) Ambrose Evans-Pritchard (more on both below). The Aldrich book trafficks in discredited rumors about Clinton's sexual behavior. Evans-Pritchard recycles the by now familiar tales about murder and drug-running. Regnery is a close friend of Kenneth Starr and, like Starr, was a lawyer in the Reagan Justice Department.

The Tobacco Companies and Kirkland & Ellis

Starr's elite Washington law firm, Kirkland and Ellis, represents the tobacco companies in the litigations brought against big tobacco by the Clinton administration. Starr worked as a lead lawyer on these cases before being made special counsel and continued working on tobacco cases long after being appointed special counsel, i.e., well into last year. This is highly unusual, as special prosecutors typically drop everything else so as to avoid even the appearance of a conflict of interest. Starr has conspicuously failed to do this. Starr is, however, sensitive to such charges and, in response, has appointed former Watergate committee counsel Sam Dash as his "ethics counsellor."

The FDA, under the Clinton administration, has shown that the tobacco companies have been engaged for decades in a conspiracy to defraud the public. It's not just that they market something that hurts people. What the Clinton FDA has shown is that they've known for years that the stuff was a) addictive and b) linked to cancer and yet they've consistently lied about such knowledge. Not only that, but they actively moved to increase the addictive elements in cigarettes and consciously marketed the stuff to kids. They are, one might say, drug lords, whose deceit has gotten a lot of people killed. (Meanwhile, recall that Ken Starr claims to be deeply disturbed that someone might lie under oath. Also, note the state—North Carolina—that Senators Helms and Faircloth represent and the industry that dominates its economy.) The tobacco companies are also among the largest contributors to the Republican party.

According to the Chicago *Tribune,* Kirkland and Ellis is currently conducting an internal inquiry into the possibility that a partner in the firm has been providing "unapproved assistance" to Paula Jones and her lawyers. The partner in question, Richard Porter, was formerly a senior aide in the Bush administration. During the 1992 presidential race, Porter handled "opposition research" for the Bush/Quayle reelection campaign. Opposition research, or "oppo," as they call it in Washington, is a polite term for dirt-digging. The oppo specialist is charged with finding material that can be used to embarrass, undermine or smear an opponent. Clinton's lawyer, Robert Bennett, has alleged that personnel at Kirkland and Ellis may have done secret, undisclosed work for Jones and her lawyers regarding their sexual harrassment suit against the president. As partners in the firm, both Porter and Starr are legally responsible for each other's work.

The Rutherford Institute

The Paula Jones case is now being funded by the Rutherford Institute, an ultra-right legal foundation that typically handles cases involving fundamentalists who want to reinstate prayer in school, etc. It is based in Charlottesville, VA, in the heart of Falwell country and is reported to have received its share of funding from the apparently ubiquitous Richard Mellon Scaife. In 1995, its founder, John Whitehead, published an editorial endorsing the anti-Clinton allegations—of murder and drug-running—promoted in Falwell's *Clinton Chronicles* video.

Whitehead is a protege of R. J. Rushdoony, head of the Chalcedon Foundation (based in Vallecito, CA) and the founder of Christian Reconstructionism, a movement dedicated to replacing secular law with "Biblical law" and secular states with "theocratic republics." Whitehead's

1977 book, *The Separation Illusion*, contains an introduction by Rushdoony. The book employs a Manichaean-sounding rhetoric emphasizing spiritual warfare between "the sons of God" and "the sons of darkness."

Though the Institute enjoys tax-exempt status, the Rutherford folk have recently blanketed the country with letters asking for money to help them fight for Jones' supposedly maligned rights. Their letter explains that funds may go to other, unspecified causes which the Institute supports. (No doubt the sons of God need new uniforms.)

The Rutherford bunch took over after Jones' previous lawyers, Gil Davis and Joseph Cammarata, quit, saying that Jones (and her conservative "advisor," platinum spokesmodel Susan Carpenter-McMillan) had gone against their advice and turned down a very generous settlement offer. The lawyers said that they could not proceed without violating ethical procedures, suggesting that their client had some agenda other than simply bringing a lawsuit. According to Davis and Cammarata, "The client persists in a course of conduct involving the lawyer's services that the lawyer reasonably believes is illegal or unjust."

Starr has now more or less hijacked the Jones case, a civil proceeding, and turned it into a federal criminal case. This, however, was not Starr's first interaction with the Jones case. Before Starr became Whitewater independent counsel, he offered to advise Jones' original legal team free of charge.

The American Spectator

The Jones story, and many of the other allegations (e.g., "Troopergate") about the sex lives of both Bill and Hillary, originated (at least in the US press) in a series of attack pieces that appeared in the *American Spectator* by David Brocke. *The Spectator* has received millions in recent years from Richard Mellon Scaife. Brocke was the lead hatchet man in the Get-Clinton publicity campaign of Clinton's first term. Brocke has since given up that post and claims to regret some of what he did. Brocke now says that he lost favor with his right-wing employers when he drew the line, in an unauthorized biography of Hillary Clinton, at absolute character assassination. Instead, Brocke settled for a simple smear: According to Brocke, his Clinton-hating superiors wanted him to call Hillary a lesbian; instead, he wrote that unidentified sources from Hillary's past had reported rumors and suspicions that Hillary might be gay. Brocke was also the source for the most sensational claim in Gary Aldrich's *Unlimited Access*. (Aldrich was a an FBI agent assigned to the White House; like Linda Tripp, with whom he is friendly, Aldrich was a holdover from the Bush administration. Aldrich has worked with literary agent Lucianne Goldberg and his book was published by Regnery.) The claim, attributed to an informed but unidentified insider, was that Bill Clinton regularly snuck out of the White House in the middle of the night for trysts at local Washington motels. The sensational claim was widely reported and dominated the Sunday chat shows for a couple of weeks in the summer of '96. Then Brocke spoke up to say that Aldrich had actually heard the story from himself and that Aldrich had gotten it wrong: The story, Brocke claimed, was just a rumor Brocke had come across which had no substance. Of course, by this time, the story had been repeated everywhere.

The Right Wing in Britain

The American Spectator is published by longtime conservative flack R. Emmet "Bob" Tyrell. Tyrell and the magazine's editorial staff have close ties to the right wing in Britain, in particular to the Hollinger Corporation's *Telegraph*, a major daily in England (where it's sometimes called the "Torygraph"). The *Telegraph* employs Ambrose Evans-Pritchard, who, up until last year, functioned as the paper's Washington bureau chief. Evans-Pritchard has written numerous articles and even a book about Clinton (published by Regnery), all of which traffic in lurid rumors and outrageous allegations. He claims to have been a close advisor to Paula Jones and her lawyers. Along with Lord William Rees-Mogg, former editor of the (Murdoch-owned) London Times and another big Tory, Evans-Pritchard has been in the forefront of the journalistic attack on Clinton. Many of the smear allegations which have surfaced in the *American Spectator* and the Washington *Times* first appeared in British stories by Evans-Pritchard and Rees-Mogg. Rees also publishes the widely read *Strategic Investment* newsletter, which for years has been full of the same mix of lurid rumor and wild allegation about Clinton.

The Tabloidization of News

The preceding list describes a complex network of associations among right-wing players with common interests. However, such groups and individuals have been aided in their efforts by certain economic structures and social trends, particularly as these affect the mass media. And even these long-term trends track back to the political right; not to a literal conspiracy, but rather to the radically laissez faire economic policies of the Reagan administration.

Key to moving the smear-Clinton campaign to the center of the national agenda has been the tabloid trend in mass media. In the early 80s, the Reagan administration deregulated the broadcast industry and inaugurated a frenzy of corporate buyouts and mergers which has yet to end. A new regime of owners took control of the networks and their news departments, a regime which took a one-dimensional view of such holdings, seeing them as profit centers and nothing more. Ever since, journalism has been increasingly handled as simply a bottom-line business. This has resulted in the utter tabloidization of all the media, even of those sectors that were once considered serious and hard news-oriented. Journalists may be reluctant to admit it, but they're now, all of them, in the entertainment business. Corporate bosses interested only in profits expect the news to produce good ratings in the same way they expect *Melrose Place* to do so. Consequently, the news is organized not to inform citizens, but to hook and titillate viewers, and tabloid formulas emphasizing sex, violence, celebrities and scandal have proven the most cost-effective means of marketing "the news."

And this was not always the case. Before Reaganomic deregulation, the major networks ran their news departments at a loss; the prevailing view was that such corporations were obligated to give a little something back to the society that gave them these (broadcast) licenses to print money. That attitude is long gone now. Economic incentives, set in motion by deregulation, have at last turned almost all forms of mass media journalism into infotainment. And the simplest, most profitable and time-tested model for infotainment is the tabloid model.

Tabloid Politics

The tabloid trend has real political effects, most of them reactionary. Its motto is "If it bleeds, it leads," and this emphasis on sensationalism not only coarsens the sensibilities of viewers; it also keeps all sorts of serious but "unsexy" topics utterly outside the frame.

Consider that staple of tabloid journalism, the crime-in-the-streets story: Typically it's dramatic, violent, personalized and easily framed in terms of good guys and bad guys, conflict and resolution. Moreover, the crime story is easily made to sound like a piece of serious, socially committed reporting: the reporter mentions public safety and gets a quote from a cop. The crime story, in other words, virtually writes itself and is a dependable rat-ings-getter.

Built around crude sensationalism and familiar stereotypes, the crime story tends to ignore the sorts of crime—i.e., nonviolent, white-collar—often committed by the upper classes and emphasizes violence in the streets, associating this implicitly with the poor and nonwhite. And though all such stories are, in this formal sense, the same, the crime story typical-ly presents an isolated incident: background or context are utterly absent. There is zero discussion of crime as related to economic factors like pover-ty, social institutions like racism or political issues like the bias of the jus-tice system in favor of the white and well-to-do. Instead, the airwaves are full of exotic-sounding, contextless accounts of mayhem in the streets.

At the same time that crime is flooding news broadcasts, it's declining in our neighborhoods. For several years now, FBI statistics have shown the national crime rate going down in all significant categories. However, polls of the electorate consistently show that people believe that the crime rate is higher than ever and that crime is peoples' main concern. Coincident with all this is a national trend that favors draconian, "tough-on-crime" politicians and which has made prison-building the country's number one growth industry. Clearly there's a disconnect between the facts about crime and peoples' perception of it. It seems safe to say that the tabloid fetishiza-tion of crime isn't helping to correct this situation.

The tabloid trend also means that there is now an enormous market for infotainment-style "news"—a ravenous beast that has to be fed 24 hours a day. Sexual allegations about, say, a president (particularly one with an already tabloidized "history" in such an area), are almost guaranteed to go to the top of such an agenda, where they will quickly take on a life of their own. As the line between entertainment and news disappears, such stories become the media's very definition of "great TV," of profitable, cheaply produced programming.

As for investigative reporting on such a matter, consider that as jour-nalism has become more and more profit-driven and profit-conscious, real investigative reporting has virtually disappeared. That kind of thing, after all, costs money, takes time and may never pan out; in financial terms, it's a risky investment that fewer and fewer press shops are willing to under-write in any serious fashion.

At the same time though, we have, particularly in broadcast news, a cadre of prominent, highly-paid reporters who like to drape themselves in the mantle of Woodward and Bernstein. These are yuppies who spend most of their time toadying to corporate power, but they pretend to be intrepid watchdogs of the public interest in order to justify their salaries and maintain their self-image. They love a sex scandal of this type not only because it's great for ratings, but also because they can pose as hard-hit-ting investigators. No matter that they do little more than report rumors or leaks from Ken Starr's office; no matter that a sex scandal is trivial com-pared to assaults on the entire political system like Watergate or Iran-Contra; Sam Donaldson is working on behalf of you and me to get vital answers to that burning question: did the president get a blowjob? Enquiring minds want to know. The people behind the various Get-Clinton smears understand such mechanisms and dynamics. One suspects that they've tailored their leaks, allegations and smear campaigns to fit the tabloidized format of contemporary mass media.

The Murdoch Method

Among the darkest stars in today's media firmament is Rupert Murdoch, the billionaire magnate behind Fox TV and films, Newscorp, the Harper-

Collins publishing empire, TV Guide and 132 newspapers, nationally and worldwide. Murdoch made his money in tabloid publishing in Australia and England, where his instinct for the lowest common denominator never failed him. (It was Murdoch who institutionalized the "page three girl" feature in British tabloids, a staple of the industry today. This stroke of sales genius consists of featuring a topless woman on page three of every issue. Meanwhile, Murdoch editors talk a lot about traditional family values.) Combining sleazy content with ruthless business tactics, Murdoch has, in the last few decades, completely taken over the newspaper business in both Australia and England. In the 70s and 80s he moved into America, buying up newspapers, movie studios, TV networks and publishing firms.

More than a businessman, Murdoch is a right-wing ideologue and he has cast himself, again and again, as a kingmaker in Australian and English elections. Murdoch has consistently favored conservative candidates and boasts openly of the power he wields over elections through his control of the press. The Murdoch method of political control in these foreign elections has been crude but effective; it typically revolves around tabloid scandals targeted against politicians of whom Murdoch doesn't approve.

Murdoch hasn't been so heavyhanded in America thus far, though he did use Harper publishing leverage to offer Newt Gingrich a bribe, in the form of a $5 miilion book deal, right after the Republican sweep of 1994. However, the classic Murdoch style—and, sometimes, Murdoch media— have figured in the campaigns against Clinton. The current scandal over alleged sex with an intern was broken on ABC's *Brinkley Show* by conservative pundit William Kristol, who edits the Murdoch-owned *Weekly Standard*. (The fact that Kristol has zero experience as a journalist didn't deter Murdoch from making him editor of this widely read conservative weekly. Apparently other aspects of Kristol's resume, like his stint as the brain trust for Dan Quayle, or the fact that he is the son of an influential neoconservative intellectual, were more impressive. In other words, Kristol might not be a journalist, but he certainly knows the conservative party line.)

Similarly, it was classic Murdoch when the New York *Post* broke the Dick Morris-with-a-call-girl story in August 1996. The story had been circulating in the tabloids for a while but had been ignored by mainstream media as too sleazy. Then the *Post*, a mainstream paper owned by Murdoch, went with the story. This move legitimized the story for all sectors of the media, including the supposedly more serious ones, and the predictable feeding frenzy ensued. On the day the story broke, Morris's boss, Bill Clinton, was being nominated for president by his party. If that was a coincidence, it's one that Rupert Murdoch relished. For what it's worth, the current scandal coincides with another Big Moment for Clinton—the State of the Union message—and threatens similar embarrassment.

Media Foodchain

In the above instance we see what a 1996 White House memo called a "media foodchain," in which rumors, allegations and sex stories begin on the fringes of the mainstream media and gradually make their way in toward the center. Often the mass media pick up such stories while trying to insulate themselves, using a sort of "second order" story model in which the focus of the mainstream story is not the sleazy-sounding rumor itself, but rather the fact that "lots of people are talking about the sleazy-sounding rumor." Technically speaking, this inoculates the mainstream story against irresponsible sleazemongering; but of course it also repeats the rumor or smear, amplifying it in the much larger and more resonant chamber of the mainstream media.

Many of the smear-Clinton stories have worked in a similar fashion, starting out on the fringes of the mainstream, in obscure right-wing journals and conservative propaganda; they then move into what we might call the para-media realms of talk radio and the Internet. Once they've stirred up enough interest in these realms, they often become legitimate topics for the "serious" sectors of the media, who can treat them according to the second-order story model described above.

A related media dynamic concerns the sheer volume of smear material. If enough smear material comes out and keeps coming out, this can have the effect of legitimizing at least some of it. Common sense tells people not to believe everything they read or hear, but if virtually everything they read or hear is negative, then they'll tend to assume that there must be something wrong somewhere. They may not have a problem with Clinton themselves, but they figure there must some sort of problem, otherwise there wouldn't be so much talk about problems. There's so much smoke, there must be fire.

This is the sort of approach the Nixon administration used in 1973 when it was engaged in overthrowing the democratically elected socialist government of Salvador Allende in Chile. The CIA waged a massive propaganda campaign in Chilean media, using rumor and innuendo to flood the airwaves with manufactured doubts about Allende's ability to govern. It's one of the standard techniques employed by such organizations to destabilize governments. In intelligence circles this sort of thing is called a "psy op," (psychological operation) or "black propaganda" campaign.

The Nixon Legacy

Regarding Nixon: his name comes up a lot these days, usually in strained comparisons with Clinton. But the real legacy of Nixon to the Clinton scandals does not concern presidential corruption so much as the scandalmongering itself. The true Nixon legacy is the conservative propaganda network described throughout this article. Nixon and many other conservatives believed (wrongly, many would argue) that the Vietnam war had been lost by the (supposedly liberal) press and that Nixon had been deposed by the (supposedly liberal) press. Nixon's message to conservatives was, "Never again." Since then, the right has poured massive amounts of money, time and energy into media work, creating a powerful and influential network of think tanks, foundations, university chairs, political action committees, opposition research orgs, media flak outfits, news outlets and broadcasting personalities. They've been aided in this by trends in media ownership: The giant corporations who own the mainstream media are inherently conservative to begin with, as big money almost always is; and deregulatory trends have produced a mainstream news profession driven strictly by profits and tabloid sensationalism and which is easily manipulated by savvy smear-meisters.

Combine this propaganda infrastructure with a tabloidized mass media and a conservative takeover of the independent counsel mechanism, and voila: White House crisis. Many of the people who seem most "out to get" Bill Clinton, including Kenneth Starr, come out of this milieu. It may not be a literal conspiracy, but it's certainly vast, and it's definitely right-wing.

Sources for information in the above include *The Nation*, the Chicago *Tribune*, the New York *Times*, *Extra!* (published by FAIR, Fairness and Accuracy in Reporting), *In These Times, Executive Intelligence Review, Esquire, Time, Fools for Scandal: How the Media Invented Whitewater by Gene Lyons,* and the distinguised investigative reporting of Robert Parry in his online *Media Consortium* and *I.F. magazine*.

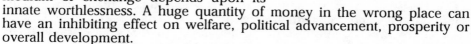

THE CRIPPLE FACTOR
By Roy Lisker
EXPORTING INAPPROPRIATE TECHNOLOGY TO THE THIRD WORLD

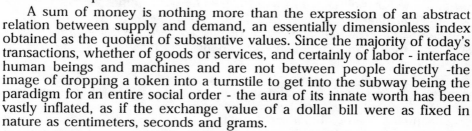

1. Oil, Weapons, And The Balance Of Payments

Money, whatever its quantity, has no intrinsic worth. Indeed, its versatility as a medium of exchange depends upon its innate worthlessness. A huge quantity of money in the wrong place can have an inhibiting effect on welfare, political advancement, prosperity or overall development.

A sum of money is nothing more than the expression of an abstract relation between supply and demand, an essentially dimensionless index obtained as the quotient of substantive values. Since the majority of today's transactions, whether of goods or services, and certainly of labor - interface human beings and machines and are not between people directly -the image of dropping a token into a turnstile to get into the subway being the paradigm for an entire social order - the aura of its innate worth has been vastly inflated, as if the exchange value of a dollar bill were as fixed in nature as centimeters, seconds and grams.

We measure wealth directly in dollars, as if all other less tangible intuitions of value might theoretically be adjusted to this universal magnitude. Observe that the Koran itself distinguishes four kinds of wealth: precious metals, lands, livestock and merchandise, and that tax structures in the traditional Islamic world were adjusted for each category. The modern and , by definition advanced, West has reduced this list to its first category of goods, then replaced even that by a promissory note which, drawn upon a government of more or less legitimacy, and by a polite fiction only, can be exchanged for them.

People are obsessed as well by the need to earn money, as if it were far more important that the things which it can (and cannot) buy. No apparent distinction is made between the paper contract, and the obligation to fulfill same: people truly believe that there are laws which oblige persons to supply merchandise whenever enough dollars are presented, as if the only obstacle to dining on lobster in the Gobi Desert is the lack of $20,000 - or whatever.

It is because of this, it should come as no surprise that there are so many people in our culture who find it difficult to understand that the many billions of petrodollars bestowed on the tiny feudal elites of the Middle East over the last half century have actually had the effect of further impoverishing these wretched lands. [1]

There are at least two ways by which the power of the dollar has been actively inhibiting and even destroying the natural wealth of this region:

(1) Its basic natural resource, the mineral wealth, is being striped away in exchange for dollars, pounds, francs and lira which have no 'kinetic worth' in the sense of energizing these societies, but only a 'potential

worth' contingent on their purchasing power. The United States has aggravated this situation because of illegal tax incentives [2] which discourage the search for domestic sources of fuel and encourages the accelerated depletion of Middle Eastern reserves.

(2) This 'potential' purchasing power is concentrated in the hands of feudal aristocracies with a strong vested interest in blocking the development of the countries they oppress. The only use they have for it is to acquire untold quantities of non-productive, advanced though generally obsolete, (no contradiction in the weapons jungle) and thoroughly inappropriate weapons technology and other military systems hardware and training. [3]

This weaponry comes from, (excepting Russia, which is self-sufficient in oil), the same nations which import its oil; the companies manufacturing it, Lockheed, Northrop, Grumman, Dassault, Vickers, are thus able to maintain employment for many thousands of workers at home who, being paid with the same dollars that were initially exchanged for Middle Eastern oil, can now freely (in the sense of the 'Free Market System'), spend them on gasoline for their cars and fuel for heating their homes.

In a nutshell: the exchange of oil for arms ties in with the balance of payments in such a way as to return vitalizing currency back to the larger society of the oil importing nations, without them having in turn to give up anything of real value . [4]

This fallacious "exchange" drives the motors of industry and eases labor discontent at home; while in the Middle East, the rusts trickling off the gargantuan stockpiles of atavistic/futuristic/obscene/obsolescent weaponry mingle their haemoglobin dyes with the desert sands to create abstract paintings which, in the dazzling heat, celebrate the spiritual and material sterility of a once great civilization. [5]

This situation is not restricted to the Middle East. Third World countries in all parts of the globe, broken by their burdens of poverty, disease, illiteracy, hunger, without communications, roads, lacking an educated class or industrial base, are still somehow managing to arm themselves from scalp to toenails with the most sophisticated modern weapons, Exocet and Stinger and Scud B and Nike-Hercules missiles, with laser guided aircraft, 'people sniffers'and other electronic sensors , fragmentation bombs, napalm, pineapple grenades, computerized surveillance networks, the gruesome chemical weapons which are a Russian speciality , biological and even nuclear weapons, and so forth [6]

The causes for this situation are not hard to seek: in the total picture, the whole world is responsible, and it is an error to blame only the European bloc of arms-producing nations, or just the United States: the appetite for aggression is not limited to one population or one part of the globe. Yet the United States, the self-styled 'arsenal of democracy' , controlling as it does.at least 50% of the world's arms trade, has joyously accepted far more than its share of blood guilt.

(a) The sale of arms, accompanied always by "loans" or "foreign aid" with which to pay for them, to a Third World country, creates a false "national debt" for the possession of useless@goods that do nothing to develop the resources by which that debt might be repaid, (save that one occasionally hears of one country, such as Saudi Arabia, selling American weapons to another, such as Egypt. Needless to say, this money is not returned, even indirectly, to the general population.) This is however an effective strategy in catastrophically subverting the international exchange rate for that nation's currency, and this opens the door for the outright exploitation of its labor force by the multi-national corporations and the rip-off of its natural resources.

Observe the ease with which the Bush administration "forgave" Egypt's 7 billion dollar military "debt" on September 2,1990. This debt had in fact been 'paid back' many times over by our exploitation of its economy. Most of the "foreign aid" which the United States gives to the Third World appears to take the form of bribes, either to the military, the ruling elite, or to a small group of private individuals. This money, ending up in Swiss bank accounts, or lubricating the gears of corruption in the government and the army, gets charged to the nation as a whole. This pattern was never so clearly present as in the Nixon administration's support of the Shah of Iran in the 70's. Aid went directly to him, his family, or the gratification of his lunatic passion for advanced fighter aircraft. The bill was, however, passed on to the Iranian people [7]

(b) It is from last cited venture that what has come to be known as the "Nixon-Kissinger" doctrine emerged, which has since had so devastating an effect on the world's military complexion and both local and global power balances. We present a number of extended quotations from Anthony Samson's "THE ARMS BAZAAR", published in 1977:

"... The arms race in the Middle East was not initiated by any perceived new threat from the East but by the commercial opportunities coinciding with the diplomacy of the Nixon doctrine and the British retreat from the Persian (or Arabian) Gulf, which had resulted in a general loss of control over arms sales..." (ARMS BAZAAR,SAMSON, pg.290) "...[in 19691 ... Nixon and Kissinger expounded the 'Nixon doctrine'. by which the United States would supply 8rna rather than troops, equi pping their reliable allies with large arsenals in crucial areas .... In 1971 the United States foreign trade balance showed a deficit for the first time since 1893-The need for exports was now far more urgent than ten years before, when McNamara and Henry Kuss had first unleashed the Pentagon's salesmen, and the aerospace slump and unemployment added to the crisis. In the White House, Nixon discussed how to redress the trade balance, and was pressed, for both political and economic reasons, to relax restrictions on arms sales..." [ARMS BAZAAR, pgs. 242-243] [19721 "...Nixon agreed to sell Iran 'virtually any conventional arms it wanted', supported by unlimited American technicians in Iran: and he personally told the Shah that he could choose between the two new-generation planes, the Tomcat and the Eagle.

It was the first time that any non-industrial country had been allowed to reach the same level as the United States in the 'state of the art'. There had been no major review beforehand and Nixon's decision was passed to the Pentagon with no chance to revise it .... There was little evidence .... that Nixon had recognised the far-reaching policy implications..." (ARMS BAZAAR, pg. 252)

We are today harvesting the fruits Of the Nixon-Kissinger doctrine throughout the world; Saudi Arabia Is military budget is about $17.8 billion a year. Its CSS-2 missiles can strike as far to the east as Bangladesh, into Ethiopia and the Sudan and as far to the north and west as Czechoslovakia, Poland and a good part of Russia. India and Israel also have missiles of great accuracy with a range of over a thousand miles, and Iraq appears to have bolstered its Russian Scud B missiles to a range of 550 miles, enabling it to strike all of Iran, Saudi Arabia, Syria, Israel and Turkey.

It certainly does not look like a mere coincidence that on the one hand,

Saudi Arabia has the materiel to devastate Europe, Asia and Africa and that, on the other hand, the United States now occupies Saudi Arabia's deserts with over 100,000 troops. One recalls that China in the 50s gave a similar reason for the occupation of Tibet: its strategic position relative to China, Russia and the rest of Asia. [8]

(c) In those countries which are in reality extremely poor though in possession of enormous though unproductive surplus worth, (the "oil rich" nations of the Middle East), then as described above, the bartering of arms for oil solves the balance-of-payments problem in the oil-importing countries, returning their currency, thus stabilizing its international exchange rate and mitigating immediate social discontent.

This dynamic cycle is something like the process of osmosis, whereby the rich become richer and the poor lose even the little that they have. The oil-Money-Arms-Cycle, is the polluting motor which drives the phenomenal prosperity of the so-called First World. It must be maintained in operation around the clock; were it to stop for even a single day, our illusions of permanent economic security and well-being would come crashing instantly about our heads. [9]

2. The Cripple Factor

An inevitable question presents itself: what makes the industrialized arms-manufacturing nations so confident that the diabolic weaponry which they sell to the rest of the world will never be used against them? This guarantee, which appears to be as pervasive in the public optic as it is in the circles of government, I have given the name of " The Cripple Factor" : the multiple, mutually reinforcing, handicap effects inherent in the export of deliberately inappropriate technology.

After stating the essential features of the Cripple Factor, I will try to show how both internal and external policy are governed by it. I will give a few examples of situations in which the Cripple Factor appears to have worked. The Vietnamese War is then presented as an example of the bankruptcy of Cripple Factor thinking; it is also envisioned as a kind of watershed, the first stage in the collapse of the hegemony of Europe over the rest of the planet, and the fading away of the mentality that has grown up with it. Finally I will show how the Cripple Factor is apparent within our own society, making us victims of our own delusions. As space is quite limited, I can only begin to sketch these ideas, but I believe that I can give,.enough here to provide the basis for further analysis by others and myself.

The doctrine of the Cripple Factor inherent in inappropriate technology transfer rests on 3 basic tenets:

I. The assumption that Third World countries lack, and always will lack the basic educational level, literacy, a leisure and educated class, a minimal standard of living, vocabulary, communication systems, industrial base and above all, a unique system of values ('free exchange of ideas', 'open channels for debate and political criticism', ecivil liberties', etc.), to ever become competent in the us of the technology of the West. [10]

II. By overloading the rest of the world with our weapons, we shackle it, both physically and mentally, to the boundary conditions of having to fight our kind of war. Clearly we cannot lose, if the battles must be fought with our methods and our equipment. [11]

III. The Cripple Factor will always work 'for us' and against them'. We will never become bogged down in our own technology; they will never learn how to use it. [12]

Let us consider each of these points in turn:

I. Almost every commentator on the subject of the Middle East and/or the larger Muslim world takes pains to remind one that because these 'oil-rich' nations are importing Western technology without the cultural values that produced it, they are living in a fool's paradise,(See for example the book by Daniel Pipes cited in the bibliography). This argument, which may be considered a weak form of the Cripple Factor theory, is valid up to a point, but is also flawed in several ways.

Clearly those values which inspire us to dump weapons on them as a way of maintaining our prosperity are not the sort that anyone else should emulate. And it is indeed doubtful that a truly free society would permit the giving away of valuable military hardware and secrets to persons such as Sadaam Hussein and the Shah of Iran. One cannot argue that the Nixon-Kissinger doctrine which has permitted this truly represents the will of the people, particularly after learning of the critical role of Lockheed contributions in the amassing of the slush funds which got Nixon re-elected and produced the Watergate scandal.

These ideas about the inability of the Muslim world to fathom our culture and therefore our technology are self-serving justifications of arising from a guilty conscience, and the terrified recognition that we have given away our security to perpetual an irresponsible way of life. Japan has been the living counter-example to these arguments for over a century, and yet we continue on in the same kind of thinking.

Japan, too, was a militarist monarchy until the end of the Second World War. Civil liberties never achieved the level they had in the West, and under the fascist dictatorship that produced the war they vanished altogether. The Japanese imported all the Western technology they could get their hands on, imitated it then produced their own, kept their own value systems, and over a 35 year period carved out a huge Asian empire. Its creation and eventual dismantling occasioned the destruction of many millions of human lives, and if the United States had not entered the war, this empire might still be intact. The Japanese have, therefore, given the decisive counter-example to the first tenet of Cripple Factor thinking in this century.

In order, then, for the Cripple Factor to continue to work in the Middle East, one needs something more than a mere estrangement of cultural values. The Arab nations must be maintained in a situation in which it is effectively impossible for them to take their destiny into their own hands. on the one hand, ruling elites have been enriched at the expense of their populations, thereby creating in them a vested interest in opposing the development of their own countries. On the other hand, national boundaries have been drawn in such a fashion as to destroy the natural economic integrity of this region. A glance at the map of the Gulf will reveal that the artificial creation of the 'nations' of Iraq, Saudi Arabia and Kuwait in the 1920s deprived Iraq of effective access to the ocean, forcing it to build long pipe lines through Saudi Arabia and Turkey for the use of which it must pay enormous rates to both these countries. The barbarity of Sadaam Hussein is not to be excused, but there can be no doubt reasons of natural political economy indicate that Iraq ought to be part of Kuwait. [13]

II. The belief here is that the ownership and use of our kinds of weapons locks alien cultures into the rut of having to fight our kind of war. Without a doubt there is some truth in this argument. Education itself can be seen as a kind of armament of the individual and it is certainly the case that much of the purpose of compulsory public education is to force a child's thinking into modes that society can control. By obliging people to think in certain ways and reject others, society sets the ground rules of the discourse. There is an apparent paradox in all this, but it seems that we send our military advisers and equipment to other countries to teach and supply them in ways that we can most easily defeat if necessary. Many authors have explored the uses of education as a liability, but few have drawn the parallel between this and the exportation of arms and the kind of military thinking they entail. [14]

Something of the same logic appears to be present in the dumping of arms and the training of the armies of the Middle East. The strategies of conventional warfare are only effective against a conventional enemy, and our conventions derive from the Second World War. The massive bombings which destroyed Germany and Japan did not have the same effect in Vietnam; the Vietnamese would not fight our kind of war and therefore we could not beat them.

The importance given to compelling one's enemy to fight one's kind of war is based on considerable historical precedent. Most of the engagements of the Hundred Year's War were unmitigated disasters for the French. Their armies were callously massacred at Agincourt, Crecy and Poitiers by the English who refused to be drawn into "conventional" engagements in which the purpose of fighting had been the capture of princes for ransom and the key personal element was the display of reckless valor for the sake of honor.

Later the English themselves lost the American Revolution partly because of their reliance on compact phalanxes of infantry moving as a block in a country where the settling of the frontier had led to the development of more flexible tactics.

Likewise, Gandhi's strategy in the Salt March thoroughly upset all conventional expectations bound up with the very concept of force. His powerful ideas have yet to be understood and assimilated in most parts of the world.

So that when Saudi Arabia for example (by which one means a royal family of about 20,000 acting in the name of 5,000,000 people living in a desert 1/3 the size of the continental United States), purchases $18 billion of military hardware each year, it is not difficult to conclude that the purpose of this is to render it functionally unable to wage war. [15]

In terms of the Persian Gulf War - the moment a genuine threat to Saudi Arabia's security presented itself- remember that this is a country with the missile capacity to devastate India, the Sudan and most of Eastern Europe - once Iraq raised the stakes above venomous sabre rattling and invaded Kuwait -the United States acted, realistically, as if all these many billions of dollars of ostentatious weaponry constituted so much kitty litter, and sent in over 100,000 troops, (the figure may be as much as 200,000) to provide real protection - not for the people of Saudi Arabia, (whose well-being it has steadfastly opposed by propping up the Saudi dynasty for more than half a century) - but for its own concessions and derricks in the endless desert, where one finds almost no people at all. It is a final irony to note that one can search our newspapers over the past month and not discover a single item about the mobilization or presence of the Saudi army, numbering about 60,000, at their own troubled borders. obviously they have been ordered to stay home: the U.S. is well aware of just how incompetent its miseducation has made them.

III. The powers that be, including the government, the arms manufacturers, the oil companies and the Pentagon, would appear to entertain an almost religious faith in the belief that the Cripple Factor will always work "against them" and "for us" . They are certain that we (the free, first, advanced, industrialized, etc.world) will never become bogged down in our own technology to the extent that our own weapons, surveillance and command systems will become fatal liabilities, or lead us along the road to catastrophe. Once again, "he Vietnamese War serves as the decisive counter-example. Here is an extended quotation from David Marr's essay , "The Technological Imperative In US War Strategy in Vietnam" (The World Military order,pg. 36). in fact the entire essay makes for valuable reading:

.. At its peak operation in 1971-72, Igloo White was a tremendously ambitious, intricate system for seeking out and destroying truck convoys,supply depots, bivouacs, anti-aircraft sites, construction crews, repair teams,and just about any other signs of life in the hundreds of miles between the Mu Gia Pass on the North Vietnamese border and the general area where the borders of Laos, Vietnam and Cambodia converge. Ground sensors, airborne 'people sniffers' , and infra-zred detection equipment pinpointed local activity and transmitted this information automatically to a battery of IBM computers in Nakorn Phanom, Thailand.Depending on the nature of the alleged target, operational commanders at Nakorn Phanom ordered B-52's , fighter bombers, transports with side-firing weapons helicopters to vector in and attack, often on the basis of automatic firing signals. Much of this activity occurred at night, without pilots ever actually seeing the target. Meanwhile, during the day, they increasingly unloaded 'smart bombs' , guided in by diverse means usually beyond the reach of the Pilot. As one commentator rhapsodised, ' The entire process, "from beep to bang ", may take less than five minutes.' The whole operation seemed like a wild scientists dream come true.

But as the 1972 Spring Offensive demonstrated, something had gone wrong with American planning . Researchers and operational commanders had failed to understand the enemy or give him enough credit for ingenuity. Once again, by making the termination or drastic curtailment of north-south traffic a pre-eminent measure of success, they had continued to ignore or downgrade other critical elements of the struggle throughout Indochina. The Ho Chi Minh Trail had become an obsession. Yet even within the terms of that obsession, US planners never fully appreciated how tens of thousands of men And women along the Ho Chi Minh Trail in 1972 could outwit the electronic battlefield or, when that failed, reconstruct with alacrity , multiply the number of roads and paths available for alternative travel, and strip the most damaged trucks for repair of the least damaged."

We do not appear to have learned the lessons that this most recent and in some sense most terrible of all American wars, has to teach us. There is great value in defeat, even more so than in victory, because there is always much to be learned from it, whereas the victor in usually not even interested in learning that he has weaknesses and blind spots. Vietnam demonstrated the bankruptcy of all three aspects of the Cripple Factor : Firstly, the Vietnamese made far more intelligent use of their technology than we did of ours. Much of this technology came from Russia or was taken off the battlefields, and it was far from primitive. Secondly, the NLF and the army of North Vietnam stubbornly refused to be dr-awn into the conventional engagements of the post-WWII period, refusing as well to yield under the massive bombing of open cities, a strategy that was condemned as the very acme of barbarity when the Germans first employed it over Rotterdam but which has since become the hallmark of what the West believes it has to contribute to the rest of mankind. Thirdly, the Cripple Factor came home to haunt us, exposing us as a nation of fools obsessed with gadgets, gimmicry, macro-technology at all costs, waste, quick solutions, comfort, fatuous rhetoric about freedom, and, it need scarcely be mentioned, hubris.

It is therefore a mistake to automatically assume that the Cripple Factor will continue to work in the Middle East, although the evidence for its continuing relevance may appear to be convincing. our military-industrial complex basks in the smug illusion that the 6-Day War has demonstrated for all time that the weaponry of the Arab Middle East can be demolished in one day's bombing raids. But one should not assume that illiteracy, poverty and general backwardness will render the Muslim world forever incapable of making us of their own stockpiles of weapons; one should not forget that modern mathematics began in 9th century Baghdad. one should also not assume that our indoctrination is more disabling to them and less disabling to us than their indoctrination: Liberty, Fraternity, Equality are as much Muslim as they are French; the cry of "Holy war" is virtually the same as the call to a "War to save civilization". Finally, we continue to seriously under-estimate the amount of damage the Cripple Factor is creating in our part of the world, as we become increasingly victim, not so much really to our own technology, as to the fatal mentality that generates it.

FOOTNOTES

[1] David Pryce-Jones, "The Closed Circle" pg. 279 "...a unique and unrepeatable fortune has been dissipated into gunsmoke in one desert after another." A few Arab writers have drawn attention to reality, among them the Lebanese Georges Corm,.who speaks with eloquence a(nd scorn of 'this oil-fired tyranny, the new scourge of the Arabs', judging the society to be 'sick with oil'. A Kuwaiti professor, Muhammad Ruhaimi, concludes his book Beyond Oil somberly. 'Vested interests' in the Gulf, he says, oppose social justice and efficiency and 'continue to block any rational or open political development .... the importation of industrial and consumer goods do not contribute to modernization but to deepening outrage and oppression.

[2] "...The use of 'national security' to obtain a fabulous tax break occurred in 1949 when King ibn Saud, still living it up and still heavily in debt, demanded that Aramco pump more and increase its royalty payments rate ... Aramco saw a way to overcome these complaints without losing a dime. But again it would need the collusion of the United States Government. Aramco leaked its U.S. income tax records to Saudi officials, who saw that whereas - in return for their precious oil - they had received $38 million in royalties from Aramco in 1949, the U.S. government, in return for no tangible quid at all - had received from Aramco $43 million in taxes. That didn't seem fair to the Saudis .... to win the hearts of the Saudi princes, the U.S. Treasury Department broke the law. Federal statutes require income taxes to be applied equally and uniformly to all businesses. But the Treasury's Internal Revenue Service ruled that. as of 1951, overseas royalty payments would be considered income taxes, even though this ruling would exclusively benefit oil companies. They were the only companies paying such royalties.

And since U.S. law forbids double taxation, these "taxes" (royalties) could be deducted, dollar for dollar, from taxes owed at home .... Thus encouraged, the U.S.-based g;-ants began turning away from domestic exploration to develop their lush foreign fields. Why not? After all, an oil company that paid $1,000 in royalties to a landowner in Texas or Louisiana could deduct only $480 as business expenses. But an oil company that paid a foreign government (and most of the foreign oil lands were owned by governments, not by private persons) $1,000 in "taxes" could deduct the full $1,000 (italics added) . The foreign tax credit was sweet indeed. (Oil Follies, 1970-190)

[3] By 1989 figures, the military capability of Saudi Arabia consists of:

10,000 National Guard 52,000 Soldiers 14 SAM missile batteries 4 AWACS 7 Squadrons of modern fighter/interceptor aircraft A naval flotilla

The 1985-86 military budget was $17.8 x 109 . The entire population of Saudi Arabia cannot be more than 5 million, of which one million are immigrant labor. This comes out to a military investment of 3,500$ per person, and over 4,000$ per citizen. (facts and figures, The Closed Circle, pg. 277)

[4] "... Diplomats and arms-makers [1976] still argued that the Arabs could not really use the weapons , or present a serious threat to the Israelis. The arsenals in the desert could be seen as another solution to unemployment and over-production in the West: their rapid obsolescence and deterioration might keep Western workers happily employed for decades ahead..." (ARMS BAZAAR, Samson, pg. 314)

[5] In the 1970's, the Arab nations exported 1,207.3 x 10/9$ in oil, and bought 604.2xlO/9$ in arms, that is to say, about 50% of the oil revenue currency returned to the industrial block, notably the U.S. which commands 50% of the world's weapons trade. (The Closed Circle, pg. 266)

[6] Scientific American, August 90, Nolan and Wheelon: " Ballistic missiles and other means of long-range destruction, traditionally limited to a handful of industrialized nations, are fast becoming a fixture in many regional conflicts. The Third World military buildup is perhaps even more worrisome than its First World prototype, for it is far more likely to find expression in war."

"...the most depressing arms race was between the countries of the world who could least afford it, who were buying weapons instead of food and welfare; among the developing countries without oil to sell, orders for American arms had gone up from $240 million in 1972 to $2.3 billion in 1976 - a nearly tenfold increase ..... Zaire and Ethiopia, both impoverished countries, followed the arms-buying spree. American sales to Black Africa - nearly all to Zaire, Kenya and Ethiopia - went up by eight hundred Percent in one year. (ARMS BAZAAR, pg. 316)"

[7] THE ARMS BAZAAR; all of Chapter 14: "The Arming Of The Shah" pgs. 241 - 259

[8] Scientific American, op. cit.

[9][1972] " In Washington the increase in the oil-price had induced a sense of near-panic about the effects on the international economy and America's balance of payments, and William Simon at the treasury was not inclined to discourage orders for arms. The quickest way to recycle oil money or to Isop up the surplus', it was said, was to sell arms in exchange - much safer and stabler than having the oil-money 'sloshing around the short-term capital markets of the world'. (ARMS BAZAAR pg. 244)

[10] "...The arms companies offered contradictory justifications for their huge sales to Iranians or Arabs; first that they were essential to Western security, secondly that they were not really dangerous, because their customers could not effectively handle them..." (ARMS BAZAAR, SAMSON pg. 311)

"...'.Levels of education and technological skill are poor, and the troops have no compensating combat experience. The vast expenditure on arms that almost certainly could not be used outside their stockpiling warehouses is only the latest instance of military modernization as practised by Ottoman and Arab despots; and it refers more to values of honor than to actual preparation for battle..." (Closed Circle, pg.277)

[11] "...In November (of 1974), Assistant Defense Secretary Ellsworth and George Vest, then director of the State Department's politico-military bureau, flew to Riyadh with the recommendation that the Saudi government spend billions of dollars over the next ten years on more aircraft, 440 helicopters, 26 new ships, tanks, other armor, and equipment to create a paratrooper brigade. These weapons, said the Pentagon survey, would give the country the capabilities to "deter aggression and defeat an enemy." That year, Arabia ordered 300 improved Hawk missile batteries, for delivery in the 1976-79 period, at a cost of $270 million..." Weapons; pg. 560-61)

"...We are selling the A model of the Maverick, which cost us under $20,000 apiece, to the Saudis for B model prices, about $46,000 apiece, apparently in order to develop and Process the C model. This type of back door financing avoids the Congressional authorization process and provides the Pentagon with an additional source of revenue. It amounts to an incentive to unload unwanted or unneeded equipment on a country that may not need it but has money to burn..." (Weapons; pg. 563; quote Ben Rosenthal, Congressional hearing,1976)

"... Each batch of weapons generated the need for more. By 1976 the Saudis had already bought 110 Northrop Tigers, and they now wanted 2,000 Sidewinder missiles which could be fired from them, together with siiteen batteries of Raytheon Hawk missiles to provide an air defence system across the nation. The Israelis were now worried about these weapons' eventual destination, and the Arms Control and Disarmament Agency in Washington questioned whether the Saudis really needed a five-fold increase in missiles. But the Pentagon insisted that they were necessary in the event of a war with Iraq; and Congress eventually agreed on the deal. Soon afterwards the Saudis asked for 2,500 Maverick air-to-surface missiles, 1,000 laser-guided bombs and 1,800 wire-guided TOW missiles. The Senate protested, but Kissinger persuaded them to allow 650 missiles, in view of the United States' dependence or. Saudi friendship. The oil was still lubricating sales..." (ARMS BAZAAR, pg. 310)

". . . No oil country could now be seen without modern arms. All down the Persian Gulf the rich sheikdoms, with Iran facing them and Saudi Arabia surrounding them, were buying fighters, tanks and ships to catch up with their neighbors. The richest of these, Kuwait, was determined to balance its purchases, buying Skyhawk planes from America, Mirage Fls from France, and Chieftain tanks from Britain; but what kind of war they visualized was hard to discover..." (ARMS BAZAAR,pg. 312)

[12] As soon as a technologically advanced weapon system has been purchased for the armed services, a chain of supplementary import demands is induced. To remain operational, modern fighter aircraft, tanks, or naval units require an extensive network of support facilities ..... The chain of demands, generally with a high import content, seems endless. Precise data is not available, of course but a few examples can convey a general impression of the ramifications of arms imports ..... The introduction of jet-fighter aircraft in developing countries requires the construction of additional airports, the extension of existing runways and the installation

of navigational and control systems; it also leads to the adoption of a cost-ly air defence system, since the inventory of aircraft has to protected while still on the ground." (The World Military Order: The Economic Consequences of the Transfer of Military-oriented Technology, Peter Lock and Herbert Wulf; pg. 213) "... At the Hilton Hotel at Anaheim, near Disneyland, I observed a bus delivering a whole load of young Iranians ... I learnt that they were working on a top-secret intelligence project called Ibex (...) run by the Rockwell Corporation at Anaheim, at an estimated cost of over $500 million ..... Ibex was described as a sophisticated electronic intelligence system to be placed along Iran's frontiers as a protection against impending aggressors: but there were suspicions among some Iranians that it also involved an extensive bugging system Whatever the full scope of the Ibex, it soon began to run into trouble .... At the Anaheim hotel, the young trainees began to have serious psychological disorders as they reached the climax of their course; eventually a psychiatric specialist from the State Department was secretly sent to advise. In Iran, as the equip-ment began to be installed, there were doubts as to whether it could be made to work at all .... The Shah suspected that he had been sold a dud system, and bitterly complained about the chicanery of Pentagon offi-cials..." (ARMS BAZAAR, pg. 256)

[14] " Attacking the Americans in this manner obviously had its liabili-ties. Casualty rates were very heavy. US forces wiped out whole villages as they tried to retaliate effectively. Par more supplies and personnel had-to come from North Vietnam, running the bombing gauntlet all the way. Most seriously, the DRV and NLF ran the risk of seeing the entire confl-ict remoulded in ways advantageous to US capital-intensive warfare and dis-advantageous to people's war, the multi-faceted political and military cam-paigns in which the KLF excelled ... (The World Military Order,pg. 30)

[15] "...Saudi Arabia, because of its huge orders for military infrastruc-ture -80 percent or more of its arms purchases -had been America's second-best arms customer, but moved into first place in 1978 .... Not surprisingly, in view of Saudi Arabia's importance as an oil supplier and a force for con-servative moderation in the area, the decision to build up the Saudi forces was as much American as Saudi Early in 1974, plans were revealed in Washington to sell the Saudis half a billion dollars worth of F-5s and naval equipment. Reporters were told that F-4s had also been offered to replace British Lightnings, but that the Saudis were hesitant about the cost; at that time, no other Arab country had the Phantom.

BIBLIOGRAPHY

1. THE ARMS BAZAAR ; Anthon Samson Viking, 1977

2. THE CLOSED CIRCLE; David Pryce-Jones Harper & Row ; 1989

3. THE SEVEN SISTERS; Anthony Samson Viking; 1975

4. IN THE PATH OF GOD; Islam & PoliticalPower Daniel Pipes; Basic Books, 1983

S. THE WORLD MILITARY ORDER; Editors, Mary Caldor, Asbjorn Eide; Praeger, 1979

6. WEAPONS: The International Game 0f Arms, Money And Diplomacy; Russell Warren Howe; Doubleday, 1980

7. THE OIL FOLLIES OF 1970-80; Robert Sherrill Anchor Press; 1983

8. THIRD WORLD BALLISTIC MISSILES; James E. Nolan and Albert D. Wheelon, Scientific American, August 1990

STEAMSHOVEL PRESS

OCTOPUS BACKDROP TO THE LEWINSKY MATTER

After reading "Matt Drudge Meets The Octopus" in the *Things Are Gonna Slide* section of the *Steamshovel* web page, a reader wrote:

"There's more on Barbara Ledeen. She's executive director of the Independent Women's Forum, yet another conservative foundation, this one focused on hijacking feminism for right-wing purposes. The friend-of-the-court brief which Ken Starr prepared for the original Paula Jones legal team was undertaken at the behest ofthe Independent Women's Forum. In the last couple of years, Ledeen has spoken out several times in support of Jones and her "cause." It's been reported that Starr's amicus curiae brief was prepared on behalf of the Scaife-funded Landmark Legal Foundation and Mark Levin, president of Landmark, has denounced such claims. Turns out that he's technically correct; the job was handled by another part of the vast right-wing network, Ledeen's IWF. This is reported in the Feb. 27 issue of the LaRouchie Executive Intelligence Review. They connect Ledeen and her husband to what they call the Bush "secret government" network, a claim which, given Iran-Contra, seems plausible enough. They also connect the Ledeens—again correctly—to the Jewish-American neoconservative movement, the group that, next to Pat Robertson's evangelicals, is the biggest American supporter of the right wing in Israel.The LaRouchies, of course, see both groups collaborating in the operation to Get Clinton."

Michael Ledeen goes after Clinton a little more in the April 6 issue of National Review, calling the president a product of small town politics that "always have a bit of the mafia about them, particularly in the south, whether it be southern Italy, southern Germany or the Southern United States." Ledeen explains at length various mafioso practices of the current administration, including making Al Gore "the bag-man in the Buddhist temple caper" because all mafioso "must be guilty of serious crimes, so that betrayal will doom them all to extended prison terms." "For outsiders who pose a danger, more explicit threast are required.," Ledeen continues with his spin on Monica Lewisnsky, "Anyone acting against the family must be destroyed (as the White house brags it is doing with Kenneth Starr), but at the same time the Godfather invariably offers such people a corrupt way out: cooperation is rewarded." He concludes noting the Clinton marriage of the Arkansas and Chicago mobs, longstanding Clinton financial ties to Asian families, and the implication that outright war would be better than Clinton corruption.

In light of all this, Steamshovel reviews here what Danny Casolaro had to say about Michael Ledeen and political corruption. The following is taken from *The Octopus: Secret Government and the Death of Danny Casolaro:*

One of the ways in which Jimmy Carter may have "bruised the Octopus", as Casolaro says, was through the imposition of a 1979 embargo on the shipment of arms to Iran. Certainly that bruise healed quickly. Octopus familiar Ted Shackley appears, after his alleged retirement from the CIA in 1979, in 1984 negotiations for the shipment of arms to Iran by the Reagan administration. Shackley passed information from Iranians General Manucher Hashemi and Manucher Ghorbanifar, who had held influential positions in the SAVAK secret police under the Shah, and now were close to the Ayatollah Khomeini, to Oliver North and alleged P2 member Michael Ledeen in the White House. The Iranians suggested that arms shipments to "moderates" such as themselves in Iran could do much to prevent the Ayatollah from taking sides with the Soviets, and could speed the release of the American hostages. The billions of dollars of arms shipments began, using Israel, Taiwan, and South Korea as middlemen, as early as 1981, with some of the profits from the Iranian shipments being diverted to help the contra cause in Nicaragua..

The National Endowment for Democracy has been alleged to be a private intelligence network with the purpose of establishing a fascist, corporatist world state, a theme which also seems to inform the movements of Casolaro's Octopus. The model of this state can be observed in Michael Ledeen's book, Universal Fascism, in which he extolls a fascist state based upon the ideals of Gabriele d'Annunzio, Mussolini's predecessor. Ledeen was connected to P 2, which was in turn connected to the NSC. Reporting directly to North (as well as being a consultant in the Pentagon and State Department) was Michael Ledeen. Ledeen was responsible for obtaining Israeli Mossad spy Jonathan Pollard his job in the Department of the Navy, for establishing a line of Israeli influence into the NSC, and is known in Italy to have been a member of the P2 (Propaganda Due) Masonic lodge. P2, with a membership believed to include Henry Kissinger and Alexander Haig, is the organization known to have taken over the highest levels of Italian government and responsible during the 70s and 80s for an attempted bankrupting of the Vatican, in an alliance that linked the P2, the KGB, and major networks of drug trade.The Wall Street Journal detailed a meeting between Alexander Haig, Michael Ledeen, and high ranking P 2 member and number two man in Italian intelligence Francesco Pazienza. Pazienza is said to have been involved in shipments of US arms to Iran arranged by the Reagan administration.

Reference: Honnegger, Barbara, October Surprise, New York: Tudor Publishing Company, 1989

(57) Honegger, p. 124; Servadio, Leonardo, "Ledeen's Spanish Connection", Executive Intelligence Review, March 20, 1987

Egypt

In 1979 Edwin Wilson and Theodore Shackley formed EATSCO, the Egyptian American Transport and Services Corporation, which according to some sources obtained an exclusive and highly lucrative Pentagon contract to ship US arms to Egypt. Wilson also included in the partnership Richard Secord, Thomas Clines, Hussein K. Salem, and Erich von Marbod (at the time Deputy Director of the Defense Security Assistance Agency in the Pentagon... Can you say, "conflict of interest"?). Secord and his partners were indicted in 1983 for $8 million in "billing abuses" to the government. Michael Ledeen, at the time a State Department advisor, stepped in, suggesting to US Attorney E. Lawrence Barcella that the overcharged funds may have been used for the funding of black operations (thus rendering them a "hands off" proposition for prosecution). Secord retired from the Pentagon in 1983, after the EATSCO scandal, then started another company, IRANSCO, with Albert Hakim, in order to ship arms to Iran. (73)

(73) Honegger, p. 81, 82.

MARK LANE ON JANET RENO AND MARTIN LUTHER KING

A *Steamshovel Press* Interview

In light of Attorney General Janet Reno's recent promise, at President Clinton's behest, to review the request by the family of Martin Luther King to create a federal commission to re-investigate King's assassination, Steamshovel pres - ents here a previously unpublished part of an interview it conducted with Mark Lane, one-time lawyer for James Earl Ray. It contains interesting observations about both Reno and the King case. Steamshovel conducted the interview just after the conclusion of a mock trial on television that acquitted Ray of the murder.

Lane: I have the greatest confidence in attorney general Janet Reno. I was involved in one professional encounter with her several years ago and I think that she showed herself to be a person of absolute integrity and commitment to the rule of law. I think she should appoint a special prosecutor to look into the Kennedy assassination and the King assassination. A special prosecutor, of course, has to have subpoena power. Call all the witnesses, look at all the evidence, present all of the relevant evidence to a grand jury. If that process were to begin today, before the year is over, those who killed President Kennedy and those who killed Dr. King could be indicted. But we can,t trust just a special prosecutor, although I have a lot of faith in Janet Reno and her concern in all of these matters

Steamshovel: Mark, let me ask you, what was your involvement with Reno? Did that have anything to do with the assassinations?

Lane: No. My involvement with Janet Reno was this: Some years ago, I read that a man named James Richardson in Florida had been convicted of murdering his seven children in a town called Arcadia, Florida. I went down to Florida, criss-crossed the state and wrote a book about it called *Arcadia*. I demonstrated, I believe conclusively, that he was innocent and a woman named Bessie Reece, in fact, was the murderer. Nevertheless, James Richardson was on death row for more than five years and in prison for more than twenty one years. Eventually, I secured the entire prosecutor,s file. It showed, to my thinking and to any reasonable person who looked at it, that it was the anatomy of a frame-up. The prosecutors not only got the wrong man, but that they knew Richardson was innocent and they framed him. I took that to Governor Martinez, the Republican governor at that time of Florida, and said appoint a special prosecutor. He appointed Janet Reno and we went to court together. I did not know what her position would be. She studied it for several weeks. In court, I said that the state had suborned perjury, the state had used perjured testimony against Mr. Richardson and the state had suppressed exculpatory evidence and Richardson should walk out of prison after twenty one years in jail. I sat down, and she said, "I agree with Mr. Lane. He,s quite right, she said, "The state did what it should not do. She said,

"Down in Miami we prosecute drug cases and sometimes we,re quite sure that we have someone and he,s guilty. Then a piece of evidence comes up and it can be very useful to the defense. We give it to the defense. We don,t even think about. It,s the law. And if we can,t obey the law, we can,t ask defendants to obey the law. She did what I don,t know any other prosecutor would do and said the state is wrong and this man is innocent. James Richardson walked out of prison that day.

Steamshovel: As you know, HBO acquitted James Earl Ray a few days ago. Did you see that and did any of your work come out in that?

Lane: Well, I know the HBO so-called "trial. I didn,t participate because I don,t believe thatI think there,s a good, important role for investigative journalists and I think that Steven Thompkins, who did this wonderful piece for the Memphis *Commercial-Appeal*, should be praised and should be given a Pulitzer Prize for that. I believe in investigative journalist report. I believe in trials also. I don,t believe that when you have a TV show you can call them trials. I,ve known Bill Pepper for many years, who was the so-called defense lawyer in that case, and he kept on telling me it was a trial. And I said, "What did Frank Holloman (director of police and fire department in Memphis at the time of King's murder) say when you questioned him? And he said, "He didn,t want to come. And I said, "Well, Bill, that,s what I mean. In a trial, you subpoena him. You don,t just find out who wants come. And he said, "Well, the other testimony was important. I said, "It wasn,t testimony. What could HBO do? Pull the cable on someone who lied on television and they can,t have HBO anymore? There is no penalty of perjury. That,s what makes it testimony. Nobody,s under oath.

But I,ll tell you an interesting thing about that that he told me and that I don,t think has been broadcast widely at all. That is, when HBOsomebody was taking that seriouslywhen HBO brought the so-called "jurors together and put them in hotel rooms, HBO discovered that FBI agents had moved into the hotel and were occupying the rooms next to the jurors. Real FBI agents! I,m not talking about Ephram Zimbalist, Jr. I,m not talking about fake FBI agents to go with a fake trial. These are real FBI agents who apparently going to bug the jurors, room.

Steamshovel: Spying on this HBO production...

Lane: Yeah, on a TV show! And so HBO heard about that. They were alarmed and moved the jurors out to another area.

Steamshovel Debris: The mock trial of James Earl Ray did have interesting legal dimensions. In 1978, an FBI informer named Oscar Patterson swore that representative of the House Select Committee on Assassinations instructed him to tell *New York Times* reporter Anthony Marro that Mark Lane was gay and had said that Raul—Jame Earl Ray's mysterious handler— didn't exist, and also to spread some lies about his brother Jerry. Lane found out about it and confronted Patterson, who then agreed to arrange a meeting with Marro at a St. Louis hotel. Marro walked into a room full of reporters and news cameras, whereupon he fled—with Lane in pursuit, demanding that Marro listen to the truth. Lane returned and conducted a press conference about HSCA's use of Patterson. A St. Louis newsman named John Auble was there for the whole thing and filmed it. He offered to testify and bring the film to Ray's television trial in 1992, but the judge said it was immaterial to the assassination. In his book *Orders To Kill*, William Pepper argues, as he did before the mock court, that it showed conspiracy to frame Ray as the lone assassin.

steamshovel press

John Judge and Dick Gregory at COPA conference in Memphis.

COPA CONFEREES CONFRONT GERALD POSNER

During the MLK conference put on by the Coalition on Political Assassinations in Memphis in April, five attendees decided to load up in a van and drive ten minutes uptown to David Kidd's mall bookstore, where Gerald Posner was signing his new book on the King assassination. Posner previously had written a deceptive and poorly researched book on the JFK murder called *Case Closed*. He generally is regarded as a disinformationist, poor scholar, bad prosecutor wannabe or incompetent armchair psychologist. As he did with Oswald in the previous book, Posner bases his King book on a psychological evaluation of James Earl Ray, which he is not qualified to give, and dismisses evidence of conspiracy in King's murder as cynical attempts to exploit the tragedy.

Ray's brother Jerry went to the signing and confronted Posner about inaccuracies, with a video camera on hand to record the exchange. The van load of COPA participants arrived shortly thereafter. One member of the group, Robin Palmer, walked up to Posner's table, thumped his hand on a copy of the book and declared, "This is a piece of shit!" and otherwise vented his anger to Posner, not violently but in a firm way and with a sense of humor. The crowd reacted as if air had been released from an over-inflated tire. Several people laughed. The suburban mall bookstore afternoon had been relieved of Posner's pomposity.

It made management nervous, of course. Several clerks and assistant managers attempted to kick Palmer out of the store. Others tried to re-route the crowd back in line. "Do you have a book to sign? Please leave if you don't have a book to sign!" As Palmer continued to argue that people shouldn't sit there quietly while Posner reaped money from his phony book, one of Posner's supporters spoke up for his first amendment right. How well that right was protected—for Posner, if not for Palmer—was soon demostrated.

Mall security cops came and physcially escorted Palmer out the door. *Steamshovel* editor Kenn Thomas joined him for more discussion about what was happening, but before long additional mall police came out and asked both to leave the entire mall. The COPA attendees had all arrived in Thomas'van, and so he was obligated to remain until all had returned. The mall cops were having none of that, though, and immediately called the Memphis police. It became a waiting game of who could make it first, the COPA gang to the van, or the real cops to the mall.

Conference participant Dick Gregory had planned to go to the Posner signing, but was delayed. Had he been there, he no doubt would have taught the COPA crowd the best means of being comfortable in jail that night. As it stood, that crowd barely made it out in time. Gregory did show up, in time to see that indeed real cops had been called out to make an arrest for the crime of literary and historical criticism.

The incident was a small one in an otherwise interesting and successful conference. The conference was highlighted by talks from Criminal Court Judge Joe Brown. Brown was removed from the attempt to grant James Earl Ray a new trial for "apparent bias" he developed as his investigation pointed more and more to conclusions of conspiracy. He addressed COPA attendees at the United Methodist Church on McLemore Street, where Martin Luther King gave his last press conference.

Ray's lawyer William Pepper was not encouraging about Ray getting a new trial at this point, but COPA organizers, John Judge, Phil Melanson and Dick Russell among them, passed a resolution to support the King family's current request for a new investigation commission. Researcher Wallace Milam gave out a point-by-point refutation of Posner's appearance with Dan Rather on *48 Hours* and said that he would provide a full analysis of Posner's King book on the web, as was done with Posner's previous book.

THE GUN SMOKES
By Len Bracken

A red light rotates outside the door to the Oval Office. The clapstick snaps shut - Scene 1, take 1. Whispered rumors from the wings about the President and his intern as the camera films his world-weary reflection in a mirror while he lolls on his sofa. But there's something strange about this mirror - a patch of silver backing is missing around the reflection of his crotch and a scene emerges through transparent glass: tones change quickly from light to dark as her long dark hair bobs back and forth. A publicity still of the President's face in ecstasy as the nation crumbles in the background. Murder on Ruby Ridge. Transshipment scenes from Mena. Cut to a montage of the young, barefoot boy coming to Washington with a hayseed in his mouth and a saxophone around his neck; then to the icing expert with such a winning smile who is all too willing to throw her weight around - a screwball comedy in the works, one that calls for a new style of acting in which people from the worlds of politics, culture and business play themselves like Howard Stern and his retinue in *Private Parts*.

These rumors about the most "decisive" person in the most delicate affairs of American political life give the West Wing an illusory quality. And these powers of illusion are so great the cast frequently loses their heads and becomes confused with other protagonists: Dick Clinton and Bill "call girl" Morris, for example, or Janet Hamrod and The Hillary We Know (as lesbians call her when she gives into sadistic urges). Paula Dumbski, Monica Jones - opportunists separated at birth? A glorious pubic feud erupts in the trailer park on Pennsylvania Avenue between Dick and his Starr-struck prosecutor, a judge intent on determining if the president would risk the world for a piece of pie.

For all we know, this infamy is precious to the president. He has assassins for friends or assassinates his friends when they become unworthy accomplices. Rumor has it he came to power thanks to a coalition of prostitutes and an appetite for glory that affords no patience for morality. An affable, even gregarious man dances on the stage of the world historic with a harem in tow. He bluffs the public about everything, including his health. And for a while he brilliantly camouflages his Casanova past and delinquent inspirations. Some see the ruin of the presidency expressed in his personal ruin; others judge him on abstract ideas about morality rather than concrete examples of injustice. Still others are reassured that Clinton has an Epicurean side to go with his insane ambition. His cult of charm is constrained by his foibles and a web of laws he only half believes. What emerges isn't the thief in tricky Dick, rather the con man, now with a big red nose - a clown who would be king. With his face in place, he openly speculates on the ignorance of the American people and its taste for scandal.

Only the latest and widest range of cinematic techniques can capture these rumors as they're transmitted around the globe like points of light from a mirror ball. But the effort and expense is justified because Washington rumors are more significant than other equally truthful and malicious rumors. The first rumors scream into view on a missile tracking camera, as if on a magic carpet, and explode in the veritable center of the universe.* Critics in future generations will debate the symbolism involved here, and it's true, it's not what you'd think. A bomb is dropped on the American psyche and the lever of war is up for grabs. Mobile production units appear on the scene to assess, and inevitably add to, the damage. Puppets with exchangeable heads swallow dictionaries and let out the story like so much gas: the pyrotechnists among them execute fireworks; those with a tendency for bombing shit their pants.

Meanwhile, rumors surface about obscure organizations in the deepest shadows of recent events. Will we have to wait for the screen credits to find out about the North American News Alliance? Rumor has it the founder of this small and obscure news agency was a high-level member of the OSS. Rumor also has it that NANA became, under Sidney Goldberg (husband of Lucy, agent to Linda Tripp), a media infiltration instrument of the CIA. And what about the tabloids' ties to the CIA? Where else would one get access to Oswald's widow? Are there not direct CIA ties to a financier of *The American Spectator*? a journal that has whipped the president with its anathema from day one. Of course all sense of fair play was abandoned as soon as Starr was appointed Independent Counsel; this same magazine financier with a pedigree going back to the OSS, the "eccentric" Richard Mellon Scaife, once paid Starr through his Landmark Legal Foundation to support Miss Jones in her case against the president. She also found inspiration in the words of Ambrose Evans-Pritchard, a crony of the crown who, like most British agents, knows how to create a sex scandal to divert attention from the most pressing issues of the day. The reaction shot of the press is priceless: blank stares accompanied by plaintive chords on the violin. The production assistants are restless as this awkward moment passes; then it's back to business as usual for reporters with the humility required to chase celebrity-commodities and stick microphones under their double chins. This is what the sponsors want - a spot news check to tell everyone what to think and feel.

What were once whispered rumors have become an alarming noise. We should recall the maternity of these rumors - Linda Tripp, whose name and appearance refuse to be confused with anyone, a high-ranking civilian with Delta Force experience, a possible Bush mole and ally of Gary Aldrich, the FBI agent who made a few scandalous claims of his own about Clinton sexual misconduct. This is the same woman who made an accusation about a Bush extra-marital affair and another about Clinton sexually harassing Kathleen Willey. As the story goes, she trips here pawn with a wire at the Pentagon City Ritz Carlton, an apparently shrewd betrayal designed to get a book deal (a book that gives every indication of having pages stuck together). Whereas many women would rather fondle Clinton's stainless steel testicles than tattle, this is not an option for the Tripp who looks too fucked even for Dick and who knows all the gossip or invents her own. As Master of Obscene Arts she unravels a thread going from FBI-military intelligence connections to Nixon's plumbers and back to the CIA.

It may not appear in their training manuals in exactly these words, but all of the those mentioned above know that rumors are the least expensive poison. Washington is not Whitman's invincible city of Friends, rather center of a society founded on deceit and perpetual illusion.

In his prime time State of the Union speech, Clinton passes the personality test by demonstrating that as individually corrupt as Americans may be, they're suckers for mass spectacles that profess respect for virtue. With slogans about surplus for social security he is the ultimate Democrat giving expression to noble sentiments about care for the elderly. The way spectators enjoy being duped is one of those little truths most people avoid telling themselves and don't want to hear from others. Clinton shares pains with his people and with future glory seekers who are sure to imitate "the Clinton bluff," which he executes with tremendous powers of suggestion and no trace of irony. It's enough to make a general cry. And like so much of what Clinton is able to do, this encounter is more illusory than real.

Indeed, the film chronicles the illusion of encounters from Monica's first White House fantasies to the moment they became all too real; from Dick's very real dreams to the illusions, no less real, crafted by the Office of the President. Will these powers of illusion be enough to cover his character flaw? Not likely. We're all destined to wage war with our weaknesses, but temptresses are especially difficult - as one poll put it: "Most men go for it." Yes, Dick is oblivious, reckless... For him sexual misconduct is something like premature ejaculation. In this sense the pair - the celebrity and his face artist - is not incongruous at all, but the script stipulates that only archival footage of them together be used. We hear them on new White House tapes as the screen splits between shots of him at the beach in the Virgin Islands, and Monica, dear Monica, in a Penthouse spread. The actors are still on good terms and therefore might have wanted to reenact these scenes. But they accept, however reluctantly, every nuance of the script. Meanwhile, Clinton pushes his agenda through the assembly of mercenaries on the Hill and has Gingrich act as his valet at the State of the Union. The stage managers and Starr system make it seem as if Clinton uses his disasters as opportunities to mistreat his opponents, but he isn't the first glory hound to fill the capital with scandal and still get his way. Whereas adultery once again saves Clinton's marriage, Dick no longer hangs out in West Wing hot-spots and lays women by the dozen. What were you thinking, Mr. President? If you can't love your wife, and only your wife, you shouldn't marry! Learn fidelity from your dog and have Hillary beat both of you when you stray. She's right, after all, if she's pointing to a vast right-wing conspiracy that coalesced in Iran-Contra operations and never demobilized or purged itself of fascists. She is obviously the most brilliant protagonist, and very brave to call these dirty tricks by their proper name. A drum roll and gunfire as prophets speak of darkness and the ghost of Jacqueline.

* Location scouts from the Washington Psychogeography Association identify a point on 16th Street NW (between Meridian Hill Park and the Diplomat condos) as the center of the city.

Len Bracken is the author of Guy Debord - Revolutionary, *the translator of Gianfranco Sanguinetti's* The Real Report on the Last Chance to Save Capitalism in Italy *and the editor of* Extraphile, *which can only be obtained by sending a 9" x 12" SASE with $2 postage, an age statement and something sumptuous stolen from work to POB 5585 Arlington, VA 22205.*

FLATLAND DISPATCH
By Jim Martin

After the wettest winter on record here in California, it's starting to feel like a new year, time to look back over the past 13 lunar cycles and see where *Flatland* stands. I think my nose just broke the surface of the water.

The new 1998 *Flatland Books* catalog is now in the mails, heading toward our customers and new recruits. *Flatland Magazine* #15 has been on the newsstands since March, and I got a lot of positive responses from readers of my interview with Dr. Lloyd DeMause, editor of *The Journal of Psychohistory*. Check out the Flatland Web Page for details about the book catalog, the new magazine, and be sure to check out Dr. DeMause's take on the Clinton-Lewinsky affair, his press release "The Phallic Presidency."

Lots of people have an opinion about Mel Gibson's latest movie, *Conspiracy Theory*, but Flatland Books is one of the few places in the world where you can buy copies of (Mel's dad) Hutton Gibson's maniacal screeds against the Vatican, which he calls "the vacancy." Mel's dad, obviously, was the original "Mad Max." A Catholic traditionalist, Hutton Gibson's books scream for blood; he calls the burning of heretics "an act of charity." Hutton's books, *Is the Pope Catholic?* and T*he Enemy is Here!* (Rome, that is) are only for the Bravehearts.

Both the new *Flatland Magazine*, as well as Len Bracken's new translation of the classic hoax, *The Last Chance to Save Capitalism in Italy*, by Gianfranco Sanguinetti (a member of the radical Situationist International) have gotten some positive early reviews. In the popular *EYE Magazine* (301 S. Elm St., Suite 405, Greensboro, NC, 27401), editor Sam Gaines embarrased me with an effusive review of *Flatland* #15, - calling *Flatland* "one of the few titans of conspiracy publications" and that "Editor/publisher Jim Martin is one of the most compelling conduits of hidden and suppressed information in the United States." Wow! "And in his newest issue," Sam wrote, "he underscores his stature with the expected eloquence." Fetch me down my ten gallon hat!

Michael Theroux, who took over Tom Brown's duties as editor of *The Journal of Borderland Research*, echoed my editorial comments about the raw deal many small press periodicals got after the Fine Print Distributors went bankrupt. The fiasco has had long-term repercussions in the scene, let me tell you.

It's good to see *Anarchy Magazine* back on the stands, as they, too, have had some financial difficulties lately. John Zerzan provided a review of *The Last Chance to Save Capitalism in Italy* in *Anarchy* #45, available from C.A.L. Press, POB 1446, Columbia, MO 65205. (Zerzan has had a bit of press recently, due to his advocacy of the Unabomber's theses against technology, and has called for the release of Ted Kaczinsky.) *Anarchy* editor Jason McQuinn is taking a lot of heat for publishing Bob Black's rants in book form, and the polemic tenor of the letters section makes for the most interesting reading, a lot of verbal swordplay.

This winter, while trying to keep dry, I've been working hard on my forthcoming book, called *Wilhelm Reich and the Cold War*. It's an investigation into the history of the late forties and fifties, tracing the travails of the late Dr. Wilhelm Reich through the treacherous by-ways of his exile to the USA, his highly placed antagonists on both sides of the Iron Curtain, his avant-guard discoveries into biophysics, weather, and UFOs, and ultimately his persecution, trial and death in prison. It's an incredible ride, and thanks to Kenn Thomas and all the others who helped me research for the book.

During the latter months of 1997, I was able to make a trip back East, to continue the research, and was delighted to meet so many helpful folks along the way: Len Bracken put me up in Washington, where I visited the FBI FOIA Reading Room, and he gave me the psychogeographical tour of the nation's capital; in Boston, I met Myron Sharaf's delightful widow, Giselle, who fixed me a delicious salmon dinner, and showed me Myron's office and papers, which have been left basically untouched since Myron, a student of Reich's, and the author of the standard biography, *Fury on Earth,* died in May 1997; in Maine I reconnoitered with my friend Eva Reich, M.D., who told me where to get a live lobster, and who ushered its soul out an open window as I dropped it into boiling water in her kitchen; In New York City, I met up with Peter Robbins, author of the fine UFO book, *Left at East Gate*, who brought me out to his home near Ithaca, where I studied the archived papers of Michael Straight at Cornell University. I am still basking in the warmth all these folks showed me, and many more that I haven't mentioned. It was a rare trip for me, and well worth it.

Readers of Caroll Quigley's *Tragedy and Hope* might recall the name Michael Straight. Quigley offered Michael Straight, then publisher of the *New Republic,* as Exhibit A for the argument that the Morgan Bank manipulated both left and right wing groups in order to keep tabs on, and control, national elections and legislation. The *New Republic*, in 1947, published an article about Wilhem Reich that led to his prosecution and imprisonment. Reich, much to the consternation of his young followers, insisted that he had been set up for a "show trial" by Communist conspirators. In my book, I intend to reveal a lot of background, for the first time, that lends credence to Reich's so-called "conspiracy theory." In the 1980s, Michael Straight went public with the information that he had been recuited into the "Cambridge Five" spy ring, which included infamous personalities sich as Guy Burgess, Anthony Blunt, Kim Philby, and Donald MacLean.

I've been interviewing Michael Straight - he's still alive - and he gave me permission to access his files at Cornell.

This angle is but one chapter of my book, *Wilhelm Reich and the Cold War,* which will also cover the background of Reich's last published work, *Contact With Space,* probably the most studiously ignored classic of all time.

Wilhelm Reich, a some of you are aware, invented a method of rainmaking. In this, he drew the attention of the government, which had already been funding people like Kurt Vonnegut's brother, Bernard, who invented silver-iodide cloudseeding. I leave you with an interesting address given to the graduating 1997 class at MIT by Kurt Vonnegut:

"Ladies and gentlemen of the class of '97:

Wear sunscreen.

If I could offer you only one tip for the future, sunscreen would be it. The long-term benefits of sunscreen have been proved by scientists, whereas the rest of my advice has no basis more reliable than my own meandering experience. I will dispense this advice now.

Enjoy the power and beauty of your youth. Oh, never mind. You will not understand the power and beauty of your youth until they've faded. But trust me, in 20 years, you'll look back at photos of yourself and recall in a way you can't grasp now how much possibility lay before you and how fabulous you really looked. You are not as fat as you imagine.

Don't worry about the future. Or worry, but know that worrying is as effective as trying to solve an algebra equation by chewing bubble gum. The real troubles in your life are apt to be things that never crossed your worried mind, the kind that blindside you at 4 pm on some idle Tuesday.

Do one thing every day that scares you. Sing. Don't be reckless with other people's hearts. Don't put up with people who are reckless with yours.

Floss.

Don't waste your time on jealousy. Sometimes you're ahead, sometimes you're behind. The race is long and, in the end, it's only with yourself.

Remember compliments you receive. Forget the insults. If you succeed in doing this, tell me how.

Keep your old love letters. Throw away your old bank statements.

Stretch.

Don't feel guilty if you don't know what you want to do with your life. The most interesting people I know didn't know at 22 what they wanted to do with their lives. Some of the most interesting 40-year-olds I know still don't.

Get plenty of calcium. Be kind to your knees. You'll miss them when they're gone.

Maybe you'll marry, maybe you won't. Maybe you'll have children, maybe you won't. Maybe you'll divorce at 40, maybe you'll dance the funky chicken on your 75th wedding anniversary. Whatever you do, don't congratulate yourself too much, or berate yourself either. Your choices are half chance. So are everybody else's.

Enjoy your body. Use it every way you can. Don't be afraid of it or of what other people think of it. It's the greatest instrument you'll ever own.

Dance, even if you have nowhere to do it but your living room.

Read the directions, even if you don't follow them.

Do not read beauty magazines. They will only make you feel ugly.

Get to know your parents. You never know when they'll be gone for good.

Be nice to your siblings. They're your best link to your past and the people most likely to stick with you in the future.

Understand that friends come and go, but with a precious few you should hold on.

Work hard to bridge the gaps in geography and lifestyle, because the older you get, the more you need the people who knew you when you were young. Live in New York City once, but leave before it makes you hard. Live in Northern California once, but leave before it makes you soft.

Travel.

Accept certain inalienable truths: Prices will rise. Politicians will philander.

You, too, will get old. And when you do, you'll fantasize that when you were young, prices were reasonable, politicians were noble, and children respected their elders. Respect your elders.

Don't expect anyone else to support you. Maybe you have a trust fund. Maybe you'll have a wealthy spouse. But you never know when either one might run out.

Don't mess too much with your hair or by the time you're 40 it will look 85.

Be careful whose advice you buy, but be patient with those who supply it. Advice is a form of nostalgia. Dispensing it is a way of fishing the past from the disposal, wiping it off, painting over the ugly parts and recycling it for more than it's worth.

But trust me on the sunscreen.

-Kurt Vonnegut, Boston, Ma. 1997"

Jim Martin Flatland Books (http://www.flatlandbooks.com) POB 2420 Fort Bragg. CA 95437 707-964-8326

Steamshovel receieved the following correspondence after posting the above.

Hi! I just thought I'd offer you (and via you, Jim Martin) a correction to part of the latest Latest Word.

The last bit, while attributed to Kurt Vonnegut, was not written by him. I've attached an article by Paul Krassner on this below.

Andrew

The Realist #137 (Autumn, 1997).
Case History of a Cyberhoax Not by Kurt Vonnegut

I confess. Although I didn't handle the technological end of the Kurt Vonnegut hoax—I've never driven a car, I don't know how to program a VCR, and I use my computer only for word-processing—the idea was mine. A friend I'll call Hacker took care of the cyberspace aspects.

I've always loved pranks. In my high school yearbook, under Hobbies, I put "Eating new recipes and playing practical jokes"—not realizing that I had unintentionally described the best way for somebody to play a nasty trick on me.

When I started publishing The Realist in 1958, I printed a rumor that IBM, whose employees sometimes seemed as standardized as the machines they sold, required all personnel to have their teeth capped by a company dentist. IBM's Medical Director wrote in response: "We do not maintain dental services nor do we provide remedial dental care." Of all the hoaxes since then, my most infamous one was "The Parts Left Out of the Kennedy Book" in 1967.

Of course, I have had pranks pulled on me in return, from an announcement of my demise in the short-lived Cheetah magazine—they rationalized that I had published a fake obituary of Lenny Bruce two years before his death (in order to call attention to his plight while he was still alive)—to an interview that I had supposedly done with Bob Dylan, which was actually made up by Marvin Garson and published in the San Francisco Express-Times. It was circulated throughout the underground press and critiqued in Rolling Stone.

When I stopped publishing in 1974, many readers thought that was a hoax. Others didn't realize publication had been suspended until it was resumed in 1985. The Los Angeles Times published a series on plagiarism by their media critic, David Shaw, and I reprinted an excerpt from it, using Pete Hamill's byline. *The Realist* was back in business.

Then along came the World Wide Web. A prank could now be communicated with greater speed and reach more people than ever before. For example, the following "Virus Alert" has been spread with altruistic intent and Malthusian multiplicity:

"Warning—If anyone received mail entitled Pen Pal Greetings, please delete it without reading it. This is a warning for all Internet users. There is a dangerous virus propagating across the Internet through an e-mail message entitled Pen Pal Greetings. Do not download any message entitled Pen Pal Greetings.

"This message appears to be a friendly letter asking if you are interested in a pen pal, but by the time you read this letter, it is too late. The Trojan horse virus will have already infected the boot sector of your hard drive, destroying all of the data present. It is a self-replicating virus, and once the message is read, it will automatically forward itself to anyone whose e-mail address is present in your mailbox.

"This virus will destroy your hard drive, and holds the potential to destroy the hard drive of anyone whose mail is in your In box, and whose mail is in their In box and so on. If this virus keeps getting passed, it has the potential to do a great deal of damage to computer networks worldwide...."

However, the Virus Alert was itself a hoax. As Hacker explains, "E-mail can't contain a virus. E-mail is pure data. A virus has to be an executable code. No e-mail can contain a virus except for e-mail with executable attachments. This includes Microsoft Word, which has a macro language that can execute immediately when you open a document. So it's possible to do great harm by opening an attachment to your e-mail, but not by reading it."

In June, a subscriber sent me several clippings, including this column by Mary Schmich in the Chicago Tribune:

Inside every adult lurks a graduation speaker dying to get out, some world-weary pundit eager to pontificate on life to young people who'd rather be rollerblading. Most of us, alas, will never be invited to sow our words of wisdom among an audience of caps and gowns, but there's no reason we can't entertain ourselves by composing a Guide to Life for Graduates. I encourage anyone over 26 to try this and thank you for indulging my attempt.

<See Above>

At a recent memorial for Allen Ginsberg in Los Angeles, Bob Weide read a statement from Kurt Vonnegut which began, "Please, stop dying." Somehow, "Wear sunscreen" reminded me of that. When I chatted with Vonnegut in New York a few years ago, I got the impression that he was saddened that young people might not be familiar with his work. The perverse motivation of my prank was to help remedy that situation.

Replacing Mary Schmich's byline and opening paragraph with "This speech was given by Kurt Vonnegut at MIT's commencement this year," Hacker proceeded to transmit the text of her column over the Internet in such a way that it could not be traced to him.

The non-commencement speech traveled fast and furiously. It was even posted to the Vonnegut Newsgroup. Many of his fans thought it was valid, including Vonnegut's wife, photographer Jill Krementz, who e-mailed it to several friends (her husband was out of town at the time). Mademoiselle magazine asked Vonnegut for permission to reprint his speech. Peter Lasally, who used to be a producer for Johnny Carson, tried to book Vonnegut on the Tom Snyder show.

Actually, the commencement speaker at MIT—five days after Mary Schmich's column had been published—was Kofi Annan, secretary general of the UN, who didn't mention sunscreen or flossing. Schmich, who had written the piece "while high on coffee and M&Ms," called Vonnegut to let him know that she wasn't behind the hoax. He said that it revealed the gullibility of people on the Internet.

Schmich traced one e-mail backward from its last recipient, a professor at Malcolm X College in Chicago. He had received it from a relative in New York, who received it from a film producer in New York, who received it from a TV producer in Denver, who received it from his sister, who received it from.... At this point, Schmich gave up her quest for the culprit.

I apologize to Vonnegut and Schmich, but I'm happy to say that the revelation that the commencement speech was a hoax reached more people than the hoax did, not only on the Internet, but also in print and electronic media. The truth had triumphed in a truly free marketplace of ideas.

So who actually wrote it? Krassner, Samitch, or "Andrew"??? No wonder the internet is confused, people don't know how to use it. I still think it's a hilarious piece, who cares if Vonnegut wrote it? What difference does it make? I'm more interested in Bernard Vonnegut, anyway, which ties into the "wear Sunscreen" angle of weather modification. I just tagged it on, because I was too lame to write my own snaps, just like everybody else on the internet.

— Jim Martin, Flatland Books (http://www.flatlandbooks.com)

Don't let anyone tell you that "Class of '97" is a hoax. It is, in fact, my finest work.

—Kurt Vonnegut (e-mail address witheld. It was not "vonnegut@aol.com")

STEAMSHOVEL PRESS

LUCIEN CONEIN AND THE PROUTY HYPOTHESIS

No word has been received that before spook Lucien Conein died in early June he confessed to involvement with the Kennedy assassination. Such a confession would have been met with great skepticism because Conein was a consummate braggart and liar, the atter a fine skill developed no doubt from occupational necessity. According to the *New York Times* obit of 6/7/98, Conein often told the story of how he lost two fingers "on a dangerous secret mission" when in fact he lost them "fixing the engine of a car carrying him and his best freind's wife to an assignation." The obit also details Conein's role in convincing South Vietnamese generals that the US wanted their leadership, the Diem brothers, assassinated. E. Howard Hunt once publicly confessed to forging cables to falsely suggest that this was Kennedy's plan. Conien's obituary notes also that Hunt tried to conscript Conein as a Watergate burglar.

↑ *Lansdale?*
↓ *Conein*

Hunt has long been suspected by some researchers as one of the tramps arrested in the railyard behind the grassy knoll. Col. L. Fletcher Prouty has suggested that Conein was there, too. The article appeared in *Steamshovel Press* #11, along with photographic support. This includes the Altgens photograph, primarily known because it shows Oswald or an Oswald look-alike named Billy Lovelady, leaving the Texas School Book Depository as someone shoots from the sixth floor. The Conein figure, in a hard hat, looks at the Oswald/Lovelady figure, which even recently has been described as "the only spectator who appears suspicious" (by John Johnson in the latest issue of *Fourth Decade. Steamshovel*

Misidentified Lucien Conein from Cecil B. Currey's book, *Edward Lansdale The Unquiet American* (Houghton Mifflin, 1988). Contrary to the caption, Conein actually appears on the right.

would submit that one other looks suspicious—the Conein character.) "Hard hat man" also appears in slides of the assassination taken by Phil Willis and Wilma Bond, showing him strolling down to the Umbrella Man and the radio controller.

Jack White wrote the article in *SP* #11 from correspondence with Prouty, noting a lack of corroborative evidence. Prouty commented that it is difficult to find a photo to make a comparison because few have been published, and one was deliberately obsfucated by mislabeling in Cecil B. Curry's book, *Edward Lansdale The Unquiet American.*

Steamshovel Press #11 is anthologized in the book, *Popular Alienation.*

steamshovel press

General George Meiring

FALSE REPORT EXPOSES THE DIRTY TRUTH ABOUT SOUTH AFRICAN INTELLIGENCE SERVICES AND BEGS MORE QUESTIONS

By Len Bracken

By all accounts no-one had heard of the FAPLA or "Front African People's Liberation Army" until news of it surfaced in early 1998. And even the first accounts of this non-existent organization were plagued by suspicion; its disclosure was in connection with a false report given to President Nelson Mandela by apartheid-era general, George Meiring.

The general, since resigned, was then head of the nation's defense forces. What he was thinking when he advanced the tainted military intelligence document to Mandela? Was he too short-sighted to foresee how averse Mandela would be to the report's coup-plotting accusations? Who wooed the general into giving Mandela the report? And who, precisely, wrote the report and what are its sources? Unnamed sources tell us that intelligence reports such as this never name sources, not even when given to the president.

Members of this illusory FAPLA, the Meiring Report flatly stated, would assassinate the president, murder judges, occupy parliament and broadcast stations and cause enough general unrest to make the country ungovernable in a way that would play into the hands of this left-wing group. A more plausible scenario holds that the report was designed as a diversion to draw attention away from the old-guard intelligence types, many of whom are sympathetic to the growing Afrikaner homeland movement and who perpetrate special operations themselves.

One-hundred and thirty names were listed as members of this mythical, coup-plotting FAPLA, including Mandela's ex-wife Winnie; the deputy chief of the defense forces, Lt. General Siphiwe Nyanda, and other "black soldiers;" the controversial diplomat Robert McBride who was apparently framed to make the report seem credible; Bantu Holomisa and other former and present African National Congress leaders. Even Michael Jackson was said to be in on the plot.

The shroud of controversy surrounding the report inevitably obligated Mandela to appoint an inquiry: judges who trashed the report as "utterly fantastic."

While explicitly denying any acknowledgment of acting wrongly or with sinister motives, on April 6, 1998, General Meiring announced that he asked President Mandela to suspend his contract at the end of May and allow him to retire on early pension without prejudice.

Back in February, when the false report was given to him, Mandela might not have given it so much thought if word of its existence hadn't leaked to the press. Parliament needed reassurances; Mandela was obligated to speak about it, and he generally gets high marks for allowing opposition leaders to read the report in his office. But a strange twist in fate for Robert McBride was keeping the story alive. While in Mozambique investigating gun-running, McBride, a notoriously dangerous man who was once sentenced for bombing a Durban beach bar and killing three women, was himself arrested on March 10. He was accused by local authorities of buying guns to smuggle to South Africa. Then, as McBride languished in a Maputo jail, reports began to surface about South African Police Superintendent Lappies Labushagne's involvement in framing McBride in concert with his Mozambiqan colleagues. Labuschagne ultimately resigned over the incident.

Nelson Mandela

Another name that emerges in connection with these dirty tricks is Hendrik Christoffel Nel, probably not the author, but quite possibly something like the editor, of the Meiring Report. South African papers paint a gruesome portrait of a man who was once a member of the Civil Co-operation Bureau (a secret hit squad that assassinated anti-apartheid activists) and who now heads the Army's counter-intelligence unit. He was reportedly involved in the shooting of an academic named David Webster and has been described as a "professional leaker." One doesn't have to be easily swayed by conspiracy-mined suspicions to question the innocence of someone who served in the infamous Directorate of Covert Collection, the veritable headquarters of apartheid-era dirty tricks that many suspect was the breeding ground for those involved in the more recent shooting of trains and in the not-so-subtle stoking of taxi violence.

President Mandela, Deputy President Thabo Mbeki and Deputy Intelligence Minister Joe Nhlanla speak of a "third force" comprised of old-guard security operatives who specialize in provocations - the type of operations that cause communities to fight without knowing why. To support their claims, they point to events such as the strange death of police assistant commissioner Leonard Radu, the most senior former African National Congress member to join the new South African Police Service. According to Justice Malala of the Financial Mail, Radu was "alleged to be on the trail of ANC leaders who spied for the National Party government." As unready to fade as these accusations of a third force are, the evidence so far is more episodic than conclusive.

Malala writes convincingly about the faction-ridden conflict resulting from the integration of South Africa's old twelve officially recognized intelligence networks into four new agencies. The National Intelligence Co-ordinating Committee, or NICOC, as its name states, coordinates the four separate agencies and advises the government on intelligence policy. According to Malala, the Meiring Report "should first have gone to NICOC, which would have forwarded it to the relevant Minister for a rigorous examination before it was sent to the Office of the President." Meanwhile, Business Day published unconfirmed reports that Meiring may have discussed the report with Defense Minister Joe Modise who may, they allege, have "deliberately allowed the general to shoot himself in the foot" by recommending that it go to Mandela. Similar logic alleges Mandela used the report as a pretext to appoint Siphiwe Nyanda to Meiring's post.

Third force or no third force, the most plausible scenario is that Meiring took his dirty document to Mandela with the expectation that the president would weaken his party by skewering members in the defense forces and intelligence services who had been named in the report. As fate would have it, it was

Meiring who fell on his sword: "My early retirement, therefore, is an effort to restore the trust in and to promote the *esprit de corps* in the South African National Defence Force." Questions linger... Are the authors of the report still at large? and if so, what is being done to stop them from perpetrating dirty tricks before their next attempt? Are more shake-outs in the South African intelligence community overdue? Tolerance of dissent is a hallmark of democracy but it is unacceptable when enshrouded in the conspiratorial form of special operations, such as this false report.

Len Bracken is the author of *Guy Debord - Revolutionary*, the translator of Gianfranco Sanguinetti's *The Real Report on the Last Chance to Save Capitalism in Italy* and the editor of *Extraphile*, which can only be obtained by sending a 9" x 12" SASE with $2 postage, an age statement and something sumptuous stolen from work to POB 5585 Arlington, VA 22205.

steamshovel press

CASTANEDA CAST OFF

Unusual that *Steamshovel* would choose writing by Richard DeMille as its send off to Carlos Castaneda, whose death in April was only recently reported in the news. DeMille used Castaneda to fight an imaginary assault on mainstream science that he thought Castaneda's work represented. It is an ungenerous and narrow minded view that *Steamshovel* certainly does not endorse. In fact, DeMille's conclusion that Castaneda and Timothy Leary competed in a marketplace of uncritical cult worshippers is presented here partly to demonstrate how wrong that view appears as these figures recede into history. Still, DeMille wrote with a sense of humor and a familiarity with Castaneda's *oeuvre* that betrays his fascination, as often happens among "skeptics". *Steamshovel* offers this for those reasons and because the essay brought to mind *Steamshovel*'s dear, departed friend, Dr. Tim, and his view that death, like life, is matter of opinion.

CREWES REVIEWED

Another member of the psuedo-skeptic press, Frederick Crewes, took shots at new books by David Jacobs, Whitley Strieber and Jodi Dean in the June 25 edition of *The New York Review of Books* ("The Mindsnatchers"). "Insofar as the UFO obsession constitutes just another form of supernatural belief, it can be regarded as a comforting hobby," he writes with apparently few clues about what it provides a comfort against. Crewes complains that Jodi Dean fails to see the scientific standards of the "majority culture" as "our common rational heritage but merely as technocratic idols to which the powerless are forced to pay homage."

*Steamshovel*lers recently attended a support group meeting for survivors of silicon breast implants who might agree with Bari. Not necessarily UFO believers, these victims have come to regard abuse by scientific industry as something less than our rational heritage. One woman, having just returned from a second radical masectomy, felt that her condition was at least exacerbated by the rather otherworldly job environment of sitting with her back to a bay of computer monitors. The *LA Times* had just printed a story dimissing such claims, insisting that genetics, diet and exercise were the sole determinants of such ill-health. Praise be to ufology if it represents dissent from such "rational" dismissal.

Greg Bishop, of *Excluded Middle* (a zine that has a new issue poised and eagerly awaited) adds some more observations about Crewes' analysis:

CREWES REVIEWES: SAME TIRED ARGUMENTS DON'T ADDRESS REAL ISSUES
Rant/ Reply by Greg Bishop

I am struck by the willingness of Crewes in his reviews of a small segment of the current UFO litera-ture to immediately adopt the arguments of people like Klass and Menzel, but to gloss over the more cogent arguments of the UFO "community" (at least the brighter members of it, who are routinely and conveniently ignored.) We never hear any opinion from Jacques Vallee, Jerome Clark, Keith Thompson, Jenny Randles, Jim Moseley, Michael Grosso, Dennis Stacy, Martin Kottmeyer, Dennis Stillings, etc. in the public discourse on the UFO subject because they're not reducible to sound-bite status, and might confuse a sim-plified subject with intelligent debate.

I too lament the sloppy thinking and sometimes loud-mouthed writings of Mack, Hopkins, Strieber, and Jacobs, but Crews throws the baby out with the bathwater. I don't think he even read the Streiber book (I haven't either, but I have talked to the doctor with whom Strieber worked) because he seems to ignore the main premise of *Confirmation*, which I assume is that anomalous objects removed from various people who have had "abduction" experiences (or believe that they have) are not always identifiable as simple fragments of glass, etc. He quotes Strieber's discussion of "bright objects" in his brain as some sort of new-age mumbo-jumbo, without bothering to mention that the term is shorthand for an anomalous object found in a CAT scan that shows up as a "bright" spot in the imaging device.

Crewes also seems to conveniently ignore the not unknown premise that the aliens (or whatever they are) may be manifested thoughtforms, human agents, products of possible neo-MKULTRA exercises, psychotechnoolgy, mind-control drugs and/ or suggestion, time-slippage perception, a revival of fairy and elf lore, or any number of other causes or combination of causes. If it's not stamped with the imprimatur of 20th century aristotelian science, or culturally and media-approved catogories, it seems that the reviewer doesn't consider it worth mention. He also writes about the "unaccountable congru-ence of detail from one account to another" and puts it down to the influence of Hollywood. What Crewes (and the abduction researchers he is talking about) fail to realize or accept is that accounts and desriptions from abductees vary all over the map. They like to throw out the data that doesn't fit with their agenda, and while this is fine in a controlled lab experiment this attitude does the phenomenon and the confused "experiencers" a disservice. Experience cannot be reduced to a few limited categories in this arena.

He wants to stick to the "if aliens are from another galaxy/ star system it would be nearly impossible for them to visit" idea. He sticks to this because it's the lynchpin of his argument. I would hasten to point out that countless physical processes and concepts were routinely used by humans before anyone knew how or why they worked. As examples; the process for making bronze, the theory of relativity, and the concept of non-locality were all eventually experimentally proven and entered into the scientific lexicon far before anyone knew how or if they "worked." In the case of non-locality the experimental evidence of atomic particles seemingly "communicating" with each other while never having been in physical contact still defies "common sense" and remains a topic of debate.

I too worry about the plight of so-called "abdcutees" at the hands of unscrupulous reseachers and hypnotists with their own agendas, but what I cry out for is someone with a comprehensive view of the entire phenomenon who actively works to pursue the root causes of the syndrome with an eye towards healing and understanding the cause or set of causes without the goal of simply adding another case to an already bulging file full of defiling aliens. This defines an agenda as well, but perhaps it could prove, disprove, or amend the current argument in which we must be in favor of or against the "alien" theory. On a public level, it's really turned into a stupid gamesaying-type discussion, and this is everyone's loss.

Like Posner (whom I haven't read much either) this guy seems like a kiss-ass and he doesn't even know it. We don't need this kind of redemption. It adds nothing to the public discourse and doesn't advance any understanding of the phenomenon, even though he insists that there is nothing there while offfering little in explanation of what he thinks is an actual cause other than vague references to sleep paralysis and hypnotic suggestion. It's the "nothing but" school of psychology, which to my mind is almost as dangerous as what Crewes is railing against. I don't see a phD after his name, so why is he practicing? There's a reason why medicine and psychology are called "soft" sciences and deal with their data by means of vast samples and meta-analysis to arrive at a best guess. This is also why medical insurance is so high (apart from the fact that people are greedy) namely, the spectrum of the natural world and of human experience are difficult to nail down into discrete categories amenable to simple answers.

Sure, everyone knows that personality and political and economic agendas are the secret templates of everyone's viewpoint, and there can never be any real objectivity, even in the cold logic of science, but the inquisition mentailty of academics like Crewes is more frightening than the popularity of the books he so vehemently denounces as the death knells of our rational culture. He doesn't care to mention that even his hero Carl Sagan thought that such subjects as reincarnation and ESP deserved serious research and said as much in his last book.

Crewes is quite right to point out that researcher/ authors are guilty of sloppy reasoning, but he hatchet-pieces them without considering an alternative viewpoint of many of their claims. Perhaps he just doesn't have time, but if that's the case, he shouldn't be writing reviews of things he doesn't care to research to any reasonable depth. He also seems inordinately interested in the subject matter to an obsessive degree, so might there be something else going on here. The subject really doesn't concern the vast majority of people to the point where it's important on a daily basis, so Crewes must have some personal hard-on for the evil mind-controller hypnotists, and little concern for other political and economic agendas and practices that have and are doing actual physical and mental harm to a great number of people around the globe. He's got the "save the heathens" mentality, and it's sort of sad to see this attitude still going strong.

A *Steamshovel* reader sent the following in response to Greg Bishop's comments:

First, about Frederick Crews: I'm in basic agreement with the guy from *The Excluded Middle*. However, a couple of points about Crews may be worth noting. He's a respected critic/professor (just retired) specializing in American Lit. Moreover, in the fifties/sixties, he was in the vanguard of a Freudian movement in criticism which applied psychoanalytic theory to textual interpretation. Then, he experienced a crisis of belief in which he rejected Freudianism as dangerous bunk. For several years now, he's been an aggressive critic of psychoanalytic thought and its popular offshoots. In particular, he's written critically and thoughtfully about the alleged phenomenon of "recovered memory" in child abuse cases, emphasizing the dubious and probably abusive role played in such cases by "therapists" using hypnotic regression techniques. More often than not, he argues, such practice amounts to a form of brainwashing in which fake memories are created according to a preset agenda, much of which is imposed or encouraged by the "therapist." The whole thing is then justified, in pseudoscientific terms, by recourse to pop Freudian notions about trauma, repression and recoverable memory, etc.

Of course the UFO abduction field is full of the same sort of therapeutic practice. It was therefore expectable that, sooner or later, Crews would write about that field as well. And, though Crews is something of a mechanistic reductionist (he once described himself as a "stone-kicking empiricist"), the field could, I think, use some strong corrective medicine. I'm most definately not a mechanistic reductionist (or an apologist for the scientific establishment), but I too think that Ufology today is in an incredibly sorry state.

steamshovel press

ILLUMINATI FOOTNOTE

By X Sharks DeSpot

The establishment scholars say that the Illuminati was founded in Bavaria, Germany, by Adam Weishaupt in 1776. Establishment histories ignore what is often said in the conspiratorial histories: that the group had predecessors. Nesta Webster, for example, claimed that Weishaupt had received instruction in Ancient Egyptian occultism from a mysterious man named Kohlmer in 1771. The implication is that an unbroken line of conspiratorial adepts going back to ancient Egypt created the Illuminati. But, of course, this avoids the obvious: where did Kohlmer get his information? Could it be he had simply read about it in books? Or again, the Abbe Augustin de Barruel claimed that the Illuminati was part of a conspiracy dating back to the Knights Templar of 1314. But did Barruel have any evidence that an unbroken line of members

extend from 1776 until 1314, four hundred and sixty two years into the past? Or did Barruel simply read about the Kniqhts Templar in a book and assume this without evidence?

The establishment scholars repeat, over and over again, that the Order of the Illuminati was disbanded in 1776. But the two major conspiracy books of the time, John Robisons' *Proofs of a Conspiracy* and Abbe Barruel *Memoirs of Jacobinism*, were actually concerned with the French Revolution of 1789-1794. The Elector of Bavaria, which ordered the closing of the German Illuminati lodges in 1785/1786, did not leave any authority in France, so obviously, if there were Illuminati lodges in France they were not in a position of getting rid of them.

Elector of Bavaria Jean Joseph Mounier, who wrote *On the Influence Attributed...* in 1801 to refute Barruel and Robison, argued that there was no correspondence between French lodges and the Bavarian headquarters in existence, and suggested that this meant there were no Illuminati lodges in France. Fair enough, but a September 1996 issue of the John Birch Society magazine *The New American* claimed that many important members of the French Revolution were recruited into the Illuminati through a convention of Freemasons attended by Honore Gabriel Riquetti Mirabeau, a leader in the States-General between 1789 -1791. If Mirabeau was recruited into the Illuminati, it would have had great influence through Mirabeau, and not needed a lodge in France. Of course, this comes from the John Birch Society. The *New American*'s attitude towards other conspiracy theories is so stupid and dishonest that I wonder if Mirabeau had even *met* a member of the Illuminati, much less *joined it*.

The *New American*'s an article about the French Revolution completely ignores the French Monarchy, which was the major source of attention throughout the time. The JBS also ignored that a restored French Monarchy under Louis XVIII was set up by the victors after the defeat of Napoleon in 1815. Considering that the execution of Louis XVI led to 22 years of war between France and England, you'd think it would have been important enough for the JBS to mention.

Which leads to another point: when John Robisons' *Proofs of a Conspiracy* was published in 1797, Great Britain was living in dread terror of a French invasion, and was recruiting a huge military to fight abroad, and at home if there had actually been an invasion. In such an atmosphere, is it surprising that a book explaining the French Revolution as the result of an evil conspiracy of hostile secret societies would sell so well? (I read in guide to used books that original editions of Robison's *Proofs of A Conspiracy* sell for $150. They must be pretty common to sell that cheaply.)

But establishment accounts of the Illuminati conspiracy theory ignore this fact. It doesn't seem to occur to establishment scholars that Robison and Barruel had an army of sales representatives in the form of the French Army pushing up book sales. They behave as though the idea of an Illuminati conspiracy to conquer the world were the results of political extremists in the United States during the 1790s. It was a reaction to the French wars for control of Europe that created an audience for Robison's and Barruel conspiracy theories.

In the Reverend Marion 'Pat'Robertson's 1991 book *New World Order*, he suggests that members of the Rothschild banking family may have been recruited into the Illuminati because they lived in Frankfurt, Germany, and the

Illuminati had a lodge there. By suggesting the Rothschild banking family joined the Illuminati, Roberston completely avoids the question of how, and even if, the Illuminati survived the order to disband. Hand the ball to the Rothschilds and every single thing the family ever did suddenly becomes an attempt to turn the world over to the Illuminati. It would make just as much sense to suggest that since Patricia Hearst joined the Symbionese Liberation Army in 1974, all Hearst newspapers are secretly manipulating the society towards a radical leftist revolution. Perhaps Robertson believes this, but his logic here leaps even farther, to the point of suggesting that all the movies director John Waters makes for the rest of his life will be covert Symbionese Liberation Army propaganda because Hearst played a part in his movie *Serial Mom*.

And, of course, Robertson does not claim to know this, just suspect it. That's because he never bothered to go to Germany and spend a few days in some archives to see if there any evidence exists that the Rothschilds and Illuminati actually met.

STEAMSHOVEL PRESS

ALLEN GINSBERG AND THE STUDENT SPIES OF CZECHOSLOVAKIA

Right and Next Page: Interestingly, this newsclip appeared in the same edition of the *New York Times* that carried on its front page photos of mind control scientiest Jose DelGado, stopping a bull with an electronic implant.

The late, great conspiracy bard Allen Ginsberg became king of the Czechoslovakian May Day festival in May 1965 and was promptly expelled from that Communist country. The circumstances of his ascension to that throne, however, only recently emerged in the current

THE NEW YORK TIMES, MONDAY, MAY 17,

Czechs Oust Ginsberg, 'Village' Poet

PRAGUE, May 16 (AP)—Allen Ginsberg, avant-garde poet of New York's Greenwich Village, has been expelled from Czechoslovakia, the youth newspaper Mlada Fronta said today.

Mr. Ginsberg was here as the elected king of Czech youths' May Day festival. He was briefly detained and his diary seized before his expulsion, Mlada Fronta said, according to CTK, the official press agency. He was ordered out of the country May 7 and left that day for London. ▼

In 1961, the State Department discouraged a visit here by the Lithuanian-Russian poet Eduardas B. Mezhelaytis, who had been in New York in 1960 and seems to have met Mr. Ginsberg then. One of Mr. Mezhelaytis's poems, with a title translated as "Howl Above Brooklyn Bridge," refers to Mr. Ginsberg's work.

Allen Ginsberg

"Allen Ginsberg" issue of *The Massachusetts Review* (South College, University of Massachusetts, Box 37140, Amherst, Massachusetts, 01003-7140.) It reprints the redacted Czechoslovakian secret police file from that time, with writer Andrew Lass' observation that "the report is accurate in most details pertaining to Allen...I know, because I was either present at some of the situations described in the report or because Allen told me about them later. But how did they know? Who among us was the mole?" The issue also includes the following 1986 exchange between Lass and Ginsberg concerning his election as May Day king:

AL: Do you remember how you actually got elected, what the procedure was?

AG: No, that I don't remember.

AL: The procedure was to measure the loudness of the applause and so there was this microphone hooked up to this enormous meter, and while you were singing I went behind this enormous thermometer-bulb meter and there were these

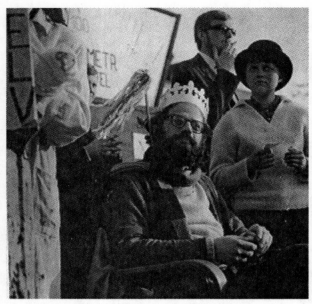

two guys looking at a little version of the meter connected to the microphone you were singing into and that was also pointing into the crowds-and these two guys would move the arrow of the meter as you were singing...

AG: According to accurate scientific method...It was a fake! Was it a fake?

AL: I have to tell you twenty-one years later that as you came out they said Ginsberg, Ginsberg sssswwwreee, and the thing went up and you became the King of May.

AG: I am totally disillusioned after this. I thought I won it fair and square.

AL: No, what this tells you is the extent to which this was a political demonstration and how important it was for the people who were arranging the parade and masterminding it to actually use you as a symbol and a vehicle and actually...

AG: Was the parade that well masterminded, managed and manipulated, do you think?

AL: I think it was.

AG: I thought it was more spontaneous than that.

AL: It was very spontaneous, but someone had to come up with the idea and get the permission and orchestrate the actual production.

AG: Who? Who were those people?

AL: I don't really know.

AG: CIA?

AL: No, no, they were students, they were students who actually then really became leaders in the student movement in '68. And some of them actually ended up in prison afterwards.

AG: So I was up on the stage with the official title of King of May on my throne and the next election was for the Queen of May. Suddenly about six big guys like the ushers came over and told me "You are no longer King of May," lifted me, lifted the entire chair and took it off the stage to the side. I said "what's going on here?" Someone said that these were sort of like the fake students that were working with the administration or the ministry of culture, who were there as ushers for the government. I assumed that since a hundred thousand people saw me as the King of May there wasn't any problem about being the King of May no matter what the government wanted to do. In fact that put a little salt and pepper into the scene. But I also realized I was now in a dangerous position and had to be very careful, very correct in my conduct at this point, lest there be real scandal, 'cause as long as I was impeccable in my behavior I was invulnerable. I'd already had the experience of being grabbed and isolated in Havana, so I was really quite apprehensive and knew what was possible. I wasn't afraid in a physical way, but I just didn't want to get into more trouble, actually. I had another week there and my plane was coming, so I figured I'll just cool it. So we took a nice long walk ... through the park.

SECOND INTERN THEORY

Right: **Matt Drudge surfaced a videotape showing a prelude to Clinton tryst with an intern other than Monica Lewinsky, from August 1993.**

The White House claims that the woman pictured in the "second intern" video recently exposed to the world by Matt Drudge is a family friend from Arkansas. Its purported date, however, August 1993, does not exclude it from consideration as showing Mary Caitrin Mahoney. Neither do the images on the videotape seen at *Steamshovel*, since they actually provide very little visual information at all.

Mahoney formerly worked as a White House intern. Her July 1997 murder at a DC Starbucks followed Drudge's early leaks of Michael Isikoff's *Newsweek* story on Lewinsky. At the time, Lewinsky was not identified by name, only as an intern who was about to go public with her story of sex with the president. Some speculated that hitmen got the wrong intern and instead killed Mahoney. Mahoney's murder is still officially unsolved. Details about the case can be found in a previous *Latest Word* column.

Limiting speculation about Bill Clinton's sexual appetite to one or even two isolated dalliances with interns is probably not the most intelligent way to look at it. Steamshovel does not offer the opinion that Mary Caitrin Mahoney is the second intern. However, it does take the opportunity to remind readers of this murder mystery and to present some interesting biographical details about Mahoney below.

Mary Caitrin Mahoney's Obituary

from *The Washington Blade* Inc. Mary Caitrin "Caity" Mahoney, 24, a founder of the Baltimore Lesbian Avengers, died Sunday, July 6, 1997, at the Starbucks coffee shop on 1810 Wisconsin Avenue, NW, in Georgetown.

Mahoney, who was the night manager at Starbucks, and two other Starbucks employees died of gunshot wounds sometime after the shop closed at 8 p.m., according to D.C. police detective Tony Patterson. Patterson said police still have no suspect in the case. The bodies of Mahoney and her co-workers were discovered early Monday morning, July 7, by an employee who was to open the store.

Mahoney was one of a core group of six women who founded the Baltimore Lesbian Avengers, a political activist group, in February 1995, according to her best friend, Mary Hall of Baltimore, Md.

"She was very passionate about everything she did, and she did everything the best she could," Hall said.

The Lesbian Avengers have a tradition of eating fire as a stunt at their actions. Hall said that once the Avengers were having a picnic at the house where she lived with Mahoney when they decided to do fire-eating for fun. Hall said Mahoney wanted to impress her girlfriend.

"She decided to show off and do two torches at once and she ended up burning her lips," Hall said.

"But she was a Leo," Hall said. "She was in her element when she ate fire."

Mahoney,s activism spanned many arenas, including founding a women,s issues discussion group at Towson State University in 1993; sitting as a board member of the 31st Street Bookstore in Baltimore, a Lesbian/feminist cooperative; and working on Bill Clinton,s presidential campaign as well as interning for the Clinton White House when he was newly elected.

In 1994, Mahoney and others raised more than $1,000 for Baltimore,s Pride festival while participating in a musical spoof of The Sound of Music known as The Camp of Music. In the musical, Mahoney played Gretel — the youngest of the "VonCamp" children.

"Her passion was contagious, she was just amazing," Hall said.

Mahoney was born July 22, 1972, in Baltimore. From the sixth grade on, she attended the McDonogh School near Pikesville, Md., where she graduated in 1991. She did a year of studies at Ithaca College in New York state, a semester at Fordham University in New York City, and then two years at Towson State University in Maryland, where she received a bachelor,s degree in women,s studies in the spring of 1995.

While studying at Towson, Mahoney worked as a shift supervisor at Cafe Diana, a Baltimore Lesbian/feminist coffee house from September 1993 to June 1995. During the summer of 1995, she worked as a cook at the City Cafe, a Gay-owned coffee house in Baltimore.

In September 1995, Mahoney moved to Washington, D.C., and took a job with Starbucks.

Mahoney,s hobbies and interests included her cat, Marlu; Lesbian and women,s rights; politics; and jogging.

"She was a wonderful person and lots of people miss her," Hall said. "She was such a sweet, kind, and generous person."

In addition to Hall, Mahoney is survived by her mother and stepfather, Mary Belle Annenberg and Barnet Annenberg, both of Baltimore; father and stepmother, Patrick Mahoney Sr. and Ginny Mahoney, both of Towson; sister, Molly Mahoney of Baltimore; brother and sister-in-law, Patrick and Lelah Mahoney of Baltimore; three stepsisters, Stacy Wenzl, Missy Gray, and Toni Hamilton, all of Baltimore; grandmother, Elizabeth H. Mahoney of Annapolis, Md.; and grandmother, Maria W. Simms of Ardmore, Pa.

She is also survived by several friends, including Beth Kuhns, Sally Franklin, Amanda Joyce, and Dawn Heddrick, all of Baltimore; as well as a number of friends she worked with at Starbucks.

Her remains were cremated. Memorial services were at the McDonogh School on July 18 and at Georgetown University on July 15.

"A Celebration of Caity,s Life" will be Saturday, July 19, at 1 p.m. at the Metropolitan Community Church of Baltimore, 3401 Old York Rd., Baltimore, Md.

The Baltimore Lesbian Avengers will hold a Caity Mahoney Memorial/Anti-Violence Vigil in front of the Starbucks coffee shop Tuesday, July 22 — Mahoney,s 25th birthday — at 7:30 p.m. Everyone is welcome to attend.

Memorial contributions may be sent to the Caity Mahoney Memorial Fund at the McDonogh School, Box 380, 8600 McDonogh Rd., Owings Mills, MD 21117.

steamshovel press

ROY LISKER TURNS SIXTY

Left: Roy Lisker, center, in 1965 with two others who protested the Vietnam War by burning their draft cards at Union Square in New York. A photograph of the burning appeared on the front page of the *New York Times* on November 7, 1965.

Steamshovel Press would call him a genius, but Roy Lisker notes in the current issue of his newsletter, *Ferment!*, the term "renders explicit the eugenic fascism which is clearly at the core of [such] observations." Nevertheless, the sometimes *Steamshovel* contributor celebrates 60 years on September 24,

and this momentous occasion cannot go overlooked at *Steamshovel*. Since he was first encountered by *Steamshovel* personnel in Boulder, Colorado in 1982 being carted off by bus depot security for chanting his poetry in the terminal, Lisker has been a constant inspiration.

Spontaneous spiral form, written on a paper plate at a St. Louis diner, July 9, 1983.

"One might posit the existence of a conspiracy in the collective unconscious, whereby society arrogates to itself the right not only to pass judgement on all matters of the heart, but to credentialize it as well, deeming illegitimate and even nonexistent all manifestations which do not conform to a deliberately reductive framework imposed by social institutions and mediated through language." —Roy Lisker, *Love and Cosmology*, April 1979

Not only a musician and math teacher, Lisker is also the consummate zinester, having for over three decades published a regular newsletter—originally entitled *New Universe Weekly*—as part of his performance arsenal. The zinelet, now called *Ferment!*, is available only by subscription or from him at one of his performances, chants or lectures, which can often be attended on street corners. An electronic version of <u>*Ferment!*</u> appears on the *Steamshovel* web site, where subscription information may also be found.

Roy Lisker, 1995

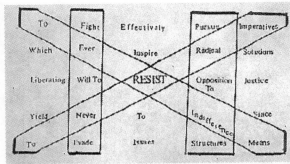

Lisker's matrix poetry.

ALIEN MATHEMATICS?

From the latest issue of *Ferment!* : "On the afternoon of January 20th, 1959, John Forbes Nash Jr., brandishing that day's copy of the *New York Times*, walked into the mathematics lounge at MIT. In a strong voice he announced that he'd discovered that the little box in the upper left-hand corner (the off-lede) carried a message from outer space aliens to the governments of Earth, which he alone was able to decipher."

Steamshovel notes that Nash, indeed, was alone among earth mathematicians to notice the subtle alien code. Witness, for instance, how the off-lede subtly changed on the day the *NY Times* began to report upon Lisker's draft resistance event of 1965. Chalk up the irregularities of box lines to printing problems, but what of the motto "All the News That's Fit To Print," slightly askew only in this edition, which included a report about how Lisker and friends added up Vietnam...

...and what to make of this? Another edition with a news story about Roy Lisker and draft resistance.

Another example:

Happy Birthday, ROY!

STEAMSHOVEL PRESS

THE BIBLE CODE OF SHAKESPEARE

The coincidence was first made public in 1900 in *The Publishers' Circular* (LXXVI, p. 30). It was observed that, in Psalm 46, the 46th word from the beginning is 'shake' and the 46th word from the end is 'spear'. In the latter calculation the word 'Selah' is omitted because it is not part of the text but a Hebrew musical notation, placed at the end of many verses in the Psalms.

Moreover, the Authorized or King James version of the Bible took six years to complete, ending in 1610 when Shakspere was forty-six years old.

In previous translations of the Bible the words 'shake' and 'spear' were differently placed in relation to the beginning and ending of the Psalm, and 'shake' had earlier been written 'shoke'.

The Authorized Version, published in 1611, was drawn up as a revision of the previous Bishops' Bible by a committee of the most learned clerical scholars in the kingdom, chosen without regard for their religious inclinations. Their work was submitted for approval to the bishops and leading theologians then to the Privy Council and finally to the King himself. Francis Bacon was not at that time a member of the Privy Council, but, as Solicitor General and adviser to King James on matters of law and state, he most probably had some part in this revision of the Bible. Baconians speculate that he was the behind-the-scenes editor-in-chief but there is no record of that.

If 'Shake-spear' was deliberately encoded in the 46th Psalm and Francis Bacon was behind it, his most likely collaborator was Lancelot Andrewes, Bishop of Winchester. He was a great friend of Bacon, who consulted him frequently about his philosophical works, and he was famous for the puns, word-play and 'verbal conceits' with which he enlivened his sermons. Andrewes was perfectly placed to doctor the Psalms if he had wanted to, for his name was placed at the head of the list of divines who drew up the Authorized Version. If there was an editor-in-chief, it was he rather than Bacon. By another coincidence, the committee consisted of 46 members.

Nothing is proved by this chain of coincidences, certainly not that the works of Shakespeare were written by Francis Bacon or any other man of mystery. It is simply a curiosity, one of the many promising clues that seem to be leading towards the centre of the Shakespeare Authorship mystery but never actually reach it.

—John Michell, *Who Wrote Shakespeare?*

STEAMSHOVEL PRESS

WILHELM REICH: THE GAYN/STRAIGHT CONNECTION

(an excerpt from *Flatland Magazine* editor Jim Martin's forthcoming book, *Wilhelm Reich and the Cold War.)*

Publication date: January 1, Y2K, This version copyright 1998 by Jim Martin

[*The story so far:* Dr. Wilhelm Reich (1897-1957) was convinced that his trial and imprisonment had been orchestrated in Moscow. Today, conventionally received "wisdom" has been shaped by those biographers of Reich who argued that the Food and Drug Agency's prosecution of Reich had its source in the antisexual, xenophobic hysteria of the "McCarthy Era." In my book, tentatively titled, *Am I a Spaceman?* we review the historical record of the late forties and early fifties, and try to locate Wilhelm Reich's actual position in the Cold War Era. We've examined the personal biographies of those people who played a hand in initiating the public damnation of

Michael Straight, in the 1930s, as a student at Cambridge, was recruited by Anthony Blunt as a mole for the Soviets. Straight gave his Soviet controller press credentials for Mark Gayn, in 1942.

Reich, such as Mildred Edie Brady, who wrote a scurrilous attack on Reich in the leading liberal "journal of opinion" (the *New Republic*) and Michael Straight, the wealthy scion of a Morgan Bank partner, who published Brady's article. Long-time *Steamshovel*lers will recall my article in issue #8 that recounted what Georgetown Professor Carroll Quigley (Bill Clinton's mentor) had to say about Straight's role in the Communist-dominated election campaign of Henry Wallace in 1947-1948, precisely at the time when Mildred Brady's article appeared in the *New Republic*. Toward the end of the research for that article, I came across the fact that Straight himself admitted, in an autobiography called *After Long Silence,* that he was in fact recruited by Soviet intelligence, back in the thirties, when he was a student at Cambridge University.

Since then, I've been able to contact Michael Straight, and interview him on several occasions. He graciously gave me personal permission to review his papers, which are under seal at Cornell University. He denies that he ever did any actual spying for the Soviets, but what he's admitted to more than confirms Wilhelm Reich's worst suspicions.

This excerpt is from a chapter that discusses the Cambridge Five Spy Ring, with which Straight was closely associated, since he had been recruited by Anthony Blunt. The American intelligence corps still does not trust the British side, not after Kim Philby - when the NSA released the highly sensitive VENONA decrypts, the Americans stood shoulder-to-shoulder with their Russian counterparts at the press conference and symposia, while the British were conspicuously absent.

I should stress here that I am not grinding a political axe, one way or another, when I point out that with the release of the archives of the former Soviet Union, and with the publication of tell-all books by some of Lyubyanka's grungiest spy-masters, some of the most far-fetched anti-communist conspiracy theories of the McCarthy "hysteria" have turned out to be true. I had no idea, when I started the research on Wilhelm Reich, that I would be led into the wilderness of Cold War espionage and the theft of atomic secrets. After studying all the recent revelations, there are few secrets left from the Cold War, and it must be said that most of them are being kept by the CIA and the NSA from American citizens. I believe one of the remaining secrets, that J. Robert Oppenheimer himself was the Soviet's main source of information about the atomic bomb, will be confirmed within a year or so. Oppenheimer was recruited while at the University of California at Berkeley, where he socialized with Mildred Edie Brady.

Okay, back to the excerpt: after a discussion of Michael Straight's confessional autobiography, *After Long Silence*, I introduce a tangent in the research that still boggles my mind. It's got to do with a tangled web between Michael Straight, his Soviet "controller" and journalist Mark Gayn. Anyone who has read Dick Russell's marvelous *The Man Who Knew Too Much* may remember Mark Gayn. I hope *Steamshovel Press* editor Kenn Thomas won't be the only reader who will appreciate the research that links the conspiracy against Wilhelm Reich to the Kennedy assassination! Comments regarding this excerpt are welcome - send them to me at flatland@mcn.org.

It wasn't until November 15, 1979 that Michael Straight's story reached the world, when Prime Minister Margaret Thatcher announced that Anthony Blunt was the "fourth man" of the Cambridge Soviet spy ring - after MacLean, Burgess and Philby. Even then, Straight's identity as the source who exposed both Blunt and a fifth man, Leopold Henry Long, as operatives for Soviet intelligence was not revealed to the public until 1981, when the Sunday Times ran a story which was confirmed in Parliament. Straight objected to press reports of his own spying on behalf of Russia, but decided not to pursue the matter beyond a letter to the *Times*, because of bad conscience.

And there ends Michael Straight's autobiographical account of his flirtations with the KGB, the CIA, and the FBI. He obliquely refers to the entire genre of literature, spy novels, counterintelligence surveys, and press accounts engendered by the revelations of the case. He succeeds in ignoring completely the implications and fall-out of the Cambridge Five's exposure of the deep penetration of the Britain's intelligence apparatus, the consequent compromise of the CIA at the highest levels, and he says nothing about the ring's role in the theft of atomic secrets.

Straight was never accused by the FBI of actively spying, and he makes every effort to make the point that the information he gave to "Michael Green," though classified, was of no strategic importance. It would appear that the most significant aid given by Straight to the Soviets was to remain silent about the covert work of Guy Burgess and Anthony Blunt, both of whom he knew to be spies. However, Straight's FBI files include reference to a meeting between Straight, "Green," and Green's wife (the niece of CPUSA leader Earl Browder) at a restaurant in New York. At Green's request, Straight provided a press credential for Mark Julius Gayn sometime in 1942. Providing press credentials to a Soviet agent is a more serious event than Straight admits to. Three years later, in June of 1945, Gayn was arrested along

with six others, including two State Department officials, Lauchlin Currie and John Stewart Service, and a young Office of Naval Intelligence officer named Andrew Roth, for possession of hundreds of highly classified documents in what would become known as "The Amerasia Case," the first inkling the American public received as to the breadth of Soviet post-war espionage reaching into top levels of the government.

The overlapping territories of journalism and intelligence work can be demonstrated by a brief examination of the career of Mark Julius Gayn. Like Kim Philby, Guy Burgess, and so many others, Gayn used journalistic cover for his activities.

The Legend of Mark Gayn

Much of the information regarding Mark Julius Gayn's early life in China can be found in a disturbing book written by his brother who remained behind after the

Journalist Mark Gayn was arrested in 1945 when the Office of Naval Intelligence discovered hundreds of secret government documents strewn around the offices of *Amerasia Magazine*. He was never prosecuted.

revolution of 1948. Sam was a translator and language teacher and suffered greatly during the Cultural Revolution. Born Mark Ginsbourg in Siberia, Mark Gayn and his brother, Sam were raised in Harbin, China amongst a small but prosperous community of Russian exiles, many of whom were Jewish refugees from Czarist pograms.

Sam's book never mentions his eldest brother by name, which is strange, since they were close. None of the names of family members are mentioned. Mark Gayn worked in the Red Army's library in Vladivistok, and majored in "pedagogy" at the Soviet "Institute for Teachers, Librarians and Propagandists" in 1926. (Later, Mark Gayn would tell FBI agents that this school was "similar to an American junior college.") A few years later, he went to Pomona College in Southern California. It's not at all clear how his family came up with the money to send Mark to California, but Sam says they did. Mark told the FBI that he worked his way through college. Dick Russell says Mark was back in Shanghai in 1939, and Sam confirms this. That same year, his mother and father relocated to "heavenly" Los Angeles, and Sam never saw them again. By then Mark Gayn had graduated from Columbia University and returned to China. "In the mid-thirties he returned to China and did editorial work on some English-language newspapers published in Shanghai. He was violently anti-Japanese and did not try to conceal it. He finally made the Japanese military black-list, on which he occupied a prominent place. He managed to escape, leaving Shanghai in the summer of 1939. Soon after arriving in the United States, he changed his name to make sure the Japanese did not take it out on me." [Wasn't this a bit late? Shouldn't Sam have changed his name? Didn't Mark change his name to hide his Soviet training in "propaganda"?]

"After victory, he was assigned to Japan as a war correspondent for one of the big American dailies. We exchanged letters. At the end of December 1946 he arrived in Shanghai. He stayed there for some weeks and then left for the Liberated Areas for some interviews with our Party leaders. (Recently he showed me a photograph of him and Liu Shaoqi taken in those days.) Not waiting for him to return to Shanghai, I went to the Shandong Liberated

Area and left him a brief note informing him of what I had done. "My departure made him unhappy. He wished I had talked things over with him before making such an important decision, of which he did not approve. "We lost all touch with each other until the late seventies." Sam's daughter went to live with Mark Gayn while she attended a university in Canada, before returning to China.

The rest of the book describes Sam losing his post as a foreign languages teacher during the succession of upheavals in China starting with the Cultural Revolution, during which he was accused of being a "Russian spy". The brutality and humiliation during this period is clear enough, but Sam is still writing confessions with a Red Guard looking over his shoulder, so he sounds a bit like Winston Smith at the end of Orwell's *1984*. He loves his country and his Party, despite its "excesses". Things are looking up. Probably, he should have talked it over with Mark first. Did Mark had an inkling of what was to come?

After graduating from Pomona, Gayn began a long career in journalism. Gayn wrote for national magazines such as Collier's and in 1934 he became the Washington Post's special correspondent in China until his return to the U.S. in 1939. Michael Straight met with his Soviet handler ("Michael Green") at Longchamps restaurant in New York sometime after November 24, 1942. In later statements to the FBI, Straight recalled that at this meeting or the one previous, Straight supplied to "Green," at his request, journalistic accreditation (i.e., journalistic "cover") for a Swedish woman journalist and Mark Julius Gayn. Why would Gayn, already a widely-published reporter, need additional accreditation from Straight? Why would "Green," rather than Gayn himself, ask Straight for these credentials? What we do know is that Mark Julius Gayn, subsequent to being accredited as a journalist for *The New Republic,* began to amass an impressive collection of classified documents from the U.S. Departments of State, War, and the Office of Strategic Services (OSS). Many of the documents dealt with "psychological warfare" and propaganda, and nearly all of them dealt with the Chinese theatre in the war against Japan. When a classified report from the OSS turned up - almost verbatim - in the pages of Amerasia, U.S. counter-intelligence agents broke into *Amerasia*'s offices and began an intensive, 24-hour surveillance of everyone connected with it, including Mark Gayn. *Amerasia* was a small-circulation, pro-Maoist journal published by Philip Jaffee and partially funded by the Institute of Pacific Relations, which in turn was financially supported by Nelson Rockefeller, Michael Straight, and a host of "philanthropic" foundations that later became the subject of a congressional investigation called "The Reece Commission."

The FBI set up a massive, round-the-clock surveillance of the spy ring, capturing on tape, via wire-taps, conversations between Mark Gayn, Phil Jaffe, and the others. Jaffe referred to the secret documents he obtained as "cigarettes" - using an inept code; "I have some fine Japanese cigarettes," etc...

The FBI files leave no doubt that Gayn was working for the Soviets.

Jaffe: It is just as you thought. She is talking all over Washington, especially in official circles, and plastering you with the good old 'red brush.'

Gayn: Me personally?

Jaffe: Yeah, you personally. Very continuous. Continuous activity on her part and you should not turn your back on her, because if you do, she will stab you.

Gayn: My turning my back or not turning my back, I have nothing to do.

Jaffe: No, nothing you can do, but run the hell out of this country and over to the Soviet Union. You will be safer there. [Uncle] Joe will protect you.

In their book *The Amerasia Spy Case, Prelude to McCarthyism*, historians

Harvey Klehr and Ronald Radosh mark the case as one of the most important in the Cold War. Coming as it did, during the last years of WWII, it set the tone for future relations between the two post-war superpowers. The investigation uncovered a network of journalists, State Department officials, and servicemen who were caught red-handed spying for Russia. The evidence against those arrested was overwhelming. However, the charges were dropped. Gayn, who was in as deep as the rest of them, was not even indicted. Klehr and Radosh suggest that a political fix crafted by none other than Michael Straight's old boss in the Roosevelt administration, Tommy "the Cork" Corcoran, worked the deal. There is also the possibility that Gayn, in particular, was let off in return for "turning" sides and becoming a double-agent. No other journalist, on either side of the Iron Curtain, could match Mark Julius Gayn's access to the highest echelons of power in Moscow, Peking and Washington, throughout the fifties.

Autumn, 1959: Mark Gayn's notebook records an exchange between Dulles and Khrushchev: "Dulles said to Khrushchev: 'You Mr. Chairman may have seen some of my intelligence reports from time to time.' Khrushchev said 'I believe we get the same reports. And probably from the same people.' Dulles said: 'Maybe we should pool our efforts.' Khrushchev: 'Yes, we should buy our intelligence data together and save money, we'd only have to pay the people once.'"

So this is a another bizarre twist, one of many in this investigation: Michael Straight gave credentials to a journalist-spy, who was subsequently cleared in what had appeared to be an open-and-shut case. While Straight was never implicated directly in the Amerasia case, it is hard to conceive some constructive purpose Straight had in mind when he provided his Soviet handler with Gayn's press credential, three years prior to Gayn's arrest. Today, Straight no longer remembers giving "Green" the credentials.

There is one final turning point in the Cold War saga of Mark Julius Gayn.

After the U.S. Attorney General declined to file charges in the Amerasia case, Gayn resumed his work in journalism. There would be no further public scandals involving Gayn, until long after he died in 1981. In 1992, journalist Dick Russell published one of the most well-documented and intriguing books ever written about the Kennedy assassination, *The Man Who Knew Too Much.* Russell unfolded the story of a Korean war-hero, former military intelligence officer in Japan, Richard Case Nagell. About a month before the assassination, Nagell said, he sent a registered letter to J. Edgar Hoover at the FBI, warning him that Lee Harvey Oswald, along with two Cuban refugees, were planning to assassinate the President. The FBI denied having received this letter when it was requested by Congressman Don Edwards (D-California) in 1974.

Nagell further stated that not only could he could prove he sent that letter, but furthermore he had a number of incriminating documents, photographs of himself and Oswald, and top-secret military intelligence reports in a Swiss safe-deposit box. Nagell was a contract agent of the CIA at that time. On September 20, 1963, Nagell walked into the State National Bank in El Paso, Texas, asked a teller for one hundred dollars in American Express travelers checks, then stepped back from the window and fired two shots from a Colt .45 pistol into the bank's ceiling, put the gun back in his belt, and calmly left the bank. He got into his car and waited until the police arrived, raised his hands and said, "I guess you've got me, I surrender." When taken into custody by the FBI, Nagell would only say, "I would rather be arrested than commit murder and treason."

Nagell's arresting officer, Jim Brunden, would later recall when interview by Russell, "When the assassination happened, I didn't think of it right away, because that was a pretty hectic time [...] Then a few days later, after Lee

Harvey Oswald was killed, what Nagell said came back to me. I thought, this had to be what he what he was talking about. How the hell would e have previous knowledge of it? How would he know what was coming down in Dallas?"

Nagell had hinted to Brunden about the coming assassination of John F. Kennedy during his arrest and trial. "I really don't want to be in Dallas," Nagell told him during the preliminary hearings.

To convince the FBI that this was not a crank letter, Nagell wrote it under an alias of a "known Communist agent" with whom he had been in contact in regard to the plot to assassinate Kennedy. This alias, "Joseph Kramer," was so well-known to the FBI that they could not have failed to realize that Nagell warning should be taken seriously, because if "Joseph Kramer" had advance knowledge of the conspiracy, then so did the Soviets. Indeed, the warning letter was so carefully worded that it ought to have led Hoover to the conclusion that a Soviet agent was planning to kill Kennedy, even though Nagell (and, most likely, Hoover) knew otherwise.

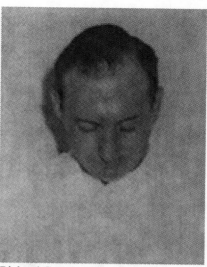

Richard Case Nagell, in a police line-up in September 1963, after his arrest in El Paso. He said he'd rather not be in Dallas.

"Joseph Kramer" was Mark Julius Gayn.

Nagell's account and Russell's investigative substantiation of it are far too complex to go into much detail here. In broad strokes, Nagell was a lifer in the ultra-secret intelligence operations of the CIA and the Pentagon. In a game played out in Korea, Japan, China, and the Philippines, intelligence officers like Nagell tried to recruit their counterparts into becoming double-agents, while knowing all the while that their counterparts on the Communist side were trying to do just the same. As deceit covered false-hoods, as lies traded with truth, men like Nagell lost touch with reality, and know longer knew who it was, exactly, that they were working for. In despair and rootlessness, they tried to forge their own guiding lights of ethics and purpose, but after so many years of military service, they were unequipped to do so. Ideals of honor, duty, country became shattered as the operatives saw hellish tours of duty filled with torture, murder, and terrorism in service to shifting geopolitical goals crafted by craven ideologues on all sides.

Nagell had found himself in a situation where he might have been in Oswald's shoes. His contact with agents on the Soviet side, while sanctioned by U.S. Intelligence, made him vulnerable to being cut loose, adrift, or framed. His principle contact with the Soviets, Nagell testified, was Mark Gayn, with whom he shared foreknowledge of multiple plots to kill the President of the United States. Nagell implied to Russell that he had been ordered to eliminate Oswald before he could pull the trigger. Nagell said this order was delivered by a Soviet agent, perhaps Mark Gayn, or, more star-tlingly, Tracy Barnes, of the CIA, Michael Straight's cousin. Recall that Straight's first approach to the US government to speak of his past, he made to his cousin Tracy Barnes.

The Amerasia Case was a *cause celebre* for the McCarthyites, yet Gayn somehow escaped prosecution even though he had been caught red-hand-ed. All evidence points to the fact that he was a double agent found useful to both sides...

steamshovel press

DR. JOHN AND THE KENNEDY VOODOO

Thanks to *Steamshovel* reader Garrick Alder

"I got shot in this finger," Mac Rebbenack, alias New Orleans music notable Dr. John, remembers in the June 13, 1998 edition of the UK's *Guardian Guide*, "and this knee; I got some buckshot in my ass and was shanked in my back. Y'know, before the words segregation and integration, when there was a law against the races minglin', there were pockets of New Orleans that was wide open, as far as race was concerned. However, in 1962 they put Jim Garrison in the district attorney's office and he started shutting all the joints down and padlocking 'em."

Jim Garrison, of course, is best known to later generations as the lawman who headed the investigation into the assassination of John F Kennedy, and Mac saw plenty of the Mob-linked corruption of the era—like David Ferrie, a local mobster Heavily implicated in the Kennedy Shooting, who died in mysterious circumstances in 1967 just before he was due to be questioned by Garrison's grand jury.

"Well, the Governor of the State of Louisiana—who at that Time was on speed and lush—used To come by our gigs, to hang with The hos and the strippers and everything, and the guys involved in the John F. Kennedy assassination used to come around there. Big guys like Ferrie used to come by when when we was workin' in Herbie Rodriguez's joint. We thought 'look at this creep,'he was like the ultimato creep of creeps. What could he do? I mean, how could he be involved in an assassination?"

JFK FROM A MARXIST PERSPECTIVE

An American Marxist historian named George Rawick wrote the following for Young Guard *from London, December 1963:*

The killing of John F. Kennedy has produced, with slight exceptions, no "witch-hunt" in the United States. Moreover, there has been a sharp turn away from the right-wing Senator from Arizona, Mr. Barry Goldwater, whose chances for the Republican presdiential nomination now seem very dim, and there has been a greater outpouring of support for Kennedy's moderate reform program.

And hardly anyone seems fully to believe that the pro-Castro Oswald was indeed the murderer. Many Americans understand that the assassination had something to do with what they call "this integration business."

But what are the specific links between the Negro revolution and this murder? Just this: Kennedy had been forced to go to Dallas in the role of

peacemaker — to make peace between the moderates and the extreme racists within the Democratic Party, even though shortly before Mr. Adlai Stevenson had been picketed and physically assaulted by white racists in that city.

That Dallas through which Mr. Kennedy drove slowly in an open automobile in an atmosphere known to be tense and dangerous is not simply a part of the South. It is one of the urban capitals of the new, industrial South. And since the events in Birmingham last May which marked the first of the massive Negro demonstrations in the industrial cities of the United States, the Negro Revolution has posed a direct threat to the American status quo. For since Birmingham the urban Negro masses have demanded not only social freedom and political rights, but equal employment rights as well.

Mr. Kennedy went to Dallas because this demand in the United States where capitalism through its use of automation has left at least four percent of the American work force unemployed — and of course Negroes are the first sacked and the last hired — has challenged capitalist society at its most vulnerable point. Either the Democratic Party in such cities as Dallas could be united to support a policy designed to placate Negroes in ways far short of effective job equality, or the Negro revolution would bring into motion far greater forces challenging the status quo. Mr. Kennedy, the American guardian of state capitalism, knew that any social upheaval that threatens the stability of the arrangement whereby the working class leadership does not challenge capitalist sovereignty at the point of production, in return for certain limited benefits of the Welfare State, was the danger to be averted.

If the Negro movement is allowed to keep going without any attempt to decapitate it by giving in at points short of meeting the demand for employment, then even the American trad union bureaucracy will have to move — or be overthrown, for Negro workers are the center of the opposition to the union bureaucracy. Therefore, Mr. Kennedy had to go to Dallas to get full support for his measures aimed at placating the Negro masses.

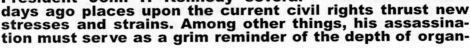

THE ASSASSINATION
AND CIVIL RIGHTS

Statement of Ernest Calloway, the First Vice-President Before The Executive Committee of the St. Louis NAACP, in a Special Meeting, November 26, 1963

Speaking from the national point of view, the assassination of President John F. Kennedy several days ago places upon the current civil rights thrust new stresses and strains. Among other things, his assassination must serve as a grim reminder of the depth of organ-

ized reaction, hate and bigotry in this country. And the bitter fruit of his assassination is picked from the same evil and blasphemous tree that produced utter contempt for federal law and moral injunction by those in high places, that produced violence and lawlessness as a substitute for community reasoning, that produced the bombs to destroy churches and innocent little girls, that produced the same rifle to assassinate Medgar Evars, that produced the evil, thunderous silence on the part of ordinary people in the face of moral disaster, and finally and inexorably, the production of a climate in which a country stands in mortal fear of itself. This all lends weight to the often repeated observation that if American democracy is ever destroyed, the destruction will come from within, rather than from without. Nevertheless, the assassination of President Kennedy and the emergence of the Johnson administration is bound to bring in its wake a new set of power forces in politics and economics. Will this emerging administration have the same sense of history and social urgency?

The present civil rights thrust has been closely identified with the Kennedy political posture. The past 1,000 days of the Kennedy administration have also been the eventful, historic days of the upsurge of a new civil rights consciousness. It was several weeks after President Kennedy's inauguration in 1961 that the historic Freedom Ride movement developed as well as a continuation of the sit-in movement that had its beginnings in 1960. In 1962 the massive assault upon the ballot box in the south began, and in 1963 the civil rights movement took on new meaning, purpose and impact with the March on Washington. All of these events took place within the short period of 1,000 eventful days, and have served as milestones in the social history or our country.

The important and significant point here is that this new thrust for the most part had the strong moral support of the occupant of the White House and key areas of his administration. Equally significant is that the Kennedy administration by its inner political nature and base sought to shift political balances within the structure of power, as a means of securing and consolidating its own built-in perception of grave national and international problems.

Consequently, it is our opinion that with the assassination of President Kennedy and his burial yesterday at Arlington Cemetery, this particular honeymoon period between the White House and the civil rights movement came to an abrupt end. Nevertheless, the present civil rights thrust will continue, but it will be naive and improper to carelessly assume that it will maintain the same ideological companionship with the White House as heretofore obtained. A new accommodation must be made within the framework of new political forces. Qualitatively such an accommodation could possibly be more fruitful from the practical legislative point of view, or it could be less. Only time and circumstances will tell.

THE EVENT THAT NEVER HAPPENED

Edited and transcribed

By William Kelly

DEALEY PLAZA MEMORIAL SERVICE - Sunday, 11/22/98 THE 35TH ANNIVERSARY OF THE ASSASSINATION OF PRESIDENT JOHN F. KENNEDY.

"Build the news upon the rock of truth and righteousness. Conduct it always upon the lines of fairness and integrity. Acknowledge the right of the people to get from the newspaper both sides of every important question." –George Bannerman Dealey, publisher of the *Dallas Morning News.*

CNN news reported that for the first time in 35 years there was to be no memorial service at Dealey Plaza on November 22, 1998, the anniversary of the assassination of President John F. Kennedy.

CBS News with Dan Rather reported that the Final Report of the JFK Assassinations Records Review Board "did find enough evidence to conclude that Lee Harvey Oswald was the only gunman," while the Final Report never concluded any such thing.

Then the Associated Press (AP) reported from Dallas on November 22 that, "JFK assassination hype fades" and that "other than the usual handful ofcurious people milling about Dealey Plaza, the day was expected to be uneventful..."

Well, what actually occured was that from noon until 1pm, the Coalition on Political Assassinations (COPA) took a break from their fifth annual conference at Union Station, two blocks away, to hold a memorial service that was attended by many hundreds of people who filled the both sides of the street of the entire plaza.

COPA is an organization composed of three independent groups - the Assassination Records and Research Center (ARRC) of Washington D.C., the Committee for an Open Archvies (COA) and the Citizens for the Truth about the John F. Kennedy Assassination (CTKA). They are professional associations interested in developing the truth about the assassination, that lobbied extensively for the passage of the JFK Assassination Records Review Act and have met with Cuban officials in the Bahamas to obtain information about the assassination from Cuban sources.

In an address before COPA the previous day, the chairman of the Assassinations Records Review Board, John Tunheim reiterated the Final Report's first paragraph that it "will not offer conclusions about what the assassination records released did or did not prove," and that significant documents were missing and some were even destroyed by federal agenecies after the board began its business of identifying and releasing records to the public.

Others who spoke at the COPA conference included Philadelphila attorney Vincent Salandria, history professor John Newman, former FBI agent William Turner and others who have been instrumental in reviewing the recently released documents and attempting to make sense of what the government wants to maintain a mystery.

At noon on Sunday, November 22, 1998, COPA board member, and Washington D.C. attorney Dan Alcorn began the memorial service at Dealey Plaza.

Dan Alcorn : The federal board - The JFK Assassination Records Review Board (ARRB) discovered that many of the records have been destroyed, and we do not have a complete record. Yet we have a much more of a documentary record than we have had ever before.

There's a memorial down on the street that has a quotation from the bible: "Ye shall know the truth and the truth shall make you free."

That quote is also enscribed on the wall of the Central Intelligence Agency headquarters in McLean, Virginia, so there is a commonality of thought there. Many of us are here today because we have never believed that the government has told us the truth about the assassination, and we believe that unless we know the truth, we are not free.

Unless we know the truth about these events we are not a free people and we have not been a free people as long as we have been lied to about the events that occured here. The spirt of our commemorative event is to take those words to heart, and until we know the truth and the full truth of what occured in the street before us today on a day very much like today, a clear, sunny day in the fall of 1963.

On behalf of our organization I will make a challenge to you. Everyone here must be here because you care very deeply about the meaning of this event and what it means to our history as a nation. I will make the challenge to you to join us in our efforts in seeking the full truth about the assassination of President Kennedy. And not just the truth as pieced together by citizens who put in the time and effort to this, but to actually cause the government to tell the truth about this event, and for the government to come forward and give us a full and truthful acounting of what happened here in 1963. Otherwise, we in fact are not the free people we want to be, have been and we should be as a nation.

You know, it is a crime for a citizen of this country to tell a lie to a federal investigator, but it is not a crime for your government to lie to you. And we feel this is an unfair relationship. If it's a crime for us to lie to our government, it should be a crime for us t o lie as well.

It is in that spirit of investigation and of honest inquiry that our organization has worked closely with the Assassinations Records Review Board to get materials out. They ran into an obstructive wall of secrecy at the federal agencies. They told us thet they ran into a Cold War system of secrecty that refused to relent on the documents and information as it related to this event. And this was thirty-five years after the event occured, and after a federal board was set up by the Congress to try to get information released about what happened here.

So we call on you to join us in our efforts. We think that great nations and civilizations cannot survive the kinds of doubt and turmoil that have been raised by the events that happened here. If you study the history of great civilizations you will find that when they lost their way in terms of truth, self-governing, democratic and republican institutions began their decline and was one of the reasons for their ultimate colapse. We do not want the decline and decay of our public and political system. We want to be a part of a healthy revival of those institutions.

We have experienced a decline in the public's trust in government since November,1963, a blimp in the charts that notes the significance of these events. Today a majority of people don't even bother to vote. The largest turnout of voters in American history was in 1960. The decline in public confidence in the government began with the ambush at Dealey Plaza and has continually declined since then. These trends are very troubling.

So we ask you to join us and support the effort we have started to try to pursue the truth of these events, to try to pursue credability, honesty and openness on behalf of our governmental institutions. And by that effort to try to turn our nation in a healthy direction, to build stronger democratic institutions, to build a stronger faith between the pubic and its government. We feel that is essential, and we call on you as free citizens of this nation to join us in that effort.

I'm going to introduce to you a series of speakers who have been very involved in this issue and can give you the benefit of their experience as well. The first is Mark Lane, one of the earliest researchers in this case who did tremendous ground-breaking work, recorded much of his work for posterity and has written extensively about this case.

Mark Lane: I remember coming here thirty-five years ago and there were no crowds on the grassy knoll. But now, after all of these years, although they have a museum over there on the 6th Floor, which is a museum dedicated to a place where nothing happened. They don't have a plaque over here, on the grassy knoll, and they should.

Thirty-five years ago today the *Dallas Morning News* published a full page ad with the sarcastic heading: "Welcome To Dallas Mr. President," and then went on to practically call him a communist and a trator. That was then.

Today's *Dallas Morning News* has an editorial: "Kennedy's Legacy - The Time Is Ripe For Idealism," with no references to him being a communist or a traitor. Now he's a great man. They'll tell us everything about John Kennedy, everything, except who killed him. Because look at the rest of the *Dallas Morning News*, thirty-five years later, when every survey in America shows that 75 to 95% of the people are convinced that there was a conspiracy to kill John Kennedy, here we go in the guise of a book review in today's *Dallas Morning News*: Oswald Alone Killed Kennedy, Oswald Alone Killed Tippit, One Man Two Murders, they're sticking with the same story. I have but one word for the *Dallas Morning News*:

Shame. Shame on you, you are discracing the city of Dallas, and it is not fair to do that.

I'll tell you where there should be plaques in this city. There were a number of brave, courageous residents of this city, longtime residents of Texas, who had the courage to speak the truth to power in the face of intimidation and threats. Right over there was Jean Hill, and she's still there thiry-five years later, one of the first to tell the truth that shots came from behind that wooden fence. And they attacked her and ridiculed her. There should be a plaque over there commemorating her right on the spot where she is standing...

The Grassy Knoll should be called "Lee Bowers Memorial Park," the railroad bridge should be the Holland-Dode-Symons Underpass - that's the monuments that should be named after the people of this state, people who had the couage to come forward with the truth, while the *Dallas Morning News* lied thirty-five years ago and continues to lie thirty-five years later.

This is the place where our leader was murdered. This is hollowed grown, and the people of this country know it. It is supose to be the largest tourist attraction in Dallas. There's people here all the time, at the grassy knoll, nobody looks for the truth from the 6th floor of the Book Depository building, because the people of America know the truth, even though the *Dallas Morning News* is unwilling to share the information with us.

That day in Dallas, in this city, at this location, when the government of the United States executed its own president, when that happened, we as a nation, lost our code of honor, lost our sense of honor. And it can only be restored when the government of the United States - and it will not do it without us insisting, and marching and fighting and voting, and putting this matter on the agenda,...but when that day comes that the government of the United States tells us the truth and all the factual details about the assassination, including their role in the murder. When that day comes, honor will be restored to this nation. Thank you.

Dan Alcorn: Our next speaker is a member of the Board of Directors of COPA, a medical doctor from San Francisco who has researched this issue and has written about it in the Journal of the American Medical Association and the Columbia Journalism Review, Dr. Gary Agular.

Dr. Gary Agular: It's hard to follow such a powerful speaker as Mark Lane and I certainly can't hope to match his eloquence, wit or command of this case, but what I can share with you is evidence...that autopsy photos are missing. This is something that you will not read in the Dallas Morning News, Time or Newsweek, but is something that is very clearly established, the ARRB releases are very clear on the point, the autopsy pathologists have described autopsy photographs that are missing. One of them defiantly stood shoulder-to-shoulder with the House Select Committee on Assassinations, which was supposed to tell us the truth about the assassination...which not only did not report that, it wasn't released until the ARRB came along.

There is enormous evidence in the forensic, in the medical area alone that indicates there was more assassin, but what is most shamefull of all is the government's willingness, even in subsequent investigations, to lie about that evidence. Thank God there was an Assassinations Records Review Board, thank God they did the work they did, because now we no longer have to rely on government appointed authorities to tell us that we can trust the government's original conclusions, because we know we can't.

We know they've destroyed evidence, not only in the medical-autopsy area, not only among photographs, we know that witnesses have been intimated, and it is ashame that you won't read about that. No credable journalist will touch the story. It is a story not unlike the story of the CIA and crack cocaine, which led to the downfall of Gary Webb, before two volumes of the CIA Inspector's Report that confirmed much more than what Gary Webb even alledged about the CIA's complicity in the cocaine importation. But you won't read about that in the Dallas Morning News. You barely get a small column about it in the New York Times after they devote many, many column inches defamind journalists who talk about the subject.

I think it is important that those of you who are here today continue to insist that your government is accountable to you and does not conduct its operations in secrecy, that it does not deny you the evidence that is collected in its investigations and that it be as accountable to us as it insits we be accountable to it.

I hope you will continue to work with us to force the goverment to be responsible and admit the full truth about the assassination of President Kennedy.

Dan Alcorn: Our next speaker is a member of the Board of Directors of COPA, a professor at Dartmouth, and the author of a number of books about the assassination, Dr. Phillip Melanson.

Dr. Phillip Melanson: Thank you. As we commemorate the 35th anniversary of this terrible political tragedy that so negatively affected our lives, our policies, our political system and our faith in our own government, we should remind ourselves that the tragedy of the President's assassination is compounded by a separate but related tragedy - the failulre of our law enforcement institutions, the failure of our political institutions and the failure of the media to affectively discover the truth of who killed President Kennedy and why. And until that happens, and it is never too late to find the truth if the citizens demand it, and until that happens the original tragedy will be compounded like a bad political debt into the next millenieum, and the faith in our political system will continue to erode.

I think also the failure to come to grips with who killed President Kennedy and why is related to the other assassinations in the 1960s, and that's why Martin Luther King's is begging the Justice Department to look for justice in that case, and we hear from Siran's lawyer in the case of Robert Kennedy.

If we had come to terms with what happened here at Dealey Plaza, discovered the truth and admitted it, the whole history of the 1960s would be different.

If the vast majority of the public believes this case is an unsolved conspiracy, who are the minority in officialdom to deny us the truth and to cling to the lone-assassin theory like it was an absolute religion in the face of overwhelming evidence to the contrary.

Thank you.

Dan Alcorn: Our next speaker is an aclaimed author and professor of history at the University of Maryland. His books include *JFK and Vietnam* and *Oswald and the CIA,* Dr. John Newman.

Dr. John Newman: I would like to say a few words about the media, and a couple of new developments for all of you gathered here. When I come here at this time of the year, I remember another place, a place connected to this place, and without the events that happened here, the other place would not exist, and that's the Vietnam Memorial in Washington D.C., which is like no other war memorial in the world. I've been to other war memorials in Russia, China and Germany, and people frequent those memorials, they eat lunch there and talk and its a nice place to be. I don't how many of you have been to the Vietnam War Memorial in Washington D.C., but nobody hangs out It's a very, very somber place because there's still something going on there, something deep, something that's still in our psyche, and our culture and it connects directly to Dealey Plaza. And I think most people know that.

I'm not going to give a speech on the Vietnam War, but I think it is clear now that John F. Kennedy was on his way to pulling us out of Vietnam when he died, and the events that happened here catapulted us to that devistating debacle called the Vietnam War.

I'd like to echo what Mark Lane said about the media. I just heard that CNN this morning said that for the first time in all these years there were no events planned for Dealey Plaza on this day. So you are not here, this gathering does not exist. Furthermore, the evening before last, none other than Dan Rather, the major icon of the network television, made the announcement that the Review Board had conducted this very large investigation and looked at all these millions of pages of documents and had discovered that the lone-nut hypothesis was true, which was attributed to Judge Tunheim. Judge Tunheim was here in Dallas and refutes this story, and all of you who have followed this story know that the Review Board has taken no such position.

But it never ceases to amaze me how the media can twist and turn and obfuscate and block this mass movement to find the truth. Let me close by giving you a few examples of the information that is flowing out of these new files, and I think these are appropate because of what happened here at Dealey Plaza. I am thinking particularly of a tape recorded conversation between President Johnson and Senator Russell, one of the Warren Commisioners. At great length they were able to save the situation and preserve the lone-nut hypthosis with that wonderful, sine qua non - CE399, the magic bullet that broke seven bones and came out prestine on a stretcher.

The newly released tape is very interesting because Sen. Russell calls the President to explain to him what this single-bullet theory is, and at the end of it he says distinctly, "I don't believe a word of it." And President Johnson said, "I don't either."

And I think that is appropriate thing to share with you the types of things that are comming out of the files. Then there is the galley proofs of the Warren Report where our estemed President Ford moved the bullet hole up, and these are the types of things that are in the newly released documents, but the mainstream media is not there to put them on page one.

Occassionally they get noted, but its like ships passing in the night. I am heartened to see by the turnout here today, that with respect to the American people, this is not passing in the night and I hope as we stand here today and think about the events that happened here, we pass the torch to a younger generation, which we are doing, our movement and our desire for the truth in this case carries on. Thank you very much.

Dan Alcorn: We are approaching the time in our program which is a memorial to the events that happened here thirty-five years ago, so for that purpose I'd like to introduce to you the executive secretary of COPA, a man who has devoted himself for a number of years to working on the projects we have as an organization, but has also done his own independent research on the assassination. I think that those who have had the experience of working with John Judge know of his serious and sincere commitment to investigating the issues that are at stake here and to his contribution that he has made to the the history of the investigation of the assassination. He has really been the heart and soul of the work we have done through COPA. He has put in a tremendous volunteer effort and sacraficed and suffered a great deal for the efforts he has made, which have gone largely uncompensated. So let me introduce to you the executive secretary of COPA, John Judge.

John Judge: It is interesting to see such a large crowd. For the better part of the last 25 years, I have come out here every year, usually with only five or six people, often in worse weather than this, with researcher and newspaper editor Penn Jones, who some of you know as having done work on the death of the witnesses, who passed on this year.

From the inception of the national security and military-intelligence state in the late 1940s, the history of this country has been a commodity that has been owned by that state. The people who don't own their own history are a conquered people.

Much of the effort I put in has to do with the idea of taking our own history back, of owning it ourselves, since much is still locked up in government vaults and hidden from us and we are really the only ones who can restore it. 35 years ago, in my view, there was a coup d'etat here in Dealy Plaza, and the government has not recovered in any significant way, towards democracy, since that day. Kennedy began to represent for many people, hope and change and a response from the top level of government to the popular movements at the time for civil rights, for arms limitations, for an end to the Cold War, and Kennedy was responding to popular movments in a way that presidents after him rarely have. So what was assassinated here that day was not just a particular man or a particular president, but a sense of hope by the American people. And I think that the government has let us know over the years, fairly consistantly, that they did kill the pesident, and they killed him from a very high level, and that if they can kill the president and get away with it that they can kill anyone of us that they would like to and that we should sit down and shut up and get out of the way.

But I'm hoping that there is enough decency left in people in America, and I see evidence of that all the time, that we can understand that there are more of us, and that we can think, and we can take back our own democracy, if we want it.

It is now 12:30, and 35 years ago President Kennedy was assassinated here, so lets have a moment of silence.

Thank you.

Peter Dale Scott, a researcher who could not be with us here today, sent an e-mail in which he said a few interesting things. He said that we've come into a new era in that one of the major tasks ahead of us right now is to focus on getting the government documents that are still locked up on the Martin Luther King assassination. The other thing he noted was a government statute that makes it illegal for a citizen of this country to lie to the government, and he suggested that a similar statute be passed that would make it illegal for the government to lie to its people.

I hope you will take this topic seriously and continue to act to get the full release of the files and to get the truth, and you are welcome to join us at COPA in fullfilling the remainder of our agenda and what is is to be done in the future. You are welcome to join us and take your democracy back.

Dan Alcorn: We have a few other speakers here, including former FBI agent William Turner, whose books have been translated into Russian, German, Japanese, French and Spanish. He is currently working on a new book entitled: "Rearview Mirror - Looking back at the FBI, CIA and Other Tails.

William Turner: Thank you Dan. It's been exactly 35 years ago and two days that I came here on assignment for a national magazine to do an article on the breakdown in security that resulted in the assassination being successful. I was assigned to it because of my background as a former FBI agent. I can tell you that when I arrived the mood was really somber, the floodlights were on, reporters from all over the world were converging, people had left floral wreaths along the curbstone where the shooting took place, and it was very erry. The headquarters of the Dallas Police Department was a feeding frenzy of reporters trying to find out what happened. I was on a very tight deadline, I could only contend with the security breakdown issue at the time, which was that Oswald had worked as an informant for the FBI and that was the reason they had not furnished his name to the Secret Service prior to the presidential visit.

One thing I remember was talking to a Dallas patrolman named Malcom Eugene Barnett who had been posted in front of the School Book Depository for crowd control at the time of the assassination. He told me that a women came running from the grassy knoll who told him that shots were fired from here. That being the case, I became very critical of the Warren Commission and when it's report came out I read it and realized it was pretty much a fairy tale. I am proud to say that I was associated with District Attorney Jim Garrison in New Orleans who tried to repopen the investigation into the assassination. Jim was a great American and was on the trail of the assassins, as his book says, when he was destroyed by the media at the Clay Shaw trial. The Garrison investigation paved the way for what we know today, and I believe that we know to a good degree of journalistic certitude what happened.

First the motives were piling up, John Kennedy had supposedly with held air cover for the Bay of Pigs, motive number one. John Kennedy had failed to invade Cuba during the Cuban Missile Crisis of October, 1962, motive number two. John Kennedy had promised to withdraw from Vietnam, motive number three. Motive number four is that John Kennedy, at the time he was assassinated, was on a second track, which was to secretly carry on negotiations with Cuba to bring about a detente. These motives piled up to the point where it became necessary to assassinate him. And I think it is very obvious with the compiliation of information that we have today that the whole mechanism of it came out of the allegiance between the CIA and the rabid Cuban exiles and the Mafia, who already had an assassination aparatus set up to kill Castro. They switched targets and hit Kennedy.

And I hope you will join us, in recognizing the significance of the events that happened here, and try to do something about it. Thank you.

STEAMSHOVEL PRESS

LETTER FROM THE UK
Robin Ramsay
Boys and their Toys 1
The Mind Control Conundrum Continues

The mind control story remains impossible to evaluate. Or it is if it's done rationally and honestly. Of course you can do what Alex Constantine does in *Virtual Government: CIA Mind Control Operations in America* (Feral Press, Portland, 1997): take the most difficult and tendentious elements of the contemporary paranoid agenda - child abuse (ritual and Satanic), alien abductions, mind control, cults and UFOs - and attribute it all to the CIA without worrying over much about evidence. It makes for an entertaining read but it isn't much help in the long, slow business of persuading the wider world that this is an area they ought to look at.

There are three distinct but presumably related areas of activity. One is the use of implants as receivers and/or transmitters. The others are the broadcasting of voices - what has been called synthetic telepathy - and the use of microwaves to influence behaviour. All seem to exist and the technology leading to them has been identified. The patents researched (some have been reported in *Lobster* —see number 34 for examples), some in *Nexus*, some in Judy Walls' excellent *Resonance* (684 C.R. 535, Sumterville, FL 33585; see number 33, for example). The technologies exist in an historical and operational framework which makes both their development, trial on involuntary subjects and eventual deployment not surprising. The opening sentence of story in *The Times* (London) was: American and Norwegian hospitals were involved in sterilisation experiments on the mentally retarded over a 20-year period up to 1994.9 US and Norway used insane for Nazi-style tests, *The Times* 29 April 1998. The bastard offspring of Sid Gottlieb and MKULTRA are among us.

This year Oak Ridge National Laboratory issued an (undated) press release on their programme developing so-called non-lethal weapons which began in 1993, headed *Physiological Responses Applicable to Development of Less-Than-Lethal Weapons*. (At point the release refers to Friendly Force!) It describes three avenues being developed based on known physiological responses to energetic stimuli, including a thermal gun, a seizure gun and a magnetosphere gun.

But this end of the subject is not yet intellectually respectable enough for the major media and/or politicians to take an interest in it. I mentioned this area recently to a friendly reporter on one of Britain's major daily papers. "Oh, that," he said. "I've had letters about that, mostly written in green ink." The green ink touch was probably an invention, a bit of baloney to convince me that the letters' authors were crazies. Press legend has it that crazies always write in green or purple ink; but I've had my share of letters from crazies and I haven't seen green or purple writing for at least a decade. But I took the hint and dropped the subject.

Since the major media won't touch this stuff yet, most of this is happening in fringe magazines and especially on the Internet in dialogue between the victims of these programmes trying to make sense of their experiences.

Microwaves

The problem for the microwave victims is that of evidence: they can produce none other than the first-hand reports of other individuals and accounts of programs being run by this or that military body. None of which would impress the legal mind. The man who first introduced me to this field, Harlan Girard, runs a group in the United States, the International Committee on Offensive Microwave Weapons, which recently tried to get a legal case going in the United States. To quote from the judgement of Gladys Kessler, a judge in the US District Court for the District of Columbia, the Committee charged that many federal departments and agencies unlawfully conduct advanced weapons research using human subjects without first obtaining their consent....that the United States, through various federal agencies, has unlawfully failed to promulgate regulations for the protection of human subjects involved in classified research.....seeks declaratory and injunctive relief, as well as costs.

Judge Kessler rejected the suit on the grounds that the Committee failed to establish standing to sue on behalf of its members, as well as making claims that are too generalized and non-specific to support a complaint.

If the first objection could be overcome, the second still looks insurmountable at present.

The most dramatic of the microwaves effects are the voices in the head. Since sounds in the head were produced using microwaves by Dr Alan Frey in 1962, this isn't terribly surprising. But until recently I had not seen anything like a plausible hypothesis of the phenomenon. But recently, one of those afflicted with the voices, Kathy Kasten, put on the Net what seem to me to be the best hypothesis about them so far.

The voices in the head are recorded

The experiences [voices in the head] the survivors report are not live ... they are recorded. The amount of electromagnetic energy that such implanted relays are capable of downlinking is so small as to have very little apparent (direct) effect, if any, upon the brain. However, over a long period of time (months or years) even that little bit of energy can be utilised to condition responses indirectly into the victims' own thinking processes.

Over a period of months and years, conditioned responses are patterned into the brain's neural pathways. This neural patterning requires millions upon millions of repetitions, but eventually the victim's brain is conditioned to produce the responses that their torturers wished to implement.....Hour after hour, day after day, year after year, the torturers broadcast weak electro-magnetic fields which emulate brain wave patterns. Sequences of these emulated patterns are then strung together to emulate a thought process. These sequences are then repeated billions of times............Over time, the neurons in the victims brains become conditioned to repeat these superimposed patterns of brain-wave activity. As time goes by, the victims "brains become the source of these broadcasts". Soon, as more neurons become more deeply conditioned, these externally patterned thought processes become more and more pronounced (louder). Ultimately, these brain wave patterns become self-sustaining.

Typically, these conditioned responses are strung together in a looped and/or cross-linked pattern so as to make these superimposed thought processes both self-sustaining and self-reinforcing. This neural patterning is usually linked to the motor and/or sensory centres of the brain in such a way as to utilise pain and pleasure to reinforce the expected responses.

Survivors may notice that when trying to suppress (resist) any of these errant, conditioned thought processes, one or more muscle spasms occur elsewhere in their bodies and these muscle spasms induce pain. The muscle spasm and its resultant pain sensations are part of the conditioned response.

The neural pathways in the victims' brains have been conditioned to induce pain if they attempt to suppress other of these conditioned thought processes. Thus, the victims' brains self-reinforce these voices, et al, in order to avoid pain. Herein lies the key to deconditioning these processes. One must learn to step outside of these errant patterns, analyse how they trigger and reinforce one another, and strategically pit them against one another.

This won't be accepted by all the victims of voices: I've met a couple who have claimed that the voices actually comment on their actions from minute to minute, suggesting constant surveillance. Of that I have always been sceptical - how is it achieved? For the moment I think Kasten has the best hypothesis. Incidentally, her account of becoming a victim of the voices is currently on the Konformist Website.

Boys and Their Toys 2

In Britain for the last few weeks we have been inundated by stories about the sex lives of members of Tony Blair's government. One member of the Cabinet was revealed to be gay after he was robbed while out cruising a public park in London. Two weeks later another came out as gay after a former lover offered to sell the story of their relationship to a newspaper. With two other Cabinet ministers, including Tony Blair's chief spin doctor, Peter Mandelson, already known to be gay, this led Britain's most powerful tabloid, the Murdoch-owned *Sun*, to ask on its front page, Is Britain being run by a gay mafia? The answer from the rest of the media, was a loud hoot of derision. The general consensus was that everybody knows that it doesn't work like that. Politicians are self-interested and ambitious and there is no way a gay network could operate at the top end of the British political system. No doubt this is true. But the *Sun's* front-page questions rested not just on the reported fact that four of the 16 male members of the Blair Cabinet are gay, but on rumours about two other senior British political figures that have never been reported but are almost universally believed by the British political media and the political system.

For several years it has been whispered that Gordon Brown, the Chancellor of the Exchequer, and William Hague, leader of the Conservative Party, are gay. The rumours have reached the level of jokes on TV and radio which only those who have heard the stories would understand. In response to the rumours, Gordon Brown creates periodic photo opportunities for himself to be photographed with a female friend, and his recent biography included an entire chapter which (not very convincingly, in my view) described his heterosexuality. William Hague went one better and got married almost immediately after he became leader of the Conservative Party. From what I have heard of the sources of the stories, I think the rumours are true, and I look forward to the day when William Hague is outed. A gay leader of the Conservative Party? Now that would really be something.

STEAMSHOVEL PRESS

THE LATE, GREAT KERRY THORNLEY REVISITED

On Nov 28, 1998, one of the truly original figures to emerge from the American landscape, Kerry Wendell Thornley, died after a long illness. Unfortunately, Thornley's passing went totally unnoticed by the mainstream press, though his death--in my opinion--was just as significant as the recent demises of such counterculture icons as Ginsberg, Burroughs, Leary, and Castaneda.

Shortly after Thornley's death, I synchronistically stumbled across a two part interview that my buddy Matt Lutz published in his zine Working Class Hero a couple years ago, and thought it a good time to bring this wonderful piece back before the general fringe public, in memoriam to our fallen comrade, the father of Discordianism, and inspiration for Shea and Wilson's Illuminatus Trilogy. My thanks to Matt for granting permission use it here. According to Matt, the new issue of Working Class Hero will be available in January '99. Copies are $2.00 ppd. from: Matt Lutz, 418 Peninsula Drive, Lot 5, Erie, PA 16505. Included in this issue are articles by Paul Rydeen, Mae Brussell and some joker named Adam Gorightly, plus an interview with Linda Thompson.

W.C.H.: You were friends with Lee Harvey Oswald in the service, and you wrote a book about this. What was your inspiration for the book?

K.T.: His defection to the Soviet Union. I was writing a novel about my experience in the military. When Oswald deserted, I pretty much understood why. At the time I was feeling pretty anti-American myself and in retrospect I realized I didn't know shit. But back then I felt I knew exactly why he did this.

W.C.H.: What, do you feel, made him want to defect?

K.T.: I thought he was disgusted with the way we (the military) behaved overseas. They think they are "concrete heroes". A generation after the war when they go to Japan, they still feel like they are concrete heroes. They're very loud, very belligerent.

W.C.H.: The "Ugly American Syndrome"?

K.T.: Right. I read THE UGLY AMERICAN the summer after Oswald defected and it was partly an inspiration for my IDLE WARRIORS. That's why my book seems so disjointed, because I felt I didn't need any unity or continuity. I just wanted to tell a bunch of different stories.

W.C.H.: When you were stationed with Oswald, did he express to you what he felt an ideal marine corp life would be like before the reality of the situation hit him?

K.T.: No, my guess was that he had come from a marine corp family. I also sensed he was disillusioned by the fucked up morale situation in the Far East. My main character was a third generation marine. As it turned out, I was pretty close; his older brother was in the service. For Lee it was a matter of being too gung ho in the beginning, in my opinion, and later becoming disheartened because things were nowhere near perfect. They were below zero. (laughs)

W.H.C.: Yes...I can understand that, I'm a vet myself. Was Lee Harvey Oswald a loner?

K.T.: He seemed to enjoy solitude. He didn't reach out to form friendships. But I didn't pay much attention to it at the time. When I was younger, I was pretty shy myself, so it wasn't anything hard for me to understand, or anything puzzling to me.

W.C.H.: So he was reluctant towards active participation?

K.T.: It seemed that way to me...I hate to reinforce anything The Warren Commission ever said, including the idea that he was a loner. But nevertheless, when you got too close he pulled away. You saw my testimony about how he spoke for the last time. I didn't actually say: "...comes the revolution"; I said something so unbearably silly that I didn't even want to tell the Commission what it was. (laughs) We were sitting there looking at this parking lot with gravel on it, and I was thinking in terms of "1984", because I was reading it at the time. Oswald loaned me his copy. So I said something about the revolutionary gravel, and Lee turned to me and said, "Not you, too, Thornley?!", then got up and walked away.

W.C.H.: Like he was pissed?

K.T.: Yes, he was quite pissed about it! To me it was a perfectly harmless statement and at the time I felt he thought I was "Red Baiting" him. If I'd known that he was going to become one of histories most interesting individuals, I would have corrected his impression. (laughs)

W.C.H.: Well, he had been in numerous misdemeanors or misconduct.

K.T.: Lee was extremely rebellious.

W.C.H.: Vying for attention possibly?

K.T.: Look, he was a C.I.D. agent. There's no possibility he was anything else. He was working for military intelligence; he was trying to identify communists in the outfit by pretending to be a communist. I'm sure of it.

W.C.H.: Which outfit? C.I.D. or C.I.A.?

K.T.: No they call them C.I.D. outfits; he went into the C.I.A. later...I don't know what C.I.D. stands for.

W.C.H.: Aaaahh...Central Intelligence Of Defense, I believe.

K.T.: Yeah, probably.

W.C.H.: I was in the Ç N.S.A. for several years.

K.T.: If you want to hear a hair raising story about that period in the marines...

W.C.H.: Love to.

K.T.: David Bucknell was in that outfit. He contacted me in 1978. And asked me if I remembered an incident that involved myself, him and Oswald. I told him I didn't remember the whole incident, except for certain highlights. All right...Bucknell made notes about this incident the next day. Oswald, Bucknell and I were called on the PA system to go into the administration office of our radar outfit on the perimeter of the base. We did, and they sent us over to base security. On our way over there Bucknell and Oswald were talking to one another and I was lagging behind about 20 feet. I caught up with them and said something. Oswald looked at me and said, "Thornley, this is a private conversation." I said, "Oh well, excuse me," dropped back and let them finish their talk. Bucknell told me what was going on was that he and Oswald were running a loan sharking operation. Bucknell was afraid that that's what the security inquiry was about and Oswald was arguing saying, "No, then why would I be involved?" We went into a room with a bunch of guys from other outfits and a captain got up and introduced this man in civilian clothes, a latin looking guy with a "DA" haircut. The captain only gave his name as "Mr. B". Mr. B said, "We've called you all together, because we understand that you're all admirers of Fidel Castro." This was right after the Cuban revolution, before Castro came out as a Marxist. They said we have reason to believe Soviet Agents have infiltrated Castro's government, and we want volunteers to help get rid to them. Then they interviewed us one at a time. Now as best I've been able to figure out, what I think probably happened is that they found out I was about to go overseas and I didn't qualify for the training program. As for Bucknell, he said he went in and talked to Mr. B privately and they filled out a little form first. A security clearance form. One thing he had to do was list 3 references. One of them he listed was a maternal grandfather of his, whose first initials were "E.H." and last name happened to be Hunt. However, Mr. B said: Who's this? Bucknell told him and Mr. B chuckled to himself. Whoever he was, he knew Howard Hunt...Now, when I went over to Atsugi afterwards, Howard Hunt was there at the same base. He was with the C.I.A. at the time. Of course, I didn't find this out until years later when I read his autobiography, so it appears to me that if Oswald was in Military Intelligence already, he was recruited at that meeting. There also was one guy in that outfit named "Delgato" and he was a fan of Castro. I remember this part too, I remember being surprised that he wasn't there. So I went back to the outfit and I said to Delgato, "I'm surprised that they didn't want to talk to you." He said,"Kerry, I think Castro's turning communist." And I said. "Oh, all right." He thought everyone was a communist; he thought Oswald was a communist. None of the rest of us took him seriously, you know? So that's the hottest piece of information I've come across about that period in the marine corp. David Bucknell, I don't know where he is, the last I heard he was living in San Francisco. There's a guy who's living in San Jose by the name of Bottello. He's a judge now. He was in the same outfit. Bucknell was going to get the three of us together. Bottello wasn't with us that day, but we were all going to get together, anyway. Bottello later told one of my friends that he didn't remember Bucknell. However, I remember Bucknell vividly ! I e Even remember his nickname; they called him "Bucky Beaver". I'm sure Bucknell was telling the truth.

W.C.H.: So, do you think that there's any connection between the Gary Powers incident and...

K.T.: Oh yeah! Very possibly. Powers said something to that effect. The U-2 used to take off and land at Atsugi all the time, and we didn't know what it was. We were told "not to even think about it," unless we wanted to get our asses in a sling. I thought it was an experimental aircraft. The U-2 incident occurred while we were over there.

W.C.H.: Do you think Oswald was set up from day one?

K.T.: Sure he was! I think they were out to set up one of us. I had a whole lot of talks with a guy I now feel was Howard Hunt. Ever since Watergate I've been ranting and raving about this everywhere, getting very few people to pay any attention to it. When I was in New Orleans after I got out of the service, I met a man who looked exactly like Howard Hunt, except he was bald. And he told me his name was Gary Kirsten and claimed he was a Nazi and had come from a family of Nazi's in the Mid-

West. He talked at great length about assassinating Kennedy...I just thought: this guy's nuts, you know? But, his idea of reality was very different from mine...As it turned out, mine was very naive! (laughs) The last thing he ever said about Kennedy--2 weeks prior to the assassination--was, "The only remaining question is, who to frame?" I said, "Why do you have to frame somebody?" "People need answers". His idea was to frame a "jail bird". I said, "Why do you want to frame a jail bird?" "Because criminals who are so stupid as to get caught, shouldn't be allowed to breed. They should be locked up, so they can't produce offspring." So I said: "I don't think you should frame a jailbird," and he asked, "Who should I frame?" And he knew what I was going to say, 'cause he was smirking so hard he couldn't look me in the eye. I said, "Why don't you frame some communist." He was setting me up. He knew then that he was going to kill J.F.K. Because one of the first things he ever said to me was, J.F.K. was a menace to the country and ought to be assassinated. Since I was into "AYN RAND" at the time--very right wing and very anti J.F.K.--I agreed with him, and we shook hands on it. My only problem was, I didn't find him very credible. What he was probably hoping for is that I would name Gary Kirsten to the Warren Commission. And that way, if they insisted Oswald had an accomplice, they would accuse this alleged Nazi from the Mid-West, who in reality was probably a KGB agent or something. I'm certain though it was Hunt or someone that looked like him--to thoroughly confuse the issue.

W.C.H.: And the final payoff was the continuation of The Vietnam War?

K.T.: Yes. His thing was, he didn't want a war with Cuba, because Castro was a "White Man". And he felt if there was to be another war against communism, it should be against an Asian country.

W.C.H.: Who felt this? Johnson?

K.T.: No, Hunt.

W.C.H.: E. Howard Hunt?

K.T.: Yes.

W.C.H.: I didn't think he had that much clout.

K.T.: I think he's an enormously powerful man. He had other people with him like Charles Cabell, John Connally.

W.C.H.: Kennedy had a lot of enemies, especially after the attempt to dissolve the C.I.A., and the plans to pull out of Vietnam.

K.T.: Well, according to Oliver Stone...I think what Stone left out was the Nazi angle.

W.C.H.: Nazi angle?

K.T.: Right. In the movie, "Mr. X" was Fletcher Prouty. Prouty is buddy buddy with Willis Carto. Carto is a raving anti-semitic who publishes the SPOTLIGHT. He also publishes some of Mark Lane's stuff and the C.I.A. renegade, Marchetti...That's the one thing that Stone did not touch upon. Mike Paine--husband of Ruth Paine, with whom Marina Oswald lived with in Sept. '63--was working for a Nazi at the time at Bell aircraft, General Walter Dornberger. There were all these ex-Nazis over here. According to Mae Brussell, there was a goddammed "WEREWOLF TEAM", a Nazi commando team. Known members of the famous Nazi werewolf commandos were in Dallas two weeks before the assassination. George DeMohrenschildt's wife admitted--when he died--that he had been a Nazi agent during World War II.

W.C.H.: Who do you think actually killed Kennedy?

K.T.: I think basically it was General Gehlen's organization, which I don't think really had an actual name to it...Gehlen defected to the Allies when the war was over and entered the U.S. Army without a reduction in rank. He was given a monopoly on the intelligence area about the Soviet Union. But he never did tell the C.I.A. who was in that outfit. (Editor's note: The Gehlen organization became the West German Federal Intelligence Agency (FIA) after his defection. During the war, Gehlen had been a member of the German General staff unde μr Hitler and was in charge of wartime intelligence for Foreign Armies East. He had been recruited into the C.I.A. by then Bonn Station Chief, Henry Pleasants. Gehlen employed many former SS and Wehsmacht intelligence officers. Gehlen's organization was not officially part of the

West German government until July of '55. Three of those former Germans e mployed by Gehlen, hence C.I.A., were Heinz Felfe, Hans Clemens, and Erin Tiebel. They actually conducted espionage against West Germany for over ten years and were arrested, tried, and convicted in July of '63.)

W.C.H.: Do you think they continued on with Bobby Kennedy, Martin Luther King and Malcolm X?

K.T.: The guy I talked to in New Orleans always said that they were going to get Martin Luther King. As for Bobby Kennedy, I don't know. There's one common thread that runs through all this stuff and that's an organization that was organized shortly after Kennedy's death and that was the PROCESS CHURCH.

W.C.H.: I'm familiar with that.

K.T.: They had tried to frame me in New Orleans for something I didn't do, which had been my actual participation in the assassination, which I didn't realize until later. They were involved in Kennedy's death somehow, I believe. That might be the link right there.

W.C.H.: They seemed to almost be a Manson like cult.

K.T.: Some of them were. Some of them were with Papa Doc Devallier, some were with Trudeau, (laughs) I forget the other name...but there were three questions to find out whether you were a Satanist, a Luciferian, and a Jehovist. The Satanist answer was Papa Doc; the Luciferian answer was Trudeau. So their politics were quite varied.

W.C.H.: It seems like the church was involved in the conspiracy.

K.T.: It's like fate, the conspiracy. There were Nazi breeding experiments which I think Oswald and myself may have been products of.

W.C.H.: Similar to the C.I.A. mind control experiments?

K.T.: That was involved also, but it was a little more complicated than that. The North Koreans had some enormously sophisticated mind control technology. As it turns out members of North and South Korea's government were part of the Japanese (column?). During the war, they were getting this technology from the Japanese, it was stuff the Germans developed unbeknownst to American Intelligence. I believe I was being mind controlled by them even before I went into the military. Then the C.I.A. got a hold of me up until the Kennedy assassination.

W.C.H.: Controlled in what manner?

K.T.: Well, it's spooky; very hard to believe.

W.C.H.: Like the Russian E.S.P. experiments?

K.T.: Very strange. They could influence my choice of words, so that it would sound like I was speaking in intelligence code. Things that I didn't realize even existed. And I think back on arguments I had with my parents, and I remember how "freaked out" they were at the time. It was like, all of a sudden one day I started speaking these double entendre sentences. Like a type of "cant" language.

W.C.H.: Like doublespeak?

K.T.: Yeah, exactly! Precisely! And my parents thought I was a "genius" (laughs) of some kind, to have figured all of this out by myself. Then later on they deduced I was being mind controlled. Also Dulles went nuts trying to figure out how the Koreans got ahold of such sophisticated techniques. Then when I got into the marines, I think Delgado at Yale planted something in my head at that point. I believe one of the purposes of the Kennedy assassination was to get those of us who had been torn out of the clutches of the Japanese by the C.I.A., back into the hands of the Japanese. (laughs)

W.C.H.: I've seen your name mentioned in Robert Anton Wilson's COSMIC TRIGGER I and...

K.T.: Everything nice Robert Anton Wilson says about me is a lie! (laughing) Especially in COSMIC TRIGGER. He was just trying to sniff out impersonators that way.

W.C.H.: Are you still in contact with him?

K.T.: He stopped speaking to me in 1976.

W.C.H.: What about Greg Hill and Bob Shea?

K.T.: I've never actually held more than a 15 second conversation with Bob Shea years ago when he was publisher of "CAVALIER", before I met Wilson. Also, Shea stopped corresponding with me around the same time I lost track of Robert Anton Wilson. They both became very strange as far as I was concerned. Greg Hill and I were in contact up until my appearance on "A Current Affair". I called him up and told him I was going to be on the show and asked if they would let them interview him. He was very pleased to hear from me, but he didn't want anything to do with Current Affair. He felt that they were "Yellow Journalists". I told him that I've been ranting and raving since 1975 about being involved with the Kennedy assassination and I haven't been able to get this stuff in front of the American public. I'm not in a position to be choosy about how I get my information across.

W.C.H.: Have you read any of Wilson's other work?

K.T.: Just THE ILLUMINATUS TRILOGY and COSMIC TRIGGER I. He changed a lot in the early 70's and sort of lost me. He was very much into politics and individualist Anarchism, Tucker Spooner, Lawrence Lapperty and all that. He converted me to a lot of their ideas. I found him a very exciting person, very knowledgeable about psychology. Then he got into magic and everything and just lost me.

W.C.H.: Right. I bought COSMIC TRIGGER II, thinking it would be a continuation of the first COSMIC TRIGGER and it was completely different.

K.T.: Wilson has gone to great lengths to avoid me, including telling Greg Hill that he didn't want me to know where he was living.

W.C.H.: I think he's in L.A.

K.T.: He just got really strange on me every time I'd bring up the Kennedy hit. Why, I don't know.

W.C.H.: That sucks. Anyway, there were a couple other things I wanted to ask you...Have you heard about Bill Cooper?

K.T.: Yeah.

W.C.H.: Have you read his book?

K.T.: No, I listened to a tape of his. He doesn't sound like a very convincing person. He's entirely misinterpreting facts.

W.C.H.: He seems to have patched together a number of different sources.

K.T.: Well, we all have to do that (laughing) when we write.

W.C.H.: He's been accusing everyone of being a C.I.A. plant.

K.T.: I know why that happens. I went through a phase of that also. There are a lot of people in the Intelligence Community and there are a lot of people, without realizing it, are working for the Intelligence Community because they're connected with organizations like the Rosicrucians and The Masons and so forth. It's very compartmentalized and they all think their working together and each group thinks they're serving that group. So it's very easy to get the idea you're surrounded by C.I.A. agents, when in fact there are agents of many, many powers. (laughs)

W.C.H.: So then you think The Illuminati and Bilderbergers are real organizations?

K.T.: Undoubtedly! Yeah, I have to deal with these people all the time. There's been some kind of misunderstanding between me and them that has been deliberately cultivated by the KKK. They're Aleister Crowley people--probably not Adam Weishaupt's Illuminati--but its inspired by similar ideas.

W.C.H.: There have been all kinds of claims about this group, fiction or otherwise. One of the claims involves satanism.

K.T.: There's a lot of satanism, because within the Catholic Church you're going to have somebody into satanism. Then you can blackmail them in the church, control them. And use them as spies within the church. So a lot of so-called "satanism" serves a purpose. It's not that people actually believe in a "devil", per se. They can be atheists and still be a satanist. Shell Oil Company is deeply involved with present day illuminati. They're not particularly into Central Ba Önking; the original conspiracy was supposed to be a conspiracy of bankers and revolutionaries.

W.C.H.: Like the Rockefellers?

K.T.: The impression I get is that these Illuminati are monetary federalists. They're against central banking.

W.C.H.: So then what's their game plan?

K.T.: To make the whole world look like the U.S.; turn it all into a Gringo Planet. (laughs)

W.C.H.: A McDonalds and Burger King on every corner? I see Coke is pretty pissed off that they can't open up shop in Vietnam.

K.T.: Shell Oil Co. has all kinds of property in Vietnam. I had a friend over there during the war and he said he saw Shell Co. property everywhere he went.

W.C.H.: I read a review of your book IDLE WARRIORS in "Anarchy", and I'm not sure if it was a direct quote from you or not, but the inference was that the Kennedy hit was a starting point to set the "New World Order" scenario into motion?

K.T.: I don't remember seeing that in the review myself; I read it, also. I can tell that guy had only read one or two chapters in the book. I can't say for sure which chapters. He didn't read the intro section; he probably read the chapter: "At Comocura", maybe one or two others. He was just faking it, basically.

W.C.H.: Really? I thought it was a good review.

K.T.: It was a nice review.

W.C.H.: What's the thrust of your books?

K.T.: All different types of things. In 1964 I wrote a book about Oswald, which I tried to explain why I thought he shot J.F.K., a non-fiction book. It was published by "New Classics House". I'm not all that proud of it, because at the time I accepted the Lone Assassin Theory", because conspiracy theories to me smacked of McCarthyism. I wanted to be an intellectually respectable right winger, not a McCarthyite. After that I wrote the IDLE WARRIORS and that was published in 1991. That same publisher (Illuminet) also put out my ZENARCHY. It basically popularizes the ideas of the beat era.

W.C.H.: Getting back to the ü Korean mind control experiments: Did you ever think you were just really paranoid?

K.T.: Oh yeah! I spent years fearing paranoia so much that I wouldn't look at the stuff at all, you know? That's why I testified the way I did at The Warren Commission, because I didn't want to look like a paranoid. I didn't even mention the guy who discussed killing Kennedy for 3 years in New Orleans. Evidently they thought I was covering up for him, or they thought that I thought I was covering up. (laughing) I was very impressed by the "Caine Mutiny" and all that stuff. I found people I thought were paranoid very entertaining and I went to great lengths to avoid actions that might be considered paranoid.

W.C.H.: A little bit of paranoia's healthy.

K.T.: Paranoia is heightened awareness, actually. A lot of paranoids are confused as to who's persecuting them, not that they aren't being persecuted. Claude Steiner, (a radical therapist) said that most people are persecuted beyond their wildest dreams. (laughs)

W.C.H.: Are you still right wing?

K.T.: No, I'm a raving left wing anarchist. I've been that way since 1969. Wilson converted me to a far left, anarchical point of view.

W.C.H.: Given that stance, what do you think about Clinton?

K.T.: He's a crypto republican. I think Nixon assassinated all the liberals in this country. A friend of mine read an article that said Nixon has assassinated 400 of his political enemies since he left office. Nixon and Hunt found out that the C.I.A. bureaucrats would sign anything that was in their "in" box without reading it, because they trusted their underlings that put the stuff there. They created their own government that way. And so on paper it all looks perfectly legal. One of the things they did was to pick certain people and said that they were assets to national security and anyone who tried to kill them could be legally killed themselves. And they used us to provoke âenemies of Nixon to try and kill us. But they were killed instead. I was one of the people used for those methods.

W.C.H.: Bill Cooper touches on that a little bit.

K.T.: Hunt, Hoover and General Gehlen were at the core of the assassination. I think they also tricked Charles DeGaulle into participating, by convincing DeGaulle that Kennedy was trying to kill him.

W.C.H.: We just saw a lecture by a guy called Jim Marrs. Are you familiar with him?

K.T.: I looked through his book.

W.C.H.: His lecture was very convincing. He came across as real down to earth, a "good ole boy" kind of guy, being from Texas and all. His contention was that a french assassin killed J.F.K.

K.T.: Frenchie they called him, yeah. I think that was William Seamore. He was an anti Castro activist at the time. I met John Stockwell (he's a renegade C.I.A. agent) when Oliver Stone interviewed me. He said that the Corsican Mafia and the French Intelligence are synonymous. There's been numerous articles indicating and linking the Corsican Mafia with the Kennedy assassination. I believe Hunt was posing as a C.I.A. agent named Maurice Brooks Gatlin Sr., who was supposed to be a legal advisor to Guy Bannister. He went over to France and gave a lot of money to some French generals who were plotting to kill DeGaulle. And they arranged for DeGaulle to be tipped off about the alleged hit. So DeGaulle thought Kennedy, through the C.I.A., was trying to kill him. So DeGaulle and The Corsican Mafia really muddied the waters, so to speak. It left all kind of evidence laying around that didn't point to Nixon, Hunt or Gehlen.

WCH: How or why do you think so many people allegedly got involved in the Kennedy hit?

KT: The guy I called "Brother-In-Law" (aka Gary Kirsten)--who I thought was Howard Hunt, that I talked to about assassinating J.F.K.--told me that he was going to talk to everybody in the country who wanted Kennedy dead. He also said to me, he thought it would be a good idea to involve a whole lot of people, who all thought they were working on other projects.

WCH: The Triangulation of Fire Theory?

KT: A maximum complicity crime. In other words, if everyone--the CIA, FBI, French or Corsican Mafia, the KGB, the Cubans--thought they were the only ones sitting around with Howard Hunt talking about killing Kennedy, then they'd all think they did it. This was the opposite approach I wanted to use, which was to use as few people as possible and to tell as few people as possible. It seemed very impractical the way he (Hunt) wanted to do it, to me at the time. I didn't understand that he was a goddamm CIA trained assassin who knew exactly how to pull these things off and how to pull off a political coup.

WCH: How feasible, do you think it is, that the possibility of a "New World Order" scenario will happen?

KT: I think...I'm not sure how you pronounce her name, Stephanie Caruana? The woman who wrote THE GEMSTONE FILES. I met her at Phenomicon. Everybody there was talking about, well, what are the plans of the New World Order, The Ideology of the Illuminati and so forth. Stephanie said, "Don't be so naive! These people don't have any ideology!" She said people with power want to keep their power and they use any ideology at hand for purposes of accumulating power. And I think that's exactly what it is. I don't think they have any particular plan for this, that or the other thing. When they take over, that's all they want to do, period.

WCH: In the Cooper book BEHOLD A PALE HORSE, there's a chapter called "Silent Weapons For Quiet Wars" which is a sort of preconditioning for a one world government. The "Mark Of The Beast" and all that.

KT: Well, the thing is they've got pretty much what they want already. A central banking system, where if someone wants to borrow money they have to pay the bankers interest for doing virtually nothing. When in fact they can issue their own money on their own collateral or their own credit. Basically, they're milking everybody for all they're worth, the poor, the middle class, even the rich to some degree. It's just a matter of them consolidating their own gains, I think.

WCH: Getting back to Clinton: Do you think he's screwed--or in the process of screwing up--the Democratic party for another 12 years?

KT: He sounds just like George Bush to me. He hasn't said anything that Bush wouldn't have said. He's been as vacillating and unprincipled as Bush, besides.

WCH: I think he has lied more than Bush.

KT: Probably so (laughs). It's really discouraging. It's really in the hands of the Rockefellers, as far as I can tell. Clinton's a Rockefeller man. Bush was a Rockefeller man. Perot's a Rockefeller man...

WCH: And Carter?

KT: Carter's undoubtedly a Rockefeller man, although personally I liked Carter. He's the only president I have liked, for that matter.

WCH: Right. You, me and about 10 other people--maybe Tip O'Neal.

KT: I had very high respect for the man, because he restrained himself so much over the hostage situation, which is where he lost everybody else. He was the first Democrat that didn't get us in a war. I'm very proud of him for that. Be that as it may, it didn't impress anybody else (laughs).

WCH: If Clinton blows it for the Democrats, who do you think will be the front runner in '96?

KT: I'm an Anarchist. To me, whoever wins, we all lose (laughs). People are so far from understanding Clinton. Man, we shouldn't be worrying about paying off the deficit, we should be canceling the National Debt and demanding reparations from bankers. (laughs) And shooting Reagan for creating such a huge deficit to begin with, putting him before a firing squad, you know? To my way of thinking, Clinton doesn't even mention anything about the banks, about the role the banks create. There's a book called THE ILLUMINATI CONSPIRACY by Donald Holmes. Read the introduction by Robert Anton Wilson if you want my view of the whole banking situation. To me, Clinton's just a pawn of the bankers, who pretty much rule the world.

WCH: The bankers being...?

KT: Not the Jewish bankers; the Templar anti-semitic bankers; the German bankers.

WCH: i.e. The Bilderbergers?

KT: Them, too. They're just some of the richest people in the world. A lot of those (German) bankers are members of the Bilderbergers. See there's a lot of bankers in Germany who proudly proclaim to be directly descended from the Templars, because the Templars were the first Christians who were allowed to practice banking and the Pope gave them a special dispensation. I believe they originated anti-semitism. They spread the ideas that Jews were stingy and so forth.

WCH: Like the "Elders Of Zion", that type of thing?

KT: Yeah! In fact the "Elders Of Zion" is supposed to be the minutes of a Templar meeting that were doctored to look like...they think they are the original Jews; they think that Europeans are the lost tribes of Israel. And they dug up some stuff on the temple mound and they thought they had recreated the original religion that preceded modern Judaism and Christianity...I think in this c ountry it's mostly the Rockefellers, the Warburgs, the Helphands. In my opinion, the Templar bankers financed both Bolshevism # Nazism and are now financing laissez-faire capitalism. Because with every laissez-faire capitalist institute you will find some revisionist historian and the revisionist historians say there was no holocaust, all of this stuff. If you read AMERICAN SWASTIKA by Charles Highams or Sandor A. Diamonds book HISTORY OF THE AMERICAN NAZI MOVEMENT, you'll find that this was the German propaganda line during the war. These days it seems laissez-faire capitalism is gaining a lot of support.

WCH: It just seems ironic in light of the rise of the neo-nazis in Germany and all of the white supremacists around the states, that lot of kids today don't study or could care less about recent history. So when they hear this revisionist bullshit, they believe it.

KT: Oh yeah, a lot of the "Nation Of Islam" people believe it, too. It's really scary, but then again look at Israel, how reactionary they are. I think Zionism might be a Nazi plot. It's very easy for Jews and Germans to pass themselves off as each other in the post war confusion.

WCH: How do you see the "Christian Right" as playing a role in the '96 election.

KT: I really don't speculate about elections that much. I don't think they make that much difference. I try not to predict the future. Cone Bendid (sp?) in his book OBSOLETE COMMUNISM speaking about the Ô68 student uprising in France said he was attending the commune meetings, the ad-hoc communes that had come together as the government was being paralyzed by the strikes. He said, you could tell they weren't ready to rule themselves because instead of talking about what they were going to do, they were saying, what's going to happen to us? To me, it's like, that's not a very fruitful area of speculation, worrying about what's going to happen. Whatever you predict, it almost never happens that way.

WCH: The only reason I say that, is growing up in the '50's #the '60's, the Cold War and all of that. It seems to me that lately there has been a definite conservative shift, or pendulum swing to the far right.

KT: I feel there's been a goddamm "war" on Cold War liberals, which involves both the extreme left #right. And in some ways, rightly so. I can see why the Communists were unhappy about the Cold War liberals and why the right wing was unhappy with them, also. Although I can see the liberals viewpoint. In the late '50's/early '60's, there were a lot of people who were totally liberal except for the fact that they hated Communists, because they didn't want to be accused of being Communist. And they went out of their way to be anti-Communist. J.F.K. was one of those "types". And I think probably Oswald. That's partially what I think the Kennedy assassination was; war on those types of liberals.

WCH: That you feel is still going on today?

KT: Oh yeah! I feel they've pretty much won by now. "Brother-In-Law" used to say the Nazis won WWII. I'm beginning to think he was right (laughs).

WCH: What I'm referring to is, oh say, the popularity of someone like Rush Limbaugh.

KT: The country's in a very strong right wing mood. It was surprising that Clinton got elected.

WCH: I was amazed!

KT: There's no doubt we're living in very reactionary times.

WCH: Now that you're on the subject of right and left extremism, it's almost turned into a sort of "Civil War"!

KT: That's very interesting! Because I was told that George De Mohrenschildt #his wife were KGB agents and by the time of the Kennedy assassination that Kruschev was trying to stir up a civil war in the U.S. And you've got everybody in this country arguing about who's straight or who's gay.

WCH: Right, all of these petty distractions from the real issues. And that's what Kennedy seemed to address, the real issues.

KT: Well in that respect, yes, but even he was appointing racist southern judges and federal judgeships up until the time he was assassinated. He was not a raving radical. He was a very pragmatic man.

WCH: Pragmatic, i.e. political. He knew which side hi ïs bread was buttered on. It just seems there is a type of Civil War going on and who's going to win?

KT: I don't think anyone wins a war.

WCH: I consider myself an anarchist, definitely leftist. Do you think there's any hope for the left?

KT: Well, I like to think there is, but I've become--in the process of dealing with the Kennedy assassination over the last 17 years--extremely cynical. Someone accused me the other day of being "a little" cynical. I said I'm not a little cynical, (laughs) I'm overwhelmingly cynical! The thing about anarchism is that it's so logical that once people understand what it is, they can usually convert to it. But until such time as anarchists take over a major media network or something, then--and only then--will there be any type of anarchist society. The other thing that worries me is the ecology. It seems to me that possibly I've misspent my life politically with all this anarchism because...the ocean for example is extremely delicate. If it ever stagnates, if the seas ever stagnate, which they very well may, that's going to be the end of human life on this planet.

WCH: That's what bugs me so much about the right. They really don't give a shit about ecological concerns. With those clowns it's money/power/industry--the ecosystem be dammed! We need jobs, now!

KT: There will probably be some enormous ecological disaster that will destroy all life on the planet before any anarchist uprising. I used to be extremely optimistic. I thought when the ILLUMINATUS TRILOGY was published that there would immediately be an anarchist revolution. (laughs)

WCH: Did you see the bombing of The World Trade Center?

KT: I heard about it.

WCH: That was leading into my question about synchronicities.

KT: Well, you know with The World Trade Center, that's the same Bloomfield/Shaw...All those people were tied into the Defense Industrial Security Command...All that Torbitt manuscript stuff. I thought that was an interesting choice of targets.

WCH: Right. It just struck me as funny. Now terrorism is starting to hit our shores.

KT: Well, it has off and on from time to time. Hijacking airplanes to Cuba used to go on all the time.

WCH: There was a long shot of the Trade Center on CNN, and in the upper left corner of the shot on the building was the #23. I saw that and my jaw hit the floor.

KT: (Maniacal laughter)

WCH: After I'd read COSMIC TRIGGER I for the second time, I started seeing 23's all over the goddammed place. I'm still seeing them to this day. And I get all these weird little synchronicities all the time, like driving over here tonight. There was this car in front of me with a mason plate on it. Does that happen to you a lot?

KT: Oh, yeah. Keep one thing in mind: If you decide 23 is a significant number, you're going to notice it every time it appears somewhere. There are two clandestine communication networks in the U.S. One of them is one the Japanese created during the war, which was a camouflaged German propaganda network. The other one is the Masons; they communicate the same way. A lot of cryptic symbolism, numbers and so forth.

WCH: I still think my "seeing" the 23's is some kind of subconscious mind trick.

KT: I have a friend who does the same thing with the number 22 (laughs). But one night I went to St. Petersburg to borrow a copy of BRAVE NEW WORLD from an assassination buff named Helen Hartman in 1969. I got home and there was a letter from Robert Anton Wilson. There was a certain passage from BRAVE NEW WORLD that I wanted to quote...about he was trying to free people, and they wanted to lynch him...basically about the slave mentality. Anyway, Wilson's letter was about the #23 and Burroughs, Capt. Clark and so on. I turned to the copy of BRAVE NEW WORLD to search for the chapter I wanted and it was on page 23, and the scene took place in the Park Lane Hospital! That was the same hospital they took Kennedy to #it rhymes with Mark Lane (laughs). I just flipped, it was very spooky.

WCH: Do you still have those types of synchronicities?

KT: Oh, all the time. Sometimes it's obviously things that couldn't possibly be anything but coincidences. I used to assume that stuff was coincidence; now I assume that it isn't, until proven otherwise. In some book I was reading, they were talking about intelligence agents and they said: Officers in intelligence are very wary of coincidence because they're usually not near as many coincidences as people have been led to believe. In fact many people, myself included, believe Jung was a raving Nazi--not a Hitler Nazi, but a raving Nazi, nonetheless. Dulles--when he was in Switzerland, striking up a deal with the S.S., trying to negotiate a secret separate peace--his principle assistant was Mary Bancroft, who was in therapy with Carl Jung. Jung's theory was: The chief problem with Nazism was the father in the German family. The authoritarianism was the problem because Germans were so male patriarch oriented. Basically, the idea was if Nazism was a matriarch it wouldn't have been so bad. I read a lot about Dulles before I came up with this idea and I mentioned it to John Stockwell, who was friends with Dulles. He said, "Kerry, that's exactly what happened, exactly!" Anyway, Jung had been accused many times of being a Nazi, plus he was the one who came up with the theory of synchronicity. Let me say something else about the #23. The code book that the Nazi's used during World War II was MEIN KAMPF. After the war, because they needed protection from the U.S. government, ex-Nazi's began to work for Communist countries, particularly North Korea, especially when we were at war with North Korea, because they were very used to working for the enemy, including my own parents. At some point they began using the "Little Red Book". All right...five was the number this guy named "Brother-In-Law" talked about. He said it was a very important number. That's why I made it the sacred number of The Discordian Society. Five in the "Little Red Book" means we must work with non party people within the intelligence community. There are three kinds of people who believe in working with non party people. One of them are the page nine people; these are people who believe history is driven forward by its contradictions and therefore they are double agents. George De Mohrenschildt and his wife are in vol. 9 of the 26 volumes. Nine signifies the middle of the roaders. Page 17 of Mao is: Reactionaries will make a last ditch effort. 17 signifies the type of page 5 people who want to work against the Communist party. And 23 says the Communist party is young #full of vigor. So 17, 9, 5 and 23 --before I ever realized this--are numbers that were being bandied about between me, Shea and Wilson. I think that was somebody's little lesson to show how the intelligence community was processing people.

WCH: Since I've been aware of the #23, I still don't fully believe it's all a mind trick.

KT: Well, nowadays it's become a fad to graffiti the #23 all over the place.

WCH: I see it in underground magazines a lot.

KT: Oh, yeah. Wilson has a lot of readers (laughs).

WCH: Bill Cooper was calling him a CIA plant.

KT: I have heard that he's a member of the Illuminati.I have heard that the "real" R.A.W. was assassinated by Gerald Ford's agents and replaced by a double. I've heard all kinds of stories like that. It's very possible that any one of those are true. I've heard that he was a Nazi all along. He's a very brilliant man, whatever he is.

WCH: That sounds like a disinformation campaign directed at him by rivals possibly.

KT: He's a very mysterious person.

WCH: When you were still conversing with him, was he a pretty regular guy?

KT: No, not at all!...What do you mean by that? To me a regular guy is somebody who's a conformist. He was very much a non conformist. He had a rather macabre sense of humor. He was just a brilliant anarchist and could explain to me what Laurence Lapperty didn't like about central banking and what Phurdome (sp?) didn't like about land monopoly. And he helped weed out all the irrationalities of "Ayn Rand".

WCH: Did you like him on a personal basis?

KT: I only met him once. That was down in Tampa in 1969. I liked him enormously. He radiated a very relaxed, very sensual...aaahhh...

WCH: Persona?

KT: Yeah, and he was very hip. He had taken acid many times by then. He seemed very unarmored in the Reichian sense. You could almost feel the sexual energy coming out of him. He had enormous sympathetic eyes, which at the time I found very reassuring, until I read the appendix in THE ILLUMINATUS TRILOGY where he was talking about making human sacrifices and identifying with the victim (laughs).

WCH: I've read that he's in so many churches, covens...

KT: He believes in being as many things as you can be and joining as many secret societies as possible.

WCH: Then at times he seems to downplay all this conspiracy stuff as if he's trying to throw people off the track.

KT: Well, yeah. He enjoys playing mind games. He eventually got me so fuckin' paranoid about him, by 1975--when I was trying to find out about all of these matters--he would write me, ever so often, and ask: "Are you getting paranoid about me yet? Because I know I say some pretty weird things in my letters to you." However, it was becoming increasingly hard not to (laughs).

WCH: Do you miss being in contact with him?

KT: Oh, hell yeah! He taught me half of everything that I now know.

WCH: That's what I was getting at. It seems like you two have so much in common that he would still be in touch with you.

KT: He was here (Atlanta) at Phenomicon a couple years ago and I had low blood pressure, because I still had my kidney condition and I couldn't stand on my feet without getting dizzy, so I couldn't go see him. But I wrote him a letter right afterwards; he never answered it, so fuck it! And that's the other thing I'm suspicious about: He has gone out of his way not to see me in person, all this time. Howard Hughes was that way and Oglesby thinks he was killed and replaced with a double. So I don't know. I think it's very possible he's not the same guy I knew back in the sixties.

WCH: Do you mean in a physical sense or a mental sense?

KT: I believe Gerald Ford killed him and replaced him with a double, at least that's what I was told. I didn't know whether or not to believe it at the time.

WCH: It sounds almost too far fetched to believe.

KT: Well evidently the ILLUMINATUS TRILOGY revealed a bunch of information which sabotaged the plans Lyndon Johnson had made to create a welfare state. A lot of people were pissed at him including a lot of left wing people. I didn't realize this until recently, so I don't know--it could have happened. I wish all of this stuff didn't sound so far out, because I know you're trying very hard to be credible with your audience. But that is why they get away with so fucking much. Did you see that movie RUBY?

WCH: No.

KT: Well, in there, Jack Ruby is dealing with a CIA agent who acts likes the comedian George Gobbels more than anybody else (laughs). And later on in the movie, Ruby is talking with one of his gangster friends and says, OYou know, I've figured out what the CIA's scheme is: They act in such a kooky way, that if you tell someone about it, they wouldn't believe you. It's a form of camouflage. It really is!

WCH: The further I delve into conspiracy work, invariably the strangest scenarios seem the most plausible.

KT: The stuff I laughed at initially was the stuff I wound up believing later on.

WCH: That's why the way out ideas and theories don't deter me from further research.

KT: I know, but you've still got your readers, you've got blue collar readers who try to work within consensus reality.

WCH: Not really. Most of the people that read this are very interested in this type of material.

KT: And I haven't even touched on the stuff they do with technology that nobody even realizes exists because it didn't have any commercial value, so they used it for political purposes.

WCH: Like What?

KT: Wireless transmission of currents, things that Nikola Tesla invented. He was a good friend of J. P. Morgan and George Westinghouse. And I believe they created the "Miracle Of Fatima" in order to blackmail the Pope. It's amazing what they could do with that technology! A lot of the things people think is magic(k) is just a bunch of German scientists with this advanced technology that nobody realizes exists...J. P. Morgan was financing breeding experiments, as well. Look at it this way, they staged the "Miracle Of Fatima", which is all stuff Tesla could have done. Tesla used to have shows on weekends where he would run thousands of volts of electricity through himself, without being hurt. Then they'd get the Pope to certify "Fatima" was a miracle and afterwards reveal to the Pope it was man-made. So the Pope is proven to be fallible, then they can blackmail him. They want the Pope to keep his mouth shut about the Nazi's, he keeps his mouth shut!

WCH: Do you ever read Mondo 2000?

KT: Occasionally.

WCH: In some of the recent issues, they'd been featuring a guy named Xandor Korzybski, who kind of goes along with what you're telling me.

KT: There's another guy (Alfred Korzybski) I laughed at until I found out what he was talking about...Tesla could make lightning strike during a storm. He figured out a way to suspend the earth's gravity. He never actually did it, obviously, (laughs) but he did figure out how to.

HOTEL KALIFORNIA REVISITED
By Wayne Henderson

"Every person, and every class and description of persons, who were at the time of the adoption of the Constitution recognized as citizens in the several States, became also citizens of this new political body; but none other..." - Dred Scott v. Sanford 19 How. 393 @405-06 (U.S. 1857)

"We think it as competent and necessary for a state to provide precautionary measures against the moral pest of paupers, vagabonds, and possibly convicts, as it is to guard against the physical pestilence which may arise from unsound and infectious articles imported." —N.Y. v. Miln 11 Pet. 102 @142 (U.S. 1837)

"The better to secure and perpetuate mutual friendship and intercourse among the people of the different States in this Union, the free inhabitants of each of these States, paupers, vagabonds, and fugitives from justice excepted, shall be entitled to all privileges and immunities of free citizens in the several states." —Articles of Confederation, Article IV (1778) [the Articles are subsumed by the Constitution, and Constitutional questions are resolved by reference to the Articles]

It has been nearly a decade since I penned the original Hotel Kalifornia; the article has seen three revisions and five reprintings, two of them overseas, and at least one of the revelations therein - of guard-instigated gladiatorial contests among prisoners - has been verified by the mainstream media, albeit eight years after I first broke the story (& do I get credited? No way) ...in the interim, much has happened, most of it bad, and as this extended visit of mine to the depths of hell nears the seventeen year mark, I felt it was time for a bit of an update.

I need hardly pontificate at any length about the psychological underpinnings of the police state; Gestapo control of our lives depends upon Gestapo control of our minds - who controls the terms of the argument controls the argument itself, and the Gestapo controls the mental viral agents ('memes') that act as substitute for actual thought: prisoners always (falsely) claim to be innocent, the accused must have done something or he/she wouldn't have been arrested, there's only a few bad cops who tarnish the rest unfairly, it's rare that the innocent are convicted,let alone executed), and ours is the best of all possible systems of criminal justice ... these assumptions are, I assure you, all lies, pathetic emotional shields for a population of frightened sheep who desperately cling to illusions of "freedom". I began this update with three quotes from the 'law of the land', something quite alien even to the better-educated among us: unless ancestors were wealthy landholders/slaveowners in the Colonies, you - yes, YOU - are one of those damned "paupers and vagabonds". You have no rights. You are not free.

"Hitler was merely the expression of the tragic-contradiction between the longing for freedom and actual fear of freedom." - Wilhelm Reich

"Our logic is at fault if we ignore the fact that right is founded on brute force, and even today needs violence to maintain it." - Sigmund Freud

The recent release of four more prisoners from Illinois' death row has received but scant mention in the mainstream media; they had been locked up about as long as I have, and, as in my own case they were convicted on the strength of lies and subterfuge by the prosecutors - a state of affairs more common than you could imagine in your worst nightmares. As with them, mine is an uphill battle: after seventeen years'incarceration, I am only now in the venue of the Federal courts, where it is theoretically possible that I might finally receive some small measure of 'justice'. It is frightening, indeed, to reflect that - if we assume a modest, conservative estimate of 5% wrongful conviction a number far too low, I assure you - I am but one of roughly 8,000 innocent people incarcerated in Kalifornia alone.

Kalifornia has recently instituted a "Mentally Disordered Sexual Predator" law, which purports to give the state the power to detain pathological rapists and child molesters beyond their release date, "for the good of the community". Hardly a law with which a reasonable person would disagree, right? Except that, buried deep in the legalese of the text, there is a provision allowing the state to apply this power to any prisoner, even those who have never even been charged with a sex offense. Am I being paranoid? I know, personally, of one case in which this law has been so used; just six weeks ago, a friend - on the day he was to be paroled and return to his family, was taken to the front gate and gaffled up into a state van, transported to a state 'hospital' for detention and observation/"treatment", which detainment, being a 'civil commitment', is of indefinite duration with no right to have an attorney or file for writ of habeas corpus; the state has ninety days to drug him into a stupor before presenting him to a "tame" judge for a "competency hearing" at which time his Thorazine-induced incoherence will be 'evidence' that he needs to be kept in the hospital for his own good, and that of the community. Worse yet, the state of Kalifornia has made it illegal for prisoners to have direct contact with the media (no telling, yet what they'll do with me, an accredited journalist), so informing the public of this might just cost me my life ... as the mainstream media can attest, this state has killed prisoners for far less. I ask again, am I being paranoid?

No matter how paranoid I am, I'm afraid I'll never be paranoid enough.

Consider: of all the criminal convictions overturned - generally at the Federal level - for criminal misconduct by the police & prosecution, just how often are these reversals followed by prosecutions of the police/ prosecutors responsible?

Consider: a partial list of those who will never be allowed to serve on a jury in a criminal trial includes the likes of Rodney King, Abner Louima, Geronimo Pratt, and myself. Why is it that any person who might see the Gestapo for what they are - an occupying army - is automatically excluded from jury duty by the prosecution - or the judge, if the prosecutor doesn't notice in time?

Consider: if just 5% - a measly 5% - of all convictions, nationwide, are tainted, then the United States currently has at least 75,000 innocent people incarcerated. You do the math. I've lived in thriving communities with smaller populations. In the face of such a national disgrace, why is it that no one so much as raises an eyebrow, yet the entire country can be paralyzed by the thought that Bill Clinton got a blowjob in the oval office?

Consider: the powers-that-be are currently involved in a feverish effort to draft legally-binding new statutes that would allow the Gestapo to take (by force, if necessary) DNA samples from everyone who is merely arrested (even if the 'charges' are dismissed the next day) and to catalog all these DNA samples into a national database, ostensibly to be used as "a tool to fight crime"... of course, much as with fingerprints, once the Gestapo have this information on file, they and their tame crimelabs can "prove" our involvement in any crime, any time, may it please the court. And remember, frightened parents practically trample each other to have their children fingerprinted and sampled, without a second thought. I hardly need illustrate the connection to the fact that our "Miranda rights" are no longer mandatory. You'll find this happening everywhere, but most particularly in Kalifornia, where an ignorant population (50th in adult literacy in the U.S., which now ranks a pathetic 47th worldwide) provides the perfect crucible for tests in social engineering, to see if fascistic new laws can be made to 'fly'. And yet, with such blatant assaults against our few remaining protections, why is it that the most spirited debate in the media in recent weeks involve Monica Lewinsky's lipstick?

It's not one damned thing after another; it's the same damned thing over and over and over again ...

Consider: John & Patsy Ramsey sexually abuse and murder their own daughter, and may dictate to the Gestapo the conditions under which they might be willing to answer a few, unthreatening questions - but not before they return from their vacation in Spain and have a chance to move across the country. Matthew Eappen's parents can abuse the poor infant - leaving many telltale injuries - and generally neglect him (what sort of parent won't feed their child, or even change the baby's diaper, before handing him off to an au pair?) - and then, when the poor tyke finally succumbs to his injuries, they have the full cooperation of the Gestapo & the prosecutor's office in blaming the tiny English slave they brought over to do their scutwork. John DuPont can murder a former national amateur wrestling champion on a whim, & is such a good friend to the Philadelphia area Gestapo that, in the face of public outcry, the worst they can think to do to him is confine him to a cushy private insane asylum, just until the heat blows over & people are focussed on another scandal-of-the-week. And yet, yours truly - able to prove that I was not even in the state of kalifornia when the crime occurred, am summarily arrested on the perjured affidavit of a pathological liar (excuse me, a brave & noble member of the Gestapo), not allowed to even present a defense, convicted & nearly sentenced to death (it was very,

very close) & must spend seventeen years fighting my way upstream to prove my innocence; not only this, but when I present evidence of the crimes of the Gestapo & prosecutors to the court, I'm summarily dismissed as one of those 'frivolous prisoner lawsuits' - let the editor of *Steamshovel Press* be my Judge; a cop of said "frivolous lawsuit" is in his possession. Do I seem bitter? A whiner, a complainer? I have reason - as do the other 75,000 innocents incarcerated in the Fascist States of Amerika.

[*Steamshovel* Debris: Copies of the legal case, clearly establishing the author's innocence, are available through *Steamshovel Press* at cost.]

QUOD LICET JOVI, NON LICET BOVI

[what is permitted to gods, is not permitted to oxen]

As a consequence of criminal conviction, the defendant has] not only forfeited his liberty, but all his personal rights, except those which the law in its humanity accords to him. He is, for the time being, the slave of the state. -Ruffin v. Commonwealth 21 Gratt. 790 (Va. 1871)

"...shall not be deprived of life, liberty, or property without due process of law..." - Amendment 14, U.S. Constitution; slavery is nowhere prohibited, only conditionally subject to "due process of law"

As stated in "Hotel Kalifornia," (*Steamshovel Press* #4; anthologized in *Popular Alienation*) amerikan prisons are the new plantation. Even with the lame, tame "unions" that spout pleasing rhetoric about protecting worker's rights from their warm, comfy position in the bosses' beds, imperial kapital demands that the 'wetware' - the drones - be less expensive, more cost-effective. Hence NAFTA, hence the rolling thunder of jobs stampeding to Third-World countries; but what about the smaller oppressors, the young, up-and-coming kapitalists? Those whose companies are not yet big enough to afford the move to friendly dictatorships where little brown people work in big brown factories? There is the domestic Third-World country the plantation: amerikan prisons. A prisoner assembles, and packages, computer components (you probably have several in your PC at work, if not at home); the bullet-resistant riot gear that the Gestapo wear when beating peaceful, unarmed protestors to a bloody pulp are made in Federal prisons by UNICOR; prisoners take your airline reservations over the phone & do telemarketing; and just recently here in kalifornia, several prisoners were transferred to the SHU at Pelican Bay - the "House Of Pain" - for revealing that they were being forced to sew "MADE IN USA" labels into sportswear trucked up from factories in Mexico. The state has no interest in "Justice"; the state's overriding interest is in profits - and prison slave labor is profitable for those who invest. Just ask former kalifornia governor Pete Wilson, part-owner in the company that provided the concrete that helped to build all the prisons he approved for construction; or ask his wife, co-owner of the company that holds the contract for producing the cheap, flimsy clothing that prisoners in this state must wear. Is it any wonder that, during a period when state workers' wages were frozen, if not declining, the powerful prison guards' union (CCPOA) was able to get juicy raises for the guards? Perhaps those millions the CCPOA donated to Wilson's political campaigns...

The horrors of which I speak are in evidence nationwide, but all stem from kalifornia, the crucible of such experiments in social conditioning & control. From the COINTELPRO experiments that produced the Manson Family, the Zebra killers, & Cinque DeFreeze of the SLA, to the social conditioning that has created the spate of gangs & serial rapists/murderers that now make up a statistically-relevant percentage of the population, kalifornia has proven to be the 'Behavioral Sink' of Skinner's theories & Calhoun's experiments; if you want to see your future, look no farther than Watts, South Central, or the gang turfs of Bakersfield and Frisco, Oakland, Fresno, and San Diego ... immense, filthy cities filled with frightened, psychotic people - all kept in their place by your friendly local Gestapo, cheerfully serving the interests of Fascism, Kapitalism, and the Amerikan Way.

Arbeit Macht Frei. Kalifornia Uber Alles.

I'm not just spouting theory, here, people; for the past seventeen years, I've been living in this hell, observing from the inside; I know the pattern of the hobnails on their boots, because I have seen their boots from underneath.

To me, the Gestapo and their machinations are all too real, all too personal. My petition for writ of habeas corpus [for those who are interested, Henderson v. Newland, docket #C.98-4837 :CW[PR], U.S. District Court, Northern District of Kalifornia and related criminal complaint against the Gestapo & prosecutors (a copy of which I've presented to *Steamshovel Press*) are currently winding their laborious way through the "criminal justice" system, the chips fall wheresoever they may; if there is any luck or injustice coming to me, I might find myself released sometime later this year. I will probably get to be the "scandal-of-the-week", albeit briefly, and then the majority of the population will change the channel stuff a few more potato chips in their mouths, and go back to their normal intellectual pursuits: Great Minds discuss ideas, admirable minds discuss events, lesser minds discuss other people, and most of the population is discussing Hulk Hogan's run for the presidency, but only during the commercials that interrupt the Jerry Springer show. The tabloidization of the Amerikan mind continues apace.

It would be nice if, just for once, the suffering of those of us who endure incarceration for crimes we didn't commit would be an impetus for broad social action, if not real change; but I will be happy to sue the state of kalifornia for everything I can get, a little something to add to my "freedom" (such as it) after seventeen years in hell. An acquaintance of mine, a fellow named Pitterman, won just such a release from incarceration; he filed suit, and the next anyone heard of him, the Gestapo "discovered" his body in an alley, a single gunshot wound to the back of his head. Naturally, the Gestapo ruled his death an "apparent suicide" (this is in San Mateo County, which is famous for such "suicides") and have closed the case, refusing to even put on a convincing show of further investigation. Not surprising in a state where prison guards can set up gladiatorial combat between prisoners, and use prisoners for target practice, with impunity.

Too many die for nothing. And of course, "it's just a few bad cops that unfairly tarnish the rest" - never mind that the rest know full well what's happening, & refuse to break the code of silence. I sometimes wonder if our species, so lacking in survival instincts, let alone enlightened self-interest, wouldn't perhaps be better off extinct; some other order of mammal could then move into our niche, and it's a safe bet that they couldn't do a worse than we have.

The most beautiful thing about us is that we are a bridge, not goal; the most frightening thing about us is that we are a bridge, not a goal. A bridge to where? I wonder; and of what shoddy manufacture? We cannot, as a species, believe that we should treat one another this way; and yet, we do ...

I hate to end an article on a negative note; so, as a personal aside to you, my gentle readers, I'd like to share: my current "job" here in prison is on what is called the "yard crew", picking up sputum-soaked cigarette butts & drippy used nosewipes without protective gear (rubber gloves are only available to staff, due to "budget constraints"), when not actively involved in the administration's laughable idea of 'landscaping' (have you ever seen *Cool Hand Luke*? It's not fiction). My current assignment, courtesy of a particularly ignorant and over-bearing facility captain, is to kill all the grass growing in a small, out-of-the-way spot, about the size of a boxing ring, near the prisoners' entrance to the visiting room. No chemical defoliants (thankfully!) just a hoe, a rake, a shovel, & me. Naturally, no matter what I do, the grass keeps coming back, greener & more luxurious each time. Life will not be denied; Mother Nature will find a way. The facility captain, of course, is apoplectic, and has not the intellect to perceive the futility of this campaign against the conquering grass; I am the slave of the state, no better (in the captain's eyes) than the offensive greenery, and so dig I must. The grass, as grass will, merely takes a deep breath and returns, as glorious as ever. I feel a kinship with the grass, a deep, blood-level bond to this defiant patch of green. It mocks all efforts at eradication; I am proud to call the grass my sister, my hero. And to the aforementioned facility captain, my message is: long after the last of your descendants to remember your name is dust, long after your bloodlines have diluted and your genes have scattered to the winds, long after the last of your children's children's children are forgotten, their very exis-tence not even a rumor in the musty corridors of time, long after the corrupt sys-tem you serve with such zeal has fallen, its ruins rediscovered by the farmer's spade and analyzed-by archaeologists who speak a tongue as yet unborn, long after all this has come to pass, captain, this grass will dance on your grave.

The grass laughs at you, captain, and frankly so do I.

You can muffle the drum, and you can cut the strings of the lyre, but you cannot command the mockingbird not to sing.
- Kahlil Gibran

Wayne Henderson 15 March 1999

steamshovel press

REVISING REALITY

A lecture by Jim Keith, delivered in Reno, Nevada, on November 29, 1998 at the Planet 9 coffeehouse.

A few weeks ago here at Planet 9, dur-ing a presentation by remote viewer Wayne Carr, I suggested to him that if remote view-ers could travel to any point in the past, present, or future — and the experimental data seems to suggest that is true — then it would be theoretically possible for those persons to revise the past, present, or future. If remote viewers have the ability to look at things without the necessity of using their bodily senses, without limitations of time or space, then they theoretically might have the power to influence those condi-tions. And if they could revise space and

Jim Keith is the author of *Mind Control and UFOs, Casebook on Alternative 3,* and other works on conspiracy and the paranormal. His books are available through Illuminet Press.

time without any limitations, then there are quite a few human problems that could be handled once and for all.

So I've been thinking about this. It could be done as a project that was roughly equivalent to the process of psychological therapy, but on a planetary or galactic scale. Remember, we're talking about remote viewers here, who are theoretically not affected by solar systems and black holes and such. The theory is that you might be able to erase events that had been harmful to or degraded consciousness or life forms on this planet, or in this galaxy or universe, and clean up the world a bit, make it a nicer place to live in, and answer all of our questions about the nature of reality, to boot.

Wayne seemed to think that was an interesting idea that I had. Actually it is something that I have been thinking about off and on for over 25 years now, spurred on in part my my involvement in Scientology 1972-82. Back in those days I thought of these possibilities in terms of "auditing," which is the Scientological term for counselling, and getting rid of traumatizing events that took place in your past. The theory is that by fully viewing something, or understanding something that has caused you trouble, you will assimilate or vanish or integrate the material, so that it no longer hangs you up. Pretty standard Freudian psychological counselling except for, of course, the fact that Scientology figures most of your problems came from previous lifetime. In order to really get out of the woods, they suggest, you have to delve into this previous lifetimes stuff and confront the "whole track"—dealing with the last 76 trillion years or so. Scientology is the last thing I would recommend that anyone get involved in, but I'm just describing the thought processes that led me to consider this possibility.

Back to remote viewing: If one can actually remote view events at a distance both in space and time, and the remote viewers say that this is so, and I personally believe the possibility exists, then you have landed smack dab in the middle of a philosophical quandary that not many remote viewers delve into, or think about, particularly. I do know that not many of them talk about it. The question is, if we can get out of the body, or at least perceive outside of the limitations of the bodily senses, what does this say about our nature, about what we really are?

If we can, as most remote viewers seem to think, travel through space and time freely and without limitation, then how does this ultimately impact on our view of what we are, who we are, what we can be? The answer, obviously, is that if remote viewing is a fact, then the strong likelihood is that our identities are not defined by our bodies. That we aren't ultimately human bodies limited to Earth and born to live out an existence of 70-odd years and then to die miserable deaths from lumbago.

If you can view things outside the limitations of the physical senses, then this suggests you are not limited by or defined by the body. Obviously, given the limitations of current technology, you can't take your physical body back to the paleozoic and cavort among the trilobites or whatever existed back then, so you are visiting these other times and places sans body. Again, this suggests that we are non-physical beings, what might be called spirits or spiritual entities. It suggests that we have for one reason or another become identified with or interiorized into a body, but also that we are ultimately not that body.

Lots of religions and philosophies have had this same view, but many of them have decided that we possess something like an "astral body" and we're linked by a silver cord to the body, and so forth. In other words, they're willing to believe that we are not composed of material substance, but they are not willing to go all the way and say that we are completely unlimited in terms of our condition and our manifestations. They probably figure this is the road to madness, to entertain the idea that you don't necessarily have any particular shape and condition and form. These religions see us as ultimately sort of ghosts with far greater powers than are normally conceived of as being possessed by humans, but still limited in certain ways. Kind of ethereal creatures. We can, they seem to think, fly around outside the bod, go through time and space, but we remain kind of coherent semi-physical packages. Many of these philosophies even believe that we exist in what they call a "subtle body" or astral body, or a condition that roughly conforms to the shape of a body, but is not limited by all of the characteristics of a physical body.

Well, who really knows about any of this stuff? Thinking logically here, it would seem to me that if we can get outside the body and still retain consciousness, then our shape, our character, our beingness, would not be limited to any body conceptions whatsoever, or any conceptions, period. We would exist in essentially whatever type of shape or condition or form that we desired... or at least that we were able to cope wth without being sent to the spin bin. We could define our nature, more or less as we pleased, so long as we had cured ourselves of the hangup of believing that the body defined our nature. Ultimately, it may be that we can define our own nature, as well as our own reality, the kind of circumstances we exist in, our lifespan or spans, and the only thing that really limits us is our own limited self conception.

This is really the first statement of these materials that I have made, and it's all rather rough-shod, and intended to be that way. Kind of a Cliff Notes version of these ideas until I have them carved on emerald tablets and all that.

As I said, I'm fantasizing about a loose-knit project for psychoanalyzing the universe and getting it back on its feet. This might involve one person doing the remote viewing, it might involve a team or teams of remote viewers. It might involve getting help from chanelled entities, for all I know, although that would really open up a bucket of worms. It isn't necessary that I describe exactly how this process would be done, just toss the idea out that it might be possible to do it, and some simple concepts about how it might be done, and then get out of the way and perhaps let this stuff percolate on its own.

In fact, a project of this nature might not even have to be put into effect for it to provide some benefits to the life forms on this world. Just the communication of the possibility that it could be accomplished might be of some help, and set people to thinking about ideas that would be liberating to them. And there is the other possibility — which may not be plain to everyone — that with the greater possibilities of mass consciousness, or higher consciousness that stands behind smaller, more limited manifestations like humanity or examples of humanity — that simply bringing the idea forward of a galactic rehab project using remote viewers — call it the Galactic Process — will set off repercussions throughout time and many dimensions.

Reality in a crude analogy, might be seen as a resonating crystal and it may be that anything that affects one part of the crystal more or less instantaneously affects every other portion of the crystal at some level. If time and space are illusions, as many physicists and mystics seem to think, there should be no problem with instantaneous information propagation in infinity, since that infinity would in truth be a single point.

What would be the basics of putting a project like this together? Who would do it? How could it be done? How would it be organized? Would you all wear little Star Trek shoulder patches? How could you make a few bucks off of it?

The first thing you would need is a technique in mind by which a remote viewer could vanish traumatic events in the past from the mass consciousness. This, I think, is do-able. There are a number of techniques that I am familiar with that might work in this respect, and certainly there is no limit on brainstorming new techniques.

What you probably don't want to get involved with is using force to handle the physical universe. In other words, let's say you determine that the big hangup in this sector is some terrible event that took place two hundred billion years ago, where aliens from the planet Mars enslaved all humanity and put implants into them to be good little boys and girls and forget all about the implant. You don't necessarily want to go back to that time and use mental energy to blow up all the aliens. You would be using force to handle force, which tends to create chaos, and actually given the nature of these aliens, each part of their body grows again and so you have lots and lots of little aliens running around.

You also probably don't want to get real creative and figure out ways to, oh, have John Wilkes Booth misplace his gun before he heads out for the Ford Theatre. You know, he gets ready to shoot Lincoln and can't find his gun and gets all flustered and asks him for his autograph instead. That kind of approach would seem to have a limited workability, too.

The basic key here — and I am open to new ideas on the subject, so feel free to offer them — is that chaotic complexes in the fabric of space and time, traumatic circumstances, can be cleared up by integrating them, by "understanding them" into the non-physical matrix of consciousness. This works on the individual level of working out all the knots in a person's brain, all the way up to the physical universe itself, by harmonizing or opening up energetic flow and limiting chaotic energy manifestations. Handling potholes in the road.

The preferred technique for handling these kinds of traumatic events, so far as I can see, is similar to the Freudian conception. By perception. Not by blasting things with energy beams. By fully perceiving the area until the "illusion" of separation falls away. This is returning to the idea that time and space are illusions. That time and space in reality are something like ideas within the cosmic mind and that, like ideas, they can be freely revised at will if you're not too neurotic on the topic. That when you perceive something fully, it vanished into the actuality of — oh, let's call it the zero point cosmic mind. That's sufficiently Buck Rogers sounding, I guess.

You would need one or more participants, who either are already capable remote viewers or would be willing to learn or open up to the possiblity of this Galactic Process. You might want to put a limited time on the project, say a year or so, and then after that you would tabulate what has been accomplished and decide where you want to go from there.

Anyway, this is the barest of bare bones on this idea, but I wanted to tell you about it while it was new and fresh in my mind.

STEAMSHOVEL PRESS

LARRY FLYNT AND JFK

By a *Steamshovel* correspondent

Larry Flynt, Ruth Carter Stapleton and Robert Groden.

In June 1997, while attending the COPA (Coalition of Political Assassinations) conference at Georgetown University in Washington, DC, a conference attendee, upon learning I was from Cincinnati, asked if I remembered a full page ad published by porn king Larry Flynt some twenty years ago in which he offered a million dollars for information about the 1963-assassination, of President John F. Kennedy.

Larry Flynt had received considerable publicity some months earlier with the release of the movie, *The People Against Larry Flynt.* The movie had been acclaimed by many critics for its artistic merit as well as the historic description of a battle for the First Amendment.

I told the conference attendee that I would look into the matter upon return to Cincinnati. The press, of personal business caused me to overlook the matter until October 1997 when Larry Flynt, eager to take on the Cincinnati establishment again, opened a shiny new *Hustler* store in the heart of the Queen City's downtown.

The media attention was enormous and police had to redirect traffic around the new *Hustler* store as I arrived and got in line with the local porn fans to get copies of *Hustler*s signed by Flynt. I opened the conversation with, "Larry, I am the only Cincinnatian who was in Judge Lance Ito's courtroom in Los Angeles in 1992 when Charlie Keating was sentenced to ten years." Larry put down his autograph pen, leaned back in his, wheel chair and laughed heartily (Keating and prosecutor Simon Leis, had pursued Flynt relentlessly back in the '70s which produced a legal battle described so colorfully in the movie).

After a few more conversational words I said: "Larry, the real reason I am here is to ask if you remember a full page ad run back in the '70s offering a million dollars for information on the JFK murder." With that, the big smile vanished and he looked at the floor and muttered: "Yeah, and I got shot right afterwards."

The next week, I went back to the Hustler store to ask Jimmy Flynt, Larry's brother and permanent manager, the date of the shooting. Jimmy responded instantly: "March 6, 1978." I then began a review of both Cincinnati newspapers, the morning *Enquirer* and the afternoon *Post,* for the two months preceding the shooting. The February 17, 1978 *Enquirer* had a large story about a Flynt press conference announcing his search for absolution to the JFK assassination. This article featured a photo of Flynt standing next to Ruth Carter Stapleton (President Carter' sister) and now prominent researcher Robert Groden.

After reviewing the newspapers back to January 1, 1978, I had not found a copy of the million dollar ad. So I returned to the *Hustler* store to seek Jimmy Flynt's assistance. Jimmy was amused and interested in the folder of clippings I had collected. I then asked, "Jimmy, can you give me a more exact date of the JFK ad?" His pleasant demeanor disappeared as he barked testily, "Look, I tried to talk Larry out of that project back in 1978 ... the man's dead, he should have left the whole thing alone!" He then stalked off leaving me open mouthed.

Conclusion: In the years after the 1978 shooting of Larry Flynt, rumors float-ed around Cincinnati that his local anti porn persecutors were behind the shooting. The suspected shooter was a "lone nut" of classic vintage. It is clear-ly obvious, however, that Larry and Jimmy Flynt believed that the shooting was directly caused by the porn king's foray into the growing field of people investi-gating that infamous day in Dallas. The CIA was in a nervous state in 1978 because of the House Select Committee's investigations; all the spooks needed was some minor character in the conspiracy to surface and take the million dol-lar bait.

A researcher at the 1999 Dallas COPA meeting perhaps summarized the Flynt episode most succinctly: "Have you ever heard of a pornographer being shot because he was in the porn business?"

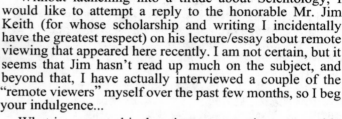

STEAMSHOVEL PRESS

REVISING KEITH
By Greg Bishop

A Commentary on Jim Keith's Lecture, "Revising Reality"

Greg Bishops edits and published *The Exculded Middle.* exclmid@primenet .com

Without launching into a tirade about Scientology, I would like to attempt a reply to the honorable Mr. Jim Keith (for whose scholarship and writing I incidentally have the greatest respect) on his lecture/essay about remote viewing that appeared here recently. I am not certain, but it seems that Jim hasn't read up much on the subject, and beyond that, I have actually interviewed a couple of the "remote viewers" myself over the past few months, so I beg your indulgence...

What is suggested is that since remote viewers are able to transcend time and space by the power of their inten-tions, and through the focusing of their mental faculties, they might be able to "fix" past events where something in our evolution or his-tory has gone wrong, thereby transforming our condition into some version of Nirvana on Earth. There are a multitude of reasons why this is not even theoret-ically possible. He also seems to fall into the peculiarly western desire to "fix" things. There is nothing in our past that needs to be "fixed." In fact, I believe that it is the point of Scientological "auditing" to remember and understand the past rather than to deny it. What Jim seems to suggest is that the collective uncon-scious needs some sort of bandage, or worse, blinders to clear us of unpleasant race memories. We are reminded of that old "Those who do not remember the past..." adage. Why as Mr. Keith suggests, would we want to "vanish traumatic events in the past from the mass consciousness"? We'd eventually commit what-ever it was all over again.

It seems odd that Wayne Carr, a claimed viewer, would not explain to Keith that given what is currently known about the process of remote viewing, that the idea of affecting distant events and times viewed is an impossibility. This is not to say that it will ALWAYS be an impossibility, but it appears to be in the realm of fiction at this time.

The first presumption Jim makes is that "we are not defined by our bodies." Fair enough. I completely agree. The argument falls apart, however as he assumes that remote VIEWING is somehow related to remote LOCATION. Just because some of us are able to separate our consciousness from our bodies does-n't mean that the consciousness is able to affect anything tangible.

Some remote viewers (Col. David Morehouse notably) have said that their viewing sessions resemble out of body experiences. From over 100 years of research and writing about OBEs, there are only a few cases where the participants were able to affect anything outside their immediate personal location. The most that anyone could ever muster was the flutter of a corner of fabric or the like. (See Hereward Carrington's The Projection of the Astral Body for more on this.) Morehouse does claim that he visited the site of a helicopter crash (backwards in time) and the recently dead soul of an Army buddy, and was able to integrate the experience and come to peace about this unfinished area of his life. He was NOT however able to prevent it. Is Keith talking about this sort of understanding? If a remote viewer is able to understand and integrate past human transgressions, how is this communicated to the population at large without the inevitable confusion and giggles?

Although rumors abound concerning research into remote influence, there is as yet no firm documentation of this. The existing literature suggests that this can only occur in the present-time is a limiting factor. Some stories from the Soviet bloc had psychics injuring or even killing subjects at a distance. Again, this is at the moment that the medium desires, not in the future or past.

Mr. Keith also assumes that causality is linear. Why time and space should be an illusion while leaving causality in an Aristotelian frame of reference is not made clear. There is growing body of theories and evidence that suggest causality depends on the meaning of the events and their effect upon the viewer (as well as the viewer's effect back upon them.) Cause does not always equal effect, sometimes the effect drops in before the cause-in our time frame. The idea has also been put forward that events are not predetermined (i.e. "fate"), and we may continually be "jumping rails" in the paths our lives, and our species take. All possibilities may be occurring simultaneously all the time, only we're just able to perceive one of them, since we are incarnate in physical bodies.

I am also forced to wonder why Jim insists that the universe needs a therapy session. Just because he's unhappy with the outcomes of many events in our particular space and time frame, doesn't mean that there is something wrong with the whole shebang. Besides, in light of the last paragraph, if the viewers went into the past and "fixed" something, the logical conclusion is that the viewer would come back to a world that didn't need fixing in the first place. The trap of linearity causes a paradox. Another, more frightening idea is that messing with causality may result in a "crash" of the viewer's reality, where ALL possible outcomes are experienced simultaneously. This is a little weird, I admit.

Perhaps I'm also going out on a limb like Mr. Keith.

Cyberculture Counterconspiracy Vol 1 • ISBN 1-58509-125-1

Cyberculture Counterconspiracy Vol 2 • ISBN 1-58509-126-X

Other Titles Available Through The Book Tree • Call For Our Free Catalog

TRIUMPH OF THE HUMAN SPIRIT: The Greatest Achievements of the Human Soul and How Its Power Can Change Your Life by Paul Tice. A triumph of the human spirit happens when we know we are right about something, put our heart into achieving its goal, and then succeed. There is no better feeling. People throughout history have triumphed while fighting for the highest ideal of all – spiritual truth. Some of these people and movements failed, other times they changed the course of history. Those who failed only did so on a physical level, when they were eliminated through violence. Their spirit lives on. This book not only documents the history of spiritual giants, it shows you how you can achieve your own spiritual triumph. Various exercises will strengthen your soul and reveal its hidden power. In today's world we are free to explore the truth without fear of being tortured or executed. As a result, the rewards are great. You will discover your true spiritual power with this work and will be able to tap into it. This is the perfect book for all those who believe in spiritual freedom and have a passion for the truth. **(1999)** • **295 pages** • **6 x 9** • **trade paperback** • **$19.95** • **ISBN 1-885395-57-4**

PAST SHOCK: The Origin of Religion and Its Impact on the Human Soul by Jack Barranger. Introduction by Paul Tice. Twenty years ago, Alvin Toffler coined the term "future shock" – a syndrome in which people are overwhelmed by the future. *Past Shock* suggests that events which happened thousands of years ago very strongly impact humanity today. This book reveals incredible observations on our inherited "slave chip" programming and how w've been conditioned to remain spiritually ignorant. Barranger exposes what he calls the "pretender gods," advanced beings who were not divine, but had advanced knowledge of scientific principles which included genetic engineering. Our advanced science of today has unraveled their secrets, and people like Barranger have the knowledge and courage to expose exactly how we were manipulated. Readers will learn about our past conditioning, and how to overcome the "slave chip" mentality to begin living life as it was meant to be, as a spiritually fulfilled being. **(1998)** • **126 pages** • **6 x 9** • **trade paperback** • **$12.95** • **ISBN 1-885395-08-6**

GOD GAMES: What Do You Do Forever? by Neil Freer. Introduction by Zecharia Sitchin. This new book by the author of Breaking the Godspell clearly outlines the entire human evolutionary scenario. While Sitchin has delineated what happened to humankind in the remote past based on ancient texts, Freer outlines the implications for the future. We are all creating the next step we need to take as we evolve from a genetically engineered species into something far beyond what we could ever imagine. We can now play our own "god games." We are convinced that great thinkers in the future will look back on this book, in particular, as being the one which opened the door to a new paradigm now developing. Neil Freer is a brilliant philosopher who recognizes the complete picture today, and is far ahead of all others who wonder what really makes us tick, and where it is that we are going. This book will make readers think in new and different ways. **(1998)** • **310 pages** • **6 x 9** • **trade paperback** • **$19.95** • **ISBN 1-885395-26-4**

OF HEAVEN AND EARTH: Essays Presented at the First Sitchin Studies Day. Edited by Zecharia Sitchin. Zecharia Sitchin's previous books have sold millions around the world. This book contains further information on his incredible theories about the origins of mankind and the intervention by intelligences beyond the Earth. This book offers the complete proceedings of the first Sitchin Studies Day. Sitchin's keynote address opens the book, followed by six other prominent speakers whose work has been influenced by Sitchin. The other contributors include two university professors, a clergyman, a UFO expert, a philosopher, and a novelist – who joined Zecharia Sitchin to describe how his findings and conclusions have affected what they teach and preach. They all seem to agree that the

myths of ancient peoples were actual events as opposed to being figments of imaginations. Another point of agreement is in Sitchin's work being the early part of a new paradigm – one that is already beginning to shake the very foundations of religion, archaeology and our society in general. **(1996)** • **164 pages** • **5 1/2 x 8 1/2** • **trade paperback** • **$14.95** • **ISBN 1-885395-17-5**

FLYING SERPENTS AND DRAGONS: The Story of Mankind's Reptilian Past, By R.A. Boulay. Revised and expanded edition. This highly original work deals a shattering blow to all our preconceived notions about our past and human origins. Worldwide legends refer to giant flying lizards and dragons which came to this planet and founded the ancient civilizations of Mesopotamia, Egypt, India and China. Who were these reptilian creatures? This book provides the answers to many of the riddles of history such as what was the real reason for man's creation, why did Adam lose his chance at immortality in the Garden of Eden, who were the Nefilim who descended from heaven and mated with human women, why the serpent take such a bum rap in history, why didn't Adam and Eve wear clothes in Eden, what were the "crystals" or "stones" that the ancient gods fought over, why did the ancient Sumerians call their major gods USHUMGAL, which means literally "great fiery, flying serpent," what was the role of the gigantic stone platform at Baalbek, and what were the "boats of heaven" in ancient Egypt and the "sky chariots" of the Bible? **(1997, 1999)** • **276 pages** • **5 1/2 x 8 1/2** • **trade paperback** • **$19.95** • **ISBN 1-885395-25-6**

SUBSCRIBE !

Steamshovel Press *is a newsstand magazine that examines conspiracy topics. Often reviled as reprehensible and irresponsible, the magazine nevertheless adheres to a standard of truth that mainstream media does not understand or appreciate. It considers itself in the tradition of such great conspiracy researchers as Mae Brussell and Ace Hayes, with articles that explore strange dimensions of current events and parapolitics made all the more bizarre by the copious documentation. Reviewed with great acclaim by the* New York Times, *the* Washington Post, *the* Smithsonian, *the* Chicago Tribune *and even* George Magazine. *"Research the mainstream press doesn't have the* cajones *to publish," says* Apocalypse Culture II *author Adam Parfrey. The* New Yorker *calls it "...on the cutting edge – and a strange place that is."* CHALLENGE CONSENSUS REALITY AND KEEP CURRENT WITH THE CONSPIRACY – SUBSCRIBE NOW.

Four Issues: $23; Single Issue: $6, post paid.
Steamshovel Press, PO Box 23715, St. Louis, MO 63121.

Name _____ Begin with Current Issue [ ]

Address _____ Begin with issue number ___

City, St, Zip _____ **www.umsl.edu/~skthoma**

Printed in the United States
114509LV00008B/164/A

9 781585 091256